THE
RIGGING OF SHIPS
IN THE DAYS OF THE
SPRITSAIL TOPMAST
1600 - 1720

R. C. ANDERSON

DOVER PUBLICATIONS, INC.

NEW YORK

Bibliographical Note

This Dover edition, first published in 1994, is an unabridged republication of the work first published in a limited edition (97 rag-paper copies) by The Marine Research Society, Salem, Massachusetts, in 1927.

Library of Congress Cataloging in Publication Data

Anderson, R. C. (Roger Charles), b. 1883.
    The rigging of ships in the days of the spritsail topmast, 1600–1720 / R.C. Anderson.
        p.   cm.
    Originally published : Salem, Mass. : Marine Research Society, 1927.
    ISBN 0-486-27960-X (pbk.)
    1. Ship models.   2. Masts and rigging.   3. Ships—History—17th century.   4. Ships—History—18th century.   I. Title.
VM298.A58   1994
623.8'62'09032—dc20   93–43440
                                                                                            CIP

Manufactured in the United States of America
Dover Publications, Inc., 31 East 2nd Street, Mineola, N.Y. 11501

PREFACE

THE production of a book on rigging by one who is neither a professional seaman nor a shipbuilder seems to require explanation, if not apology. The justification lies in the fact that a knowledge of rigging of any date before the introduction of wire-rope and other modern improvements is more a matter of historical research than of personal experience. The "old sailor" has a knowledge of the rigging of his own time at sea far more thorough and more practical than anything that can be obtained from the study of books, pictures and models; but for the ships of a century or more before his time he is a very dangerous guide. Many a model has been spoilt by being rigged or restored by a man whose experience at sea belonged to quite a different period to that of the model. To give a very simple example, it is difficult to persuade a modern seaman that ships of 1650 had no bobstays, and yet we know that this was the case. I myself parted company with one quite able rigger over this very question; he insisted that he had been at sea and his father and grandfather before him and that there had always been a bobstay in their time — therefore there must have been one from the beginning of things.

As I have said, the study of rigging for any time before the middle of the 19th century is a matter of historical research. It involves the comparison of all sorts of authorities, some easily available and some rare. Books, manuscripts, pictures, prints, models, all have to be examined and weighed in the balance. Some are more useful than others, but almost any scrap of real contemporary evidence has its value. A list of some of those authorities which have been continually in use during the preparation of this book is given on a later page, but one or two deserve more particular mention here.

A Treatise on Rigging, written about 1625 and printed for the first time by "The Society for Nautical Research," in 1921, is by far the fullest account of rigging of the early part of the 17th century. A German book, *Der Geöfnete See-Hafen,* published at Hamburg in 1700, is even more thorough in its description of rigging of the end of the century. Battine's manuscript lists of the gear of English ships exist in several copies; the earliest is dated 1684, but the copy in my own possession belongs to 1689. I believe the various copies to be very nearly the same and I have quoted Battine as evidence for the year 1685, though actually using my own copy of four years later. A similar work was prepared in 1675, by Kelt-ridge, who was also responsible for the drawings of 4th-Rates and smaller ships which are reproduced in Charnock's *Naval Architecture.* As far as I know my own copy of this manuscript is the only one.

The most useful of all authorities — at least for the end of the period under consideration — has been the model of the English 90-gun ship *St George,* of 1701. This model, the gem of the famous Sergison collection, has contemporary rigging in almost perfect condition. The same claim has been made for other models of earlier date, for the French *Royal Louis,* of 1692, the Dutch "*William Rex,*" of 1698, and the Dutch model, of 1665, in Berlin, and even for the Danish *Norske Löve,* of 1654, but I doubt very much if it could be substantiated for any of them to the same extent as for the *St George.*

Fortunately, from my point of view, this model, with the rest of the Sergison collection, was actually in my charge for some two years or more and I was able to study it in such detail that my notes, drawings and photographs, together with a complete full-sized rigging plan prepared by Mr. L. A. Pritchard, are even more useful for quick reference than the model itself.

To the model-maker who uses this book as a guide, I have one request to make. That is that he should read the book right through before starting work. It has proved impossible, or at any rate undesirable, to stick rigidly to the order in which the work should be done, when it came to describing it. To some extent I have done this; for instance, spars come before standing rigging and this comes before running rigging; but I must admit at once that the book is not as easy to use as a "cookery book," where each operation is described in its proper place and one has only to follow instructions. If it had been a matter of describing the rigging of one particular model of a definite date and country, it might have been done; but with fittings and leads varying with nationality and with date, it would be almost impossible.

A few words seem needed to explain the choice of dates for the beginning and end of this study. I chose 1600 for a start for two reasons: first, because it marks about the furthest limit of our knowledge of rigging in any detail; secondly, because it is the earliest date to which that characteristic 17th century fitting, the spritsail topmast has yet been traced; and my end date, 1720, was roughly the time when it was finally superseded by the jib boom and when 17th century rigging may be said to have given place to that of the 18th century.

American readers will perhaps be disappointed to find

that there is no mention of American practice. English, Dutch, French, and to a less extent other European methods have been described, but nothing has been said as to what ought to be done in the case of a model of American origin. To be perfectly frank, this omission is due to ignorance. As far as I know there is no evidence of what was American practice. I should imagine that American-built ships followed the fashions of those countries with which their builders and owners were most closely related; that the ships of the English colonies followed English fashions and so on. A study of 18th and 19th century rigging would make up for this neglect, for then American ships had a character of their own and American improvements were often first in the field; but for the 17th century it was England, Holland and France that led the way and it is their ships which are most important from the historical point of view.

I have no doubt that there are omissions and mistakes in this book. A first attempt could hardly escape either. I hope, though, that they are not very serious and that a model rigged in accordance with the instructions I have given will satisfy all but the few experts and will strike even them as not far from the truth.

TABLE OF CONTENTS

ENGLISH 100-GUN SHIP "ROYAL GEORGE," 1715
From the model in the Techniches Hofschule, Hanover

LIST OF PLATES

6 FRENCH MAN-OF-WAR BUILT IN HOLLAND IN 1626.

From a print published by H. Hondius, at Amsterdam. Five ships and some small craft were built in Holland for the French Navy in 1626. This is probably the *Saint Louis*. A copy of this print was used in error as the basis for the modern model of the *Couronne* of eleven years later. This is an early example of a large ship without the bonaventure mizzen. The whole rigging is much less complicated than in the Danish ship in Plate 5.

7 ENGLISH 100-GUN SHIP "SOVEREIGN," 1637.

From a print by J. Payne. The most remarkable feature about this print is the presence of fore and main royals and of a mizzen topgallant sail. These sails were not adopted officially till more than a century later, but there is no doubt that they were occasionally in use in the first half of the seventeenth century. The *Sovereign* was probably the first large English ship to dispense with the fourth mast. It will be noted that there are martnets on the main topsail and leechlines on the fore.

8 DANISH SHIP "NORSKE LÖVE," BUILT IN 1634.

From the model in Rosenborg Castle, Copenhagen. The actual ship was built in 1634, but the model was not completed till 1654. It is probable that the model shows a mixture of styles of the two dates. Some portions of the rigging have been replaced wrongly.

9 ENGLISH RIGGING-PLAN OF 1655.

From Miller's "Complete Modellist." This book is really concerned with the drawing of rigging-plans and their use in cutting the rigging to the right length. The plate is taken from the second edition of 1664, but there is little doubt that it had been used in the first edition which must have been printed about 1655. Each yard is shown twice, in the hoisted and lowered position. This is necessary to get the full lengths of the different ropes. For example, the lifts are at their longest when the yard is lowered, whereas the opposite is the case with the braces.

10 DUTCH MEN-OF-WAR, ABOUT 1655.

From an etching by R. Nooms (or Zeeman) showing "Two new frigates equipped for war against the Parliament of England." This refers to the first Anglo-Dutch war of 1652-4. Fore and main "preventer stays" are shown at a date when they are hardly to be expected. Probably they were fitted as a precautionary measure before going into action.

11 DUTCH MAN-OF-WAR OF 1665.

From a model made as a half-size copy of the large Dutch model in the Hohenzollern Museum in Berlin. The rigging, carried out by Miss B. P. Derrick, under the supervision of the Author, is based partly on photographs of the original (which has sails) and partly on other Dutch authorities of the same period. The hull and spars were made exactly half the size of the original and are by Capt. W. Brandt, formerly of the Imperial German Navy. Official photograph, South Kensington Museum.

1. DUTCH SHIP OF THE END OF THE SIXTEENTH CENTURY
From a print by W. Barentsoen, 1594

2. LARGE MAN-OF-WAR OF THE BEGINNING OF THE SEVENTEENTH CENTURY
From a Dutch print of 1613

3. English Merchantman of the beginning of the Seventeenth Century

From the model of an "English Merchantman of the size and date of the *Mayflower*"

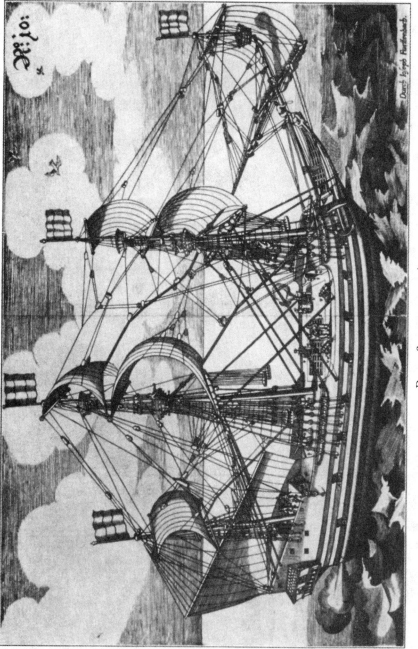

4. Dutch Ship of about 1620
From Furttenbach's "Architectura Navalis," 1629

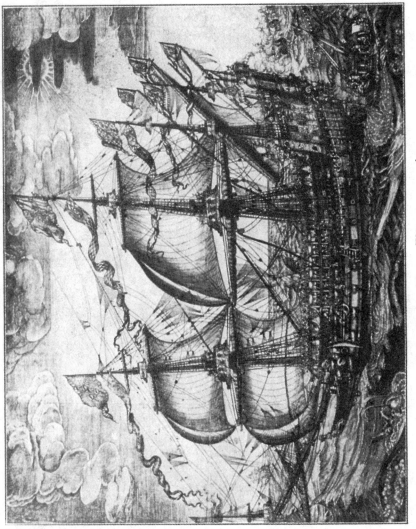

5. Large Danish Man-of-War of about 1625
From a print by C. Möller

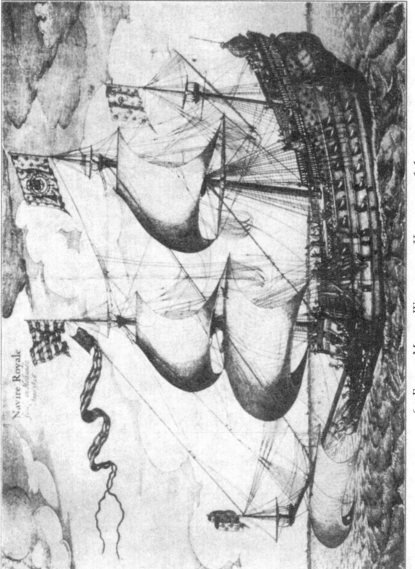

Navire Royale

6. FRENCH MAN-OF-WAR BUILT IN HOLLAND IN 1626
From a print published at Amsterdam by H. Hondius

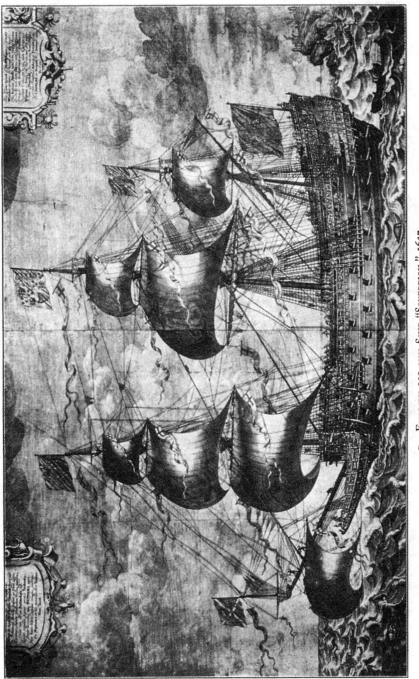

7. English 100-gun Ship "Sovereign," 1637
From a print by J. Payne

8. Danish Ship "Norske Löve," built in 1634
From the model in Rosenborg Castle, Copenhagen

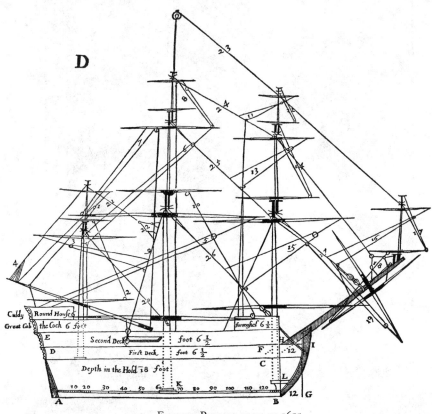

D

Cuddy
Great Cab
Round House 6
the Coch 6 foot
E
Second Deck
foot 6½
D
First Deck
foot 6½
Depth in the Hold 18 foot
forecastel 6½
H
F
C
I
12
L
A
10 20 30 40 50 60 70 80 90 100 110 120
K
B
12 G

9. ENGLISH RIGGING-PLAN OF 1655
From Miller's "Complete Modellist"

. Twee Nieuwe Fregatten. geruft ten Oorloogh. tegen t' Pademont van Engelandt, 23

10. DUTCH MEN-OF-WAR, ABOUT 1655
From an etching by R. Nooms

11. Dutch Man-of-War of 1665

From the model in the Science Museum, South Kensington

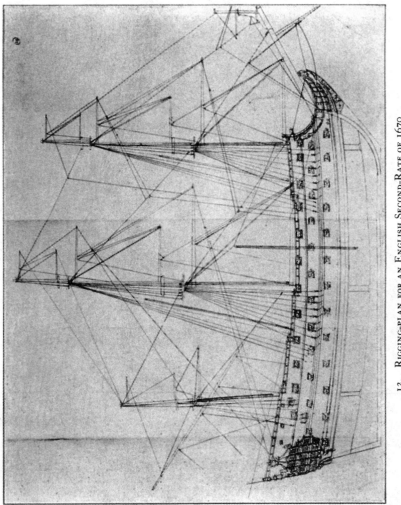

12. RIGGING-PLAN FOR AN ENGLISH SECOND-RATE OF 1670
From a manuscript in the Pepysian Library, Magdalene College, Cambridge

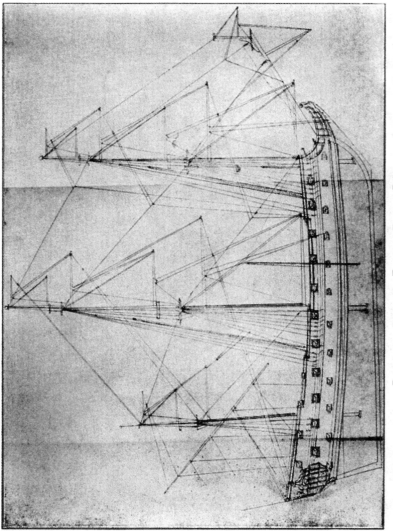

13. Rigging-plan for an English Fourth-Rate of 1670
From a manuscript in the Pepysian Library, Magdalene College, Cambridge

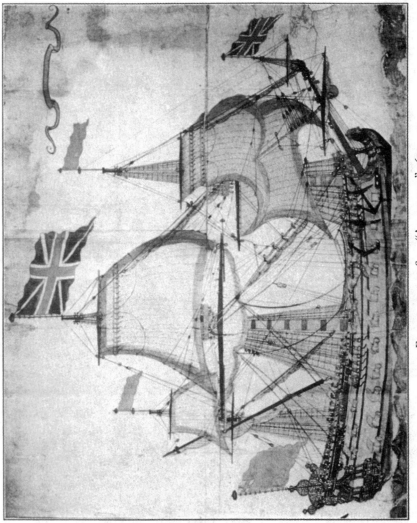

14. English 50-gun Ship "Assistance," 1673
From a colored drawing in the British Museum

15. ENGLISH MERCHANTMAN OF 1673
From a colored drawing in the British Museum

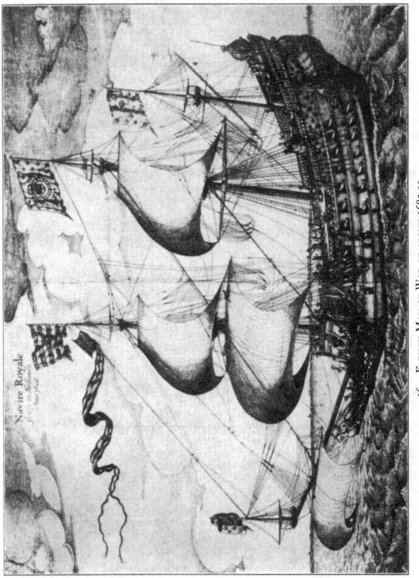

Navire Royale
...

16. FRENCH MAN-OF-WAR OF ABOUT 1685-90

From a drawing ascribed to Puget, in the Naval Museum at the Louvre, Paris

17. ENGLISH MAN-OF-WAR OF ABOUT 1690
From a drawing by C. Bouwmeester

18. RUSSIAN MAN-OF-WAR "PREDESTINATSIA," 1701
From an engraving after a print of 1701

19a. FORETOP OF THE "ST GEORGE" MODEL, 1701
From the Sergison Collection at Cuckfield Park, now owned by Col. H. H. Rogers of New York

19b. MAINTOP OF THE "ST GEORGE" MODEL, 1701
From the Sergison Collection at Cuckfield Park, now owned by Col. H. H. Rogers of New York

Fig. 1.

Main Mast

Fore Mast

Mizzen Mast

Bow-sprit

20. English Rigging-plan of about 1700

PLATE 20. KEY
(*Spelling as in original*)

MIZZEN MAST AND RIGGING:

1. Mizzen Mast
2. Yard and Sail
3. Sheet
4. Shrouds and Laniards
5. Bowlines
6. Brayles
7. Jeer
8. Peak Hallyards
9. Crossjack Yard
10. Lifts
11. Braces
12. Puttock Shrouds
13. Mizzen top
14. Top Armour
15. The Capp
16. Crowfoot
17. Stay and Sail
18. Halliards

MIZZEN TOP MAST AND RIGGING:

19. Topmast
20. Yard and Sail
21. Braces
22. Lifts
23. Shrouds
24. Halliards
25. Backstays
26. Bowlines
27. Sheets
28. Clewlines
29. Stay
30. Crosstrees
31. Cap
32. Stump
33. Stay
34. Truck
35. Spindle
36. Vane
37. Slings of the Crossjack Yard

MAIN MAST AND RIGGING:

38. Main Mast
39. Runners and Tackles
40. Tackle
41. Shrouds and Laniards
42. Stay and Sail
43. Staysail halliards
44. Yard and Sail
45. Jeers
46. Sheets
47. Tacks
48. Buntlines
49. Bowlines
50. Braces
51. Leachlines
52. Puttock Shrouds
53. Crowfoot
54. Lifts
55. Top
56. Top armour
57. Top rope
58. Cap
59. Mainyard Tackles

MAIN TOP MAST AND RIGGING:

60. Main Topmast
61. Tackles
62. Shrouds
63. Back Stayes
64. Halliards
65. Stay and Sail
66. Staysail halliards
67. Yard and Sail
68. Braces
69. Bowlines
70. Sheets
71. Clewlines
72. Lifts
73. Runner
74. Buntlines
75. Crosstrees
76. Cap
77. Stump
78. Stay
79. Truck
80. Pendant

FORE MAST AND RIGGING:

81. Foremast
82. Runner and Tackles
83. Tackle
84. Shrouds and Laniards
85. Stay
86. Yard and Sail
87. Sheets
88. Tacks
89. Braces
90. Bowline
91. Buntlines
92. Leachlines
93. Yard Tackle
94. Jeers
95. Puttock Shrouds
96. Crowfoot
97. Top
98. Top Armour
99. Top Rope
100. Lifts
101. Cap

FORE TOP MAST AND RIGGING:

102. Fore Topmast
103. Tackles
104. Shrouds
105. Back Stays
106. Halliards
107. Stay and Sail
108. Halliards
109. Yard and Sail
110. Runner
111. Lifts
112. Braces
113. Bowlines
114. Sheets
115. Clewlines
116. Buntlines
117. Crosstrees
118. Cap
119. Stump
120. Stay
121. Truck
122. Spindle
123. Vane

BOWSPRIT AND RIGGING:

124. Bowsprit
125. Horse
126. Yard and Sail
127. Lifts
128. Sheets
129. Clewlines
130. Braces
131. Bobstay
132. Top
133. Top Armour

SPRITSAIL TOPSAIL AND RIGGING:

134. Topmast
135. Shrowds
136. Halliards
137. Craneline
138. Yard and Sail
139. Braces
140. Lifts
141. Sheets
142. Crosstrees
143. Cap
144. Jackstaff
145. Truck
146. Jack
147. Best Bower Buoy
148. Cable

HULL:

A. The Cutwater
B. Stem
C. Hassholes
D. Catthead
E. Wastecloths
F. Fore Channel
G. Main Channel
H. Mizzen Channel
I. Chestree
K. Entering Port
L. Head
M. Gallery
N. Taffarell
O. Poop Lanthorns
P. Ensign Staff
Q. Truck
R. Ensign

21. DUTCH RIGGING-PLAN OF ABOUT 1700
From a print in "Dictionnaire de Marine," 1702

PLATE 21. KEY

A. Keel
B. Stem and Sternpost
C. Rudder
D. Counter
E. Gallery
F. Taffrail
G. Ensign-staff
H. Poop
I. Spare Topsail Yard
K. Half-deck
L. Forecastle
M. Cathead
N. Beak
O. Wales
P. Ports
Q. Chesstree
R. Anchor
S. Hawse-holes
T. Cable
V. Buoy
W. Mizzen Mast
X. Main Mast
Y. Fore Mast
Z. Bowsprit
a. Mizzen Topmast
b. Main Topmast
c. Main Topgallant Mast
d. Fore Topmast
e. Fore Topgallant Mast
f. Spritsail Topmast
g. Pendants
h. Flag at the Main
i. Ensign
k. Jack

1. Mizzen Yard
2. Crojack Yard
3. Mizzen Topsail Yard
4. Main Yard
5. Main Topsail Yard
6. Main Topgallant Yard
7. Fore Yard
8. Fore Topsail Yard
9. Fore Topgallant Yard
10. Spritsail Yard
11. Spritsail Topsail Yard
12. Mastheads
13. Caps
14. Tops
15. Topmast mastheads
16. Upper Caps
17. Mizzen Shrouds
18. Mizzen Channels
19. Main Shrouds
20. Main Channels
21. Fore Shrouds
22. Fore Channels
23. Mizzen Stay and Sail
24. Main Stay and Sail
25. Fore Stay
26. Mizzen Topmast Shrouds
27. Main Topmast Shrouds
28. Fore Topmast Shrouds
29. Main Topgallant Shrouds
30. Fore Topgallant Shrouds
31. Spritsail Topmast Shrouds

22. ENGLISH MEN-OF-WAR OF ABOUT 1720
From a print by J. Sartor, after T. Baston

32. Mizzen Brails
33. Main Clewlines
34. Fore Clewlines
35. Spritsail Clewlines
36. Mizzen Sheet
37. Main Sheet
38. Fore Sheet
39. Spritsail Sheet
40. Mizzen Tack
41. Main Tack
42. Fore Tack
43. Mizzen Bowline
44. Main Brace
45. Fore Brace
46. Spritsail Brace
47. Mizzen Lift
48. Main Lifts
49. Fore Lifts
50. Spritsail Lifts
51. Main Leechlines
52. Fore Leechlines
53. Main Buntlines
54. Fore Buntlines
55. Spritsail Buntline
56. Mizzen Topsail Sheet
57. Main Topsail Sheet
58. Fore Topsail Sheet
59. Main Topgallant Sheet, or Main Topsail Lift
60. Fore Topgallant Sheet, or Fore Topsail Lift
61. Spritsail Topsail Sheet, or Spritsail Lift
62. Mizzen Topmast Stay
63. Main Topmast Stay and Sail
64. Fore Topmast Stay and Sail
65. Main Topgallant Stay
66. Fore Topgallant Stay
67. Spritsail Topmast Backstay
68. Bowsprit Horse

69. Main Topmast Backstay
70. Fore Topmast Backstay
71. Crojack Brace
72. Mizzen Topsail Brace
73. Main Topsail Brace
74. Main Topgallant Brace
75. Fore Topsail Brace
76. Fore Topgallant Brace
77. Spritsail Topsail Brace
78. Mizzen Topsail Clewline
79. Main Topsail Clewline
80. Fore Topsail Clewline
81. Main Topgallant Clewline
82. Fore Topgallant Clewline
83. Spritsail Topsail Clewline
84. Mizzen Topsail Lift
85. Main Topgallant Lift
86. Fore Topgallant Lift
87. Spritsail Topsail Lift
88. Mizzen Topsail Bowline
89. Main Bowline
90. Fore Bowline
91. Main Topsail Bowline
92. Main Topgallant Bowline
93. Fore Topsail Bowline
94. Fore Topgallant Bowline
95. Flag Halliards
96. Mizzen Tie and Halliards
97. Main Tie and Halliards
98. Fore Tie and Halliards
99. Mizzen Topsail Halliards
100. Main Topsail Halliards
101. Fore Topsail Halliards
102. Main Topgallant Halliards
103. Fore Topgallant Halliards
104. Spritsail Topsail Halliards
:-: Main Tackles
-:- Fore Tackles

X... Draught Mark on the Stem

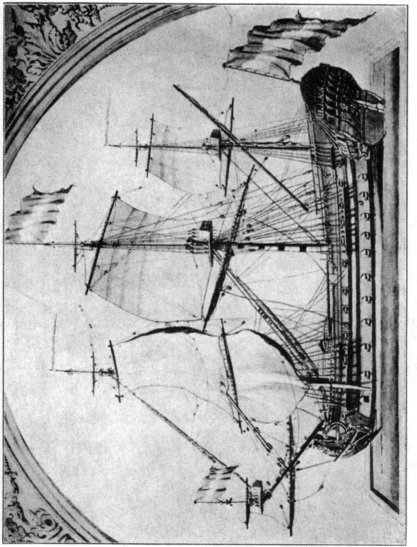

23.   Dutch East-Indiaman "Gertruda," 1720
From a plate in Adm. de Paris' "Souvenirs de Marine"

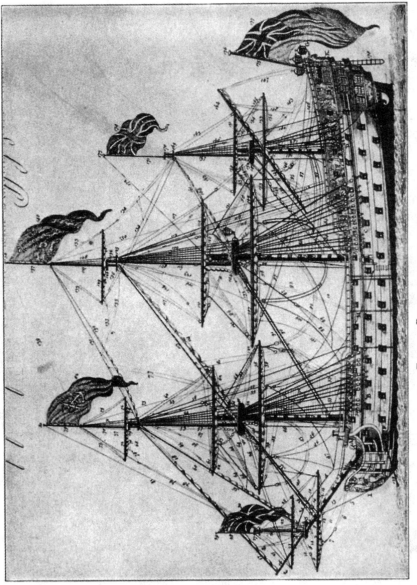

24. ENGLISH RIGGING-PLAN OF ABOUT 1720

PLATE 24. KEY

(Spelling as in original)

1. BOWSPRIT
2. Yard and Sail
3. Gammoning
4. Horse
5. Bobstay
6. Spritsail Sheets
7. Pendants
8. Braces and Pendants
9. Hallyards
10. Liffts
11. Clewlines
12. Spritsail Horses
13. Buntlines
14. Standing Liffts
15. Spritsail Top
16. Flying Jibboom
17. Flying Jibb Stay and Sail
18. Hallyards
19. Sheats
20. Horses

21. SPRITSAIL TOP MAST
22. Shrouds
23. Yard and Sail
24. Sheats
25. Liffts
26. Braces and Pendants
27. Cap
28. Jack Staff
29. Truck
30. Jack Flag

31. FORE MAST
32. Runner and Tackle
33. Shrouds
34. Lanyards
35. Stay and Lanyard
36. Preventer Stay & Lanyard
37. Wooldings the mast
38. Yard and Sail
39. Horses
40. Top
41. Crowfoot
42. Jeers
43. Yard Tackles
44. Liffts
45. Braces and Pendants
46. Sheats
47. Fore Tacks
48. Bowlines and Bridles

49. Fore Buntlines
50. Fore Leechlines
51. Fore Toprope
52. Puttock Shrouds

53. FORE TOP MAST
54. Shrouds and Lanyards
55. Yard and Sail
56. Stay and Sail
57. Runner
58. Backstays
59. Hallyards
60. Liffts
61. Braces and Pendants
62. Horses
63. Clewlines
64. Bowlines and Bridles
65. Reeftackles
66. Sheats
67. Buntlines
68. Crosstrees
69. Cap

70. FORETOPGALLANT MAST
71. Shrouds and Lanyards
72. Yard and Sail
73. Backstays
74. Stay
75. Liffts
76. Clewlines
77. Braces and Pendants
78. Bowlines and Bridles
79. Flagg Staff
80. Truck
81. Flagg Staff Stay
82. Flagg Lord High Adml.

83. MAIN MAST
84. Shrouds
85. Lanyards
86. Runner and Tackle
87. Pendant of the Gornet
88. Guy of Do.
89. Fall of Do.
90. Stay
91. Preventer Stay
92. Stay Tackle
93. Woolding the mast
94. Jeers
95. Yard Tackles

(PLATE 24 KEY, CONTINUED)

96. Liffts
97. Braces and Pendants
98. Horses
99. Sheats
100. Tacks
101. Bowlines and Bridles
102. Crowfoot
103. Toprope
104. Top
105. Buntlines
106. Leechlines
107. Yard and Sail

108. MAIN TOP MAST
109. Shrouds and Lanyards
110. Yard and Sail
111. Puttock Shrouds
112. Backstays
113. Stay
114. Staysail & Stay & Hallyard
115. Runners
116. Hallyards
117. Liffts
118. Clewlines
119. Braces and Pendants
120. Horses
121. Sheats
122. Bowlines and Bridles
123. Buntlines
124. Reeftackles
125. Crosstrees
126. Cap

127. MAINTOPGALLANT MAST
128. Shrouds and Lanyards
129. Yard and Sail
130. Backstays
131. Stay
132. Stay Sail & Hallyards
133. Lifts
134. Braces and Pendants
135. Bowlines and Bridles
136. Clewlines
137. Flagg Staff
138. Truck
139. Flagg Staff Stay
140. Flagg Standard

141. MIZON MAST
142. Shrouds and Lanyards

143. Pendants and Burtons
144. Yard and Sail
145. Crowfoot
146. Sheat
147. Pendant Lines
148. Peckbrails
149. Stay Sail
150. Stay
151. Derrick and Span
152. Top
153. Cross Jack Yard
154. Crossjack Liffts
155. Crossjack Braces
156. Crossjack Slings

157. MIZON TOP MAST
158. Shrouds and Lanyards
159. Yard and Sail
160. Backstays
161. Stay
162. Hallyards
163. Liffts
164. Braces and Pendants
165. Bowlines and Bridles
166. Sheats
167. Clewlines
168. Stay Sail
169. Crosstrees
170. Cap
171. Flagg Staff
172. Flagg Staff Stay
173. Truck
174. Flagg Union
175. Ensigne Staff
176. Truck
177. Ensigne
178. Poop Ladder
179. Bower Cable

HULL
A. Catt head
B. Fore Channells
C. Main Channells
D. Mizon Channells
E. Entring Port
F. Hause holes
G. Poop Lanthorns
H. Chesstree
I. Head
K. Stern

THE
RIGGING OF SHIPS IN THE DAYS OF
THE SPRITSAIL TOPMAST
1600-1720

THE
RIGGING OF SHIPS IN THE DAYS OF
THE SPRITSAIL TOPMAST

CHAPTER I

THE LOWER MASTS AND BOWSPRIT

I. Their Positions

WHEN what may be described as a ready-made model is to be rigged, the positions of the masts are decided beforehand and there is nothing to do except to conform to what one finds. The same holds good if one builds a model from drawings which have the masts marked. On the other hand, if drawings have to be made, the positions of the masts have to be settled early in the process, because many other details of the hull depend on them.

The first and most natural tendency is to say that the mainmast should be amidships. Within reasonable limits this is true enough, but on investigation it will be found that the matter is not quite so simple. Thomas Miller, who wrote a small book on rigging under the deceptive title "The Complete Modellist," in 1655, is very emphatic in saying that everyone knows the mainmast should be stepped in the middle of the keel, but plans both before and after his date are equally emphatic in contradicting him. Sir Anthony Deane, one of the leading English shipbuilders, prepared a manuscript on shipbuilding for Samuel Pepys, in 1670, and in all his plans (Plates 12 and 13) he puts the mainmast either at the middle of the gundeck or about its own diameter further aft. This means that the mast is well before the

middle of the keel, because the gundeck obviously over-
hangs the keel far more forward than aft. Another plan
of similar date published in "The Mariner's Mirror" in
1925 also shows the mainmast about its own diameter
abaft the middle of the gundeck. Still, there are cases
where it is stepped at the middle point of the keel. I
have two models in my own collection where this is so;
one, a 3-decker of about 1670-5, has had too much done
to her at various times to be a very reliable authority;
but the other, a 2-decker of about 1695, is quite con-
vincing. Later on, about 1720, English plans put the
mainmast about 1/25 of the length of the gundeck abaft
its middle point. Even then it is well before the middle
of the keel.

Really this is a question to which it is impossible to
give a definite answer. One can say that the middle of
the gundeck marks the forward limit and the middle of
the keel the after; one can also say that in a general
way the mast moved aft as time went on, but the exceptions must always have been numerous and it would
only be misleading to lay down a hard and fast rule of
any kind.

With foreign ships the matter is a little different. In
them the length was nearly always measured between
perpendiculars dropped from the heads of the stem and
sternpost. Witsen, whose book on Dutch shipbuilding,
published in 1671, is one of the classics of the subject,
contradicts himself a good deal, but does say clearly that
the step (in his typical ship of 134 ft. long) should be
5½ or 6 ft. abaft the middle of the ship. This agrees with
his plan, though there the mast is shown with the incredible rake of about 1 in 5. Van Yk, in 1697, says the
mainmast should be exactly amidships, but the so-called

"William Rex" model of a year later and Allard's section of a Dutch 3-decker of the same period, both show it about 1/20 of the length between perpendiculars further aft. This is a trifle more than the proportion in Witsen's ship or in the Dutch model of 1665 in the Hohenzollern Museum in Berlin (Plate 11), in which it works out to about 1/22 of the length abaft the middle point. Probably, therefore, this position, about 1/20 to 1/25 of the length abaft the middle point between stem and sternpost was normal in Dutch ships for a long time.

For other countries there is not so much information. The *Couronne* of 1638, the French reply to the famous *Sovereign of the Seas,* seems to have had her mainmast just abaft the middle point and the *Royal Louis* model of 1692, in the Louvre, shows it about 1/20 of the length abaft the middle. In Furttenbach's German book of 1629, the fore side of the mainmast is just abaft the middle point between stem and sternpost (Plate 4). Against this Dassié, writing of French naval architecture in 1677, shows the mast about its own diameter *before* the middle point. I doubt if this is correct. I fancy it would be safe to look on a point half way between the stem and sternpost as the forward limit for foreign ships and a point about 1/20 of the length further aft as marking the after limit.

The foremast changed its position very decidedly in the course of the 17th century. The change was not quite as great as appears at first sight, because it is exaggerated by the reduction in the rake of the stem. The foremast might stay at the same distance from the stemhead and yet seem to move aft because of the gradual extension of the keel forward. Still, there is no doubt that it did move aft. The well-known engraving of the

Sovereign, of 1637 (Plate 7), shows it so close to the
stem-head that it must have met the stem very little
below the waterline.   Plans of 1670 and thereabouts
show the foremast roughly half way between the end of
the keel and the stem-head, a trifle further aft in the
bigger ships (Plates 12 and 13).   By 1720, with the
shortening of the fore rake, the foremast, without moving further from the stem, came rather less than ⅓ of
the way out from the end of the keel to the stem-head.
If we put it ⅔ of the way out along the stem in 1630,
half way in 1660, ⅓ of the way in 1700 and rather less
after that, we shall not be far wrong.

Dutch fashions followed much the same course.   An
engraving of a French ship built in Holland in 1626
(Plate 6), shows the foremast quite as far forward as in
the *Sovereign*.   Witsen speaks of the foremast as being
stepped 1/11 of the ship's length abaft the stem-head,
but shows it in his plan rather more than 1/9; this
seems to indicate that he was preparing his book in a
time of change.   With the *"William Rex"* model of 1698
and Allard's section of a 3-decker of a year or two earlier,
the proportion rises to ⅛ or 2/15.   It must, by the way,
be noted that Dutch ships had usually much more upright stems than English, so that a position of the foremast which would have brought it on to the stem in an
English ship might leave it well on the keel in a Dutchman.

No doubt other foreign nations did the same as the
Dutch and English.   Furttenbach, in 1629, shows the
foremast more than half way out along the stem; in fact,
he shows it stepped on the lower deck, as it probably was
before it began to be an important mast at all (Plate 4).
Dassié in 1677 and the *Royal Louis* model of 1692, agree

in putting the foremast about 1/9 of the length abaft the stem-head. These two examples show very well how the keel grew forward underneath the mast, for the earlier ship has the mast very distinctly above the stem, while the other has it exactly above the junction of the stem and keel.

When we come to the mizzen, a quotation from Miller's book of 1655 may serve to show the difficulties. "Now in placing your missen-mast, your judgment must be better there, then about any mast: because there is no just Rule to be given, but only your eye must be your best Rule." To make things worse there is the fact that large ships in the first quarter of the 17th century usually had two mizzens. Probably few people will be bold enough to attempt a model of a big ship of this date; still, the double mizzen cannot be altogether ignored.

There are a few good authorities for the appearance of early 17th century ships with two mizzens. There is a plan in a manuscript in the Pepysian Library at Cambridge, England; personally I believe this to represent a Mediterranean vessel of about 1610, though others well able to judge think it is an English ship of ten or twenty years earlier. There is a fine print of a Danish ship of uncertain date but presumably between 1600 and 1630 (Plate 5). There are some paintings by Vroom, particularly those of Houtman's return from the East Indies and of the arrival of the English *Prince Royal* at Flushing, in 1613. There is also an ivory model of 1620 at Dresden.

These representations differ widely. The Pepysian plan shows the after or "bonaventure" mizzen just about over the top of the sternpost and the main mizzen nearly half way from there to the mainmast. The Danish print has the after mizzen, if anything, further aft still and the main mizzen very much nearer to it than to the mainmast. This ship, by the way, has her mainmast very far aft and her foremast very far forward. The German model also has the bonaventure mast as far aft as it can possibly go, but its main mizzen is not nearly so far aft as in the Dane. Vroom, on the other hand, puts his after mizzens well inboard.

How late one should go on fitting two mizzens I do not know. It would almost certainly be safe to do so up to 1620 and I think it would be wrong to do so after 1630, but I will not pretend to be sure. The *Sovereign* of 1637 and the *Couronne* of 1638 both had single mizzens in spite of their great size. So, too, had the French ships built in Holland in 1626. These were not such large ships, but they were quite big enough to have had two mizzens in the old days. It may be mentioned that a list of masts and yards for the whole English fleet, in 1640, shows no sign of the survival of the second mizzen.

As far as one can judge from the print, the *Sovereign* had her mizzen nearly as far from the taffrail as it was from the mainmast. Under the Commonwealth the mizzen moved aft a little. In a model of mine, that can hardly be later than 1660 and may be earlier, the mizzen is placed exactly 2/5 of the way from the taffrail to the mainmast. In Deane's plans of 1670, the proportion varies between 2/5 and 3/7 (Plates 12 and 13). On the other hand, the model of the *Prince,* of the same date, a ship built by Deane's rival Pett, has its mizzen almost exactly half way between the mainmast and the taffrail. The *St George* model of 1701, now in the collection of Col. H. H. Rogers, has its mizzen very little more than ⅓ of the way from the taffrail to the mainmast, while plans of 1719 show it a little less than half way; about 8/17 or something of that sort.

As in the case of the mainmast, it is possible to give some sort of limits between which the mizzen ought to be stepped, but that is all. One can say fairly safely that it ought to be not less than ⅓ or more than half way from the taffrail to the middle of the mainmast. Whether there was any system in its movements is very doubtful; they seem to have depended on individual fancy rather than on any gradual change of fashion.

Dutch mizzens moved almost as irregularly as English, but they tended on the whole to be stepped rather further forward. The Dutch-built Frenchman of 1626 (Plate 6), had her mizzen about half way from the taffrail to the mainmast, while the *Prins Willem* model of 1651, has hers little more than ⅓ way. This suggests that the mizzen began by moving aft as it did in English ships. After this it settled down somewhere about half way; sometimes it was less, as in the *"William Rex"* model of 1698 or in the model of about 1665 in the Scheepvaart Museum in Amsterdam; sometimes it was distinctly more, as in my own model of a Dutch 3-decker of about 1690 or in the Berlin model of 1665 (Plate 11); sometimes it was exactly half way, as in Allard's section of a Dutch 3-decker. On the whole, for the period 1660-1700, half way between the taffrail and the mainmast is the safest rule.

At first, French ships seem to have carried their mizzens rather far aft. In the *Couronne* of 1638, the mizzen was 50 ft. from the mainmast and 36 ft. from the stern; this was certainly much further aft than in her English contemporary the *Sovereign*. After this, French shipbuilding underwent an eclipse until 1670 or thereabouts. A drawing of the early years of the revival shows the mizzen about 5/11 of the way from the taffrail to the mainmast. Dassié (1677) puts it at 4/9 and the *Royal Louis* model of 1692 has it very nearly half way — 16/33 to be precise. In the Danish *Norske Löve* model, made in 1654 but representing an old ship, the mizzen is just before the half-way point.

Turning to the bowsprit we find a new difficulty. So far we have been dealing with one dimension only. The masts were all in the same plane as the stem and stern-post and it is only a matter of fixing their fore-and-aft positions in that plane. The bowsprit was not always in that plane, at least not in English ships. For the greater part of the 17th century it was stepped to one side of the stem and the foremast — always, I think, the starboard side. Exactly when it moved to the central position on top of the stem-head is hard to say. Probably 1675 would not be far wrong for big ships. The model of the *Prince* of 1670, in South Kensington Museum (one of the most satisfactorily identified of 17th century models), has its bowsprit beside the stem. On the other hand, the model in the New York Yacht Club, apparently an early design for the ships of 1677, has the bowsprit central. Drawings do not help as much as they might, because the ship must be named or dated and must be drawn from the right point of view — requirements which are not often satisfied at the same time. Deane's plans of 1670 are rather vague; some have the bowsprit clearly to one side and some are uncertain. Probably the change came in the smaller ships first and probably it was complete by 1675; that is as definite as I dare to be.

The sideways position of the bowsprit was closely re-

lated to the design of the bow and the resulting position
of the bowsprit in an up-and-down direction. We will
consider big ships first. In the *Prince Royal* of 1610,
the stem-head rose about as high as the middle-deck
guns and between it and the beakhead bulkhead there
was a deck about the same height as the middle deck or
a little higher. The bowsprit was well above this deck
and entered the ship through the bulkhead rather above
the level of the middle-deck guns. As far as the stem
was concerned there was nothing to prevent the bowsprit from being stepped centrally; it was only the fact
that its heel went past the foremast that made it necessary to put it to one side. With the *Sovereign,* in 1637,
the stem-head rose a little and at the same time the bowsprit was lowered; it passed close beside the stem-head
and went into the ship just about where the beakhead
bulkhead met the prow deck, which may have been a
foot or two above the middle deck (Plate 7).

Such a design made it possible for both upper-deck and
middle-deck guns to fire directly forward through ports
in the bulkhead. In spite of the gradual shortening and
raising of the head, the essential features of this design
remained the same till about 1670. Deane's plans of
that year show the 1st-Rate with a bulkhead deep enough
for middle-deck guns to fire forward. On the other hand,
the model of Pett's *Prince,* of 1670, has the prow deck
raised enough to make this impossible. If I am right in
believing the New York Yacht Club model to date from
about 1676, it must be one of the last examples of the
old fashion.

With these two changes accomplished, the bowsprit
central and the beakhead bulkhead stopping above the
level of the middle-deck ports, the method of stepping

the bowsprit became standardised. The prow deck was either level with the upper deck or a little below, and the bowsprit passed into the ship through this piece of deck, close to the bulkhead when the prow deck was dropped and close to the stem when it was on a level with the upper deck.

In smaller ships the change to a centrally stepped bowsprit may perhaps have taken place sooner, though Deane's detailed design of 1670 certainly has it to one side. In them the prow deck was usually a foot or two above the level of the upper deck, but occasionally — for instance, in some of Deane's plans — it was simply an extension of the upper deck. The variation in level had the same effect as in bigger ships in determining how far aft the bowsprit would pass into the ship.

When the bowsprit was central there were sometimes two heavy, upright timbers on either side of it just abaft the stem. These were at first carved into human heads, but later they were left plain. They were not always fitted. A drawing of the *Britannia*, of 1682, shows them and the model of that ship as rebuilt in 1700 also has them; but the *St George* model, of a year later, has none. In the 18th century they usually had a cross-piece between them, shaped to fit the upper side of the bowsprit.

Dutch ships had their bows differently designed. In them the beakhead bulkhead was usually further aft and the stem-head less prominent. The bowsprit was stepped on top of the stem and entered the ship as far forward as possible. The Dutch-built French ships of 1626 may have had their bowsprits beside the stem, but I think not. Certainly from 1650 onwards models and drawings show bowsprits stepped centrally. For other countries there is not so much evidence and what there is is rather contradictory. An early 17th century French head, 1625 or thereabouts, shows the bowsprit on top of the stem and apparently the same is the case in the big Danish ship of about the same date in the print already mentioned. Against this, Furttenbach's ship, probably drawn from a model, shows the bowsprit beside the stem and the beautiful ivory model of the Danish *Norske Löve*, of 1634, has it in the same position. This model was not made till 1654 and does not agree very well with the known dimensions of the ship, but it is perhaps worth mentioning that she was built by a Scottish builder who may have been following English practice. Towards the end of the 17th century there is no doubt that all bowsprits, English and foreign, were on the middle line.

II. *Their Angles*

THE "rake" of the masts and the "steeve" of the bowsprit are important matters. Here, again, things may be settled beforehand by the build of the model, though a little variation can be managed by paring down one side of the spar in its inboard portion or even (in extreme cases) by making a spar with a kink in it.

As a matter of fact, the rake of the masts is a very uncertain matter. Normally the foremast was vertical, the mainmast raked aft a little and the mizzen a little more. The foremast might even rake forward very slightly. This effect is very well shown in the print of the *Sovereign of the Seas* (Plate 7). Exact figures are difficult to give; photographs of models are of very little help because of the probability that the camera is off the straight; even actual contemporary rigging on a model may be deceptive, because the masts may have warped or have been pulled crooked by the shrouds or stays.

Again, the matter is complicated by the question of the trim of the ship. Most ships trimmed by the stern and models usually look best that way; naturally this affects the look of the masts. Deane (1670) shows foremast and mainmast about vertical and the mizzen raking aft about 1 in 16; this is with the keel horizontal (Plates 12 and 13). A plan of the *Prince George*, of 1723, has the foremast at right angles to the keel, the mainmast raking aft about 1 in 25 and the mizzen about 1 in 20. Some Dutch ships had more raking masts. The plans of the *"William Rex,"* of 1698, show the foremast raking aft about 1 in 28, the mainmast 1 in 16 and the mizzen 1 in 20. The Berlin model of 1665 is an extreme case; her mainmast rakes aft nearly 1 in 12 and her mizzen even more (Plate 11).

The angle of the bowsprit is similarly defined by the build of the model, in particular by the height of the figurehead. In my experience the difficulty is usually to keep it down enough. In a general way it may be said that the bowsprit rose as time went on — within limits. In the 16th century it had sloped steeply upward, but with the coming of long, low beakheads it took up a position much more nearly horizontal. As far as one can judge from the print, the *Sovereign's* bowsprit rose at an angle of about 24°. In the Deane's plans the angle is 30°. Rigging plans of 1719 show an angle of 36° and the *Prince George*, of 1723, is about the same. In foreign ships, the print of a Dutch-built Frenchman, of 1626, shows an angle of about 20°, the *Prins Willem* model of 1651, gives about 28°, the Swedish *Amarant* model of 1653, 33° and Dutch models of about 1665, 40°. This was probably about the maximum, for the *"William Rex"* of 1698 and Allard's section of a Dutch 3-

decker of the same period, agree in showing only about 35°. This seems also to have been the normal angle for French ships at the end of the 17th century.

III. Their Lengths

WHEN once the positions and angles of the masts are settled, one can get on to a consideration of their lengths. The first measurement, on which everything else depends, is the length of the mainmast. This was just less than 2½ times the Beam in large English ships and might be as much as three times the Beam in small ships. Manwayring, in about 1623, says it should be 12/5 of the Beam or 2.4 B. and the known figures for both the *Bear,* in 1618, and the *Sovereign,* in 1640, work out to 2.43 B. Miller (1655) gives 2.5 B. as the proper proportion, while the new 70-gun ships of 1678 had a value of 2.38 B. When the Beam began to be very much increased, as happened soon after 1700, the mast became rather shorter in comparison; the value for the *Prince George,* a 90-gun ship of 1723, was 2.25 B. On the other hand, the class of *Lion's Whelps,* small ships of 1627, had had mainmasts very nearly three times their Beam.

Foreign ships observed very much the same proportion. The French *Couronne,* of 1638, had a mainmast only 2.15 times her Beam; but she was an exceptional ship. Dassié, in 1677, makes the proportion for the *Victorieux,* 2.44. Witsen, writing of Dutch ships in 1671, says the mast ought to be twice the sum of the Beam and the Depth in Hold. In a normal Dutch ship the Depth was about 2/5 B. so that his value would be equivalent to 2.8. It is doubtful if this proportion was ever used for ships of any size. Even Witsen, himself, makes the mast of his typical ship 80 ft. when it should be 84 ft. by the formula he gives. It must also be re-membered that Dutch ships measured their Beam in-side the planking, whereas English ships were measured outside. Allowing for this, the proportion in Witsen's ship, a small 3rd-Rate, according to English ideas, would be about 2.65 B. In one case, the model of the 50-gun *Amarant,* of 1654, in Stockholm, the mainmast is almost exactly in accordance with Witsen's formula. Against this, the Berlin model of a 70-gun Dutch ship, of 1665, has a mainmast only about 2.2 times her Beam. Span-ish ships had mainmasts of 2⅔ the Beam (inside plank-ing) in the early part of the 17th century and about 2½ B. after 1670. On the whole, for 3-deckers and 2-deckers, both English and foreign, 2½ Beams is about reasonable for the mainmast all through the 17th cen-tury. For ships of the early 18th century, the propor-tion should be dropped to about 2¼.

Models are not always strictly to scale and in a case of doubt it may be best to take the length rather than the beam as a guide. Looked at in this way it can be said that the mainmast ought to be from 3/5 to ⅝ of the length from stem to sternpost.

Another point that needs consideration is how the mast is stepped. In some models there is a proper step made to scale, but more often the foot of the mast goes right down to the floor timbers, while in some cases, par-ticularly in block or dug-out models, the mast cannot go home far enough. It is therefore necessary to allow for the depth of an average step, so as to get the top of the mast at the right height above the top of the keel; such a step might raise the mast as much as four feet in big ships and perhaps two feet in small vessels.

This uncertainty as to the stepping of the masts makes

actual lengths for the foremast and mizzen of little value. Particularly is this the case with the mizzen, because it was sometimes stepped in the hold at an uncertain height above the keel and sometimes on the lower deck. It is best, therefore, to make the mainmast first (or to draw it on a plan) and to find the lengths of the foremast and mizzen by getting their caps at the right height compared with that of the mainmast.

To do this satisfactorily one must first settle the length of the main masthead, from the lower side of the trestle-trees to the top of the mast. This length was a steadily growing fraction of the total length of the mast. In a plan of about 1600, the masthead is about 1/15 of the mast; by 1670 it was 1/9, in 1700, ⅛ and in 1723, 2/15.

The foremast gradually became more and more nearly equal to the mainmast in length. For instance, Manwayring, in 1623, says it should be 4/5 M.; Miller, in 1655, says 8/9; and Battine, in 1684, says 9/10. The greater part of this increase was caused by stepping it further aft, so that its step moved by degrees down the curve of the stem. Still, its cap did rise as compared with that of the mainmast. About 1600 it was level with the lower side of the main trestle-trees; by 1670 it was about half way up the main masthead; in 1723 it was ⅔ of the way up.

The cap of the mizzen came about half way up the fore masthead. To make this information of value one must have some idea of the length of the fore masthead as compared with the main. Take it as ⅘ in 1620, 9/10 in 1670, and 11/12 in 1720 and one will not be far wrong. For the mizzen masthead take ⅗ or ⅔ of the main.

Some figures may be given as an example. Suppose

a ship of 1670 with a beam of 40 feet. Her mainmast will be 100 ft. long and will rise about 103½ ft. above the top of the keel. The masthead will be 11 ft. and the cap of the foremast will thus come 103½ — 5½ = 98 ft. above the top of the keel. Its masthead will be 10 ft. and this will put the cap of the mizzenmast 98 — 5 = 93 ft. above the keel; 7 feet will represent the masthead of the mizzen.

This same relation of the three mastheads was about normal for foreign ships as well as English. Dutch ships sometimes, but by no means always, had the foremast and particularly the mizzen rather longer, so as to bring the three tops (using the word in the technical sense of the platforms on the trestle-trees) almost into line. Van Yk (1697) says that this should be so, but the model of the *William Rex,*" of the same date, shows practically the English system. On the other hand, the model of the *Prins Willem*, of 1651, has the three tops very nearly in line. French ships tended in the other direction and had rather short mizzens with the cap not higher than the main top; their foremasts were about on the English standard, but shorter rather than higher. Danes and Russians, as far as I can judge, had short foremasts and mizzens with their caps about level with the main top. Spanish drawings of 1691 show rather long foremasts and short mizzens.

In the length of the mastheads there was not much difference between English and foreign ships, but, if anything, foreign mastheads were longer. Two Dutch models of about 1665 show mastheads rather more than ⅛ of the mast and the *William Rex,*" of 1698, has them about 1/7. No doubt they were shorter in the first half of the 17th century; the *Prins Willem* of 1651 has mast-

heads less than ⅛ of the masts. Van Yk (1697) gives
1/10, but is careful to say that this is a minimum. In
the French *Royal Louis,* of 1692, the mastheads are ⅛.

For the bowsprit it is again not much use to give mere
figures of length because of the difficulty in knowing how
far inboard its heel will go in any particular case. The
important point is to know how far it should project
beyond the stem-head. In the early years of the 17th
century, when the bowsprit was as long as the foremast
and when its heel went only a little way abaft a foremast
that was stepped very far forward, it must have had
about ¾ of its length outboard. Even in Miller's plans
(1655), ⅔ of the bowsprit is before the stem and the
whole bowsprit is equal to the foremast of 8/9 of the
mainmast (Plate 9); the projection of the bowsprit is
thus 16/27 or practically ⅗ of the length of the mainmast. Dean's plans of 1670 show less projection; in the
1st-Rate it is only just half the length of the mainmast.
The same proportion holds good for a 50-gun ship of
about 1700 from the Cuckfield collection, now the prop-
erty of Col. H. H. Rogers, but the bowsprit of the *St
George,* a 90-gun ship of the same period, has a slightly
longer projection, about .54 of the mainmast. In the
Prince George, of 1723, another 90, the proportion of
half the mainmast is exactly followed.

Foreign bowsprits were usually shorter. In the Dutch
"*William Rex*" and the French *Royal Louis,* which are
roughly contemporary with the *St George,* the projection
of the bowsprit is respectively about 3/7 and 4/9 of the
length of the mainmast. In Dutch models of about 1665,
rather earlier than Deane's plans, it is about 7/15. The
Prins Willem, of 1651, agrees roughly with Miller's proportion of ⅗. The Danish and Swedish models of 1654,

the *Norske Löve* and *Amarant,* differ very widely in this respect. The Danish ship has a projection of very nearly ⅔ of the mainmast, while the Swede has less than ½. It must, however, be remembered that the *Norske Löve* was twenty years old when the model was made.

IV. Their Thickness

Unless there is something in the model to prevent this, the thickness of the masts has to be determined from their length. Speaking generally, a diameter at the deck of one inch for every three feet of the length was about the normal proportion for both English and foreign ships. Various allowances were made; for instance, Sutherland, writing in 1711, explains that a 9 inch Gothenburg tree was equal to one of 10½ inches from Riga or 12 inches from New England. I am sorry to have to mention this, but perhaps the fact that there is no reference to a home-grown English tree may make the statement less insulting. Again, a single-stick mast, when it could be obtained, might be thinner than a "made" mast; still, the proportion of one inch to a yard for big ships and perhaps ¾ in. for small, is about right. If the length of the foremast and mizzen cannot be got directly, make the thickness of the foremast about 9/10 of the main — rather less for the early part of the 17th century and rather more after 1700. The mizzen should be about ⅗ of the mainmast or rather less and the bowsprit at the stem should be as thick as the foremast or a trifle thicker.

Then comes the question of the amount of taper on these masts. According to Keltridge and Battine, who wrote manuscripts on shipbuilding and equipment about 1680, the fore and mainmasts should have their extreme heads ⅔ of their diameter at the deck. Keltridge adds to this that the diameter at the "hounds," just below the trestle-trees, should be ¾ of the maximum. From there down to the deck, the taper should be an arc of a circle; in other words, the taper should be imperceptible at the deck and should gradually get steeper towards the top.

Van Yk, in his Dutch book of 1697, says that the diameter beneath the hounds should be ⅘ of the maximum and that the mast should be a true cylinder from the deck upwards to a point ⅕ of its length below the hounds; at the same time he mentions that the more general rule was to make the diameter at the hounds ¾ of the maximum. Keltridge and Van Yk agree that the bowsprit should taper at its end to half its diameter at the stem, but the former makes the taper follow an arc of a circle all the way, whereas Van Yk prefers to leave a short, cylindrical portion both inboard and outboard of the stem-head. In a model, the difference would be negligible. The mizzen should taper to half its maximum diameter, with a diameter of ¾ of the maximum at the hounds.

V. Their Construction

No model maker is likely to want to go in for such refinement as building up an exact miniature of a "made" mast. It ought to satisfy all reasonable requirements if the mast, after being painted and varnished, looks right from the outside.

Masts, like most other things, varied according to date and country. The exact date and nature of the various changes are not easy to decide. Drawings seldom show enough detail to help; models are not over trustworthy and often have their mastheads so much obscured by rigging that it is difficult to make out what they are really like. The following description is intended to refer to English masts of the end of the 17th century and the beginning of the 18th. Such differences in the practice of earlier dates and of other countries, as I have been able to note, will be mentioned later.

Start, then, by cutting the mast the right length and by making it perfectly round from end to end and tapered as already laid down. The diameter at the bottom, by the way, should be about ⅔ of that at the deck level. Whether there should be any sort of tenon at the foot, and if so what its shape should be, depends entirely on how the step is made, if there be one. Normally it should be a square almost as big as can be cut from the circular section and with two sides running fore and aft.

Mark off the length of the masthead, found as already explained, and also the same length less an amount equal to half the diameter of the mast at the cap. These two marks will give the levels of the lower and upper edges of the trestle-trees. From the top of the mast to the upper mark, cut the mast-

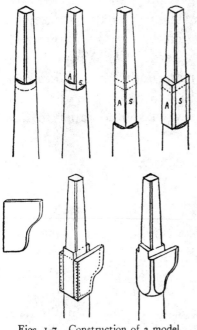

Figs. 1-7. Construction of a model masthead

head square, leaving the square a bit bigger than the true inscribed square, so that its corners are just blunted by the remains of the original rounding (Fig. 1).   Continue two opposite sides of this squared portion down as far as the lower line, with the same amount of taper as before, and mark these two sides as the port and starboard sides of the mast (Fig. 2).   From the lower line mark off, downwards, a distance equal to half its distance from the top of the mast and continue the squared portion downwards as far as this line, with parallel cuts without taper; this portion will be the least trifle bigger athwartships than fore and aft (Fig. 3). Mark the levels of the top and bottom of the trestle-trees in again.   Pad out the fore and after sides of the mast from the bottom of the parallel cuts, as far as the upper side of the trestle-trees, with two strips of wood exactly the same width as the parallel portion is athwartships and just thick enough to come flush with the round part of the mast at the middle of their lower ends (Fig. 4). This will make the section of this part of the mast into a rectangle with its two long sides running fore and aft. Take two more pieces, long enought to reach up to the *lower* side of the trestle-trees, of a thickness equal to half the thwartship measurement of the rectangular portion, just mentioned, and a width equal to twice its fore and aft measurement. Shape them as shown in Fig. 5 and fit them to the mast with their straight sides flush with the after side of the rectangular portion (Fig. 6). Ease off corners and edges as indicated, so that this structure appears to grow gradually out of the round of the mast (Fig. 7).

Dutch ships, towards the end of the 17th century, still had their mastheads left round, as had probably been the case everywhere at the beginning of the century. This left less room for the shrouds between the masthead and the heel of the topmast and made it necessary

to pad out the fore side of the lower mast more than was
the case with a square masthead. Van Yk, whose book

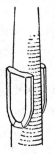

was published in 1697, shows the part of the
mast just below the trestle-trees as roughly
square in section, but says it might well have
its edges taken off to make it octagonal. He
shows no "bibs," as the projections before the
mast were called. The *"William Rex"* model
shows bibs, but still has the round mastheads.
Earlier Dutch masts seem to have been left
round everywhere and then to have been flattened enough on the sides to allow of the attachment of two large cheeks which projected

Fig. 8.
Cheeks of a
Dutch
seventeenth-
century mast

a little forward and aft (Fig. 8). Room for the shrouds
was secured by fitting a crosspiece between the trestle-
trees to keep the heel of the topmast forward.

English masts must have been somewhat similar to
this at one time. In the early part of the 17th century,

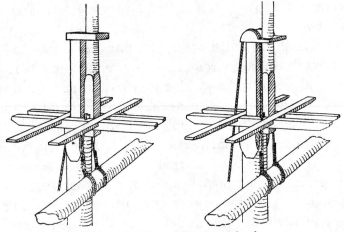

Fig. 9. English and Dutch mastheads

one of the chief differences between English and Dutch
rigging was that the "ties," the double rope which car-

ried the weight of the yard, went up over the cap in Dutch ships, but passed through "hounds" in the cheeks of the mast in English ships (Fig. 9). These cheeks had, therefore, to be of a shape and size suitable for admitting a large sheave; there can hardly have been anything in the nature of a bib attached to them. When the double ties and single halliard were superseded by double "jeers" working in blocks slung from the masthead, the cheeks would no longer require hounds in them and would have only the one duty of supporting the trestle-trees.

This substitution of jeers for ties and halliards was, no doubt, a gradual process. As far back as 1625, at least, jeers of some sort were in use as auxiliaries to the ties. As the century went on the jeers became more elaborate and more important till they were able to take over the whole work of hoisting the yard. This change will be discussed in detail under the head of "Running Rigging." At the moment it will be enough to note that in 1655 some of the larger new ships had jeers only and that in 1675, Keltridge makes no mention at all of ties and halliards.

The French, like the Dutch, kept round mastheads after they had disappeared in England. They also followed the Dutch practice of hoisting the lower yards by means of ties passing over the caps. Probably the construction of their masts was very like the Dutch. The *Royal Louis* model of 1692 has what may be described as the English method of construction modified to suit a round masthead. This means that the trestle-trees are necessarily further apart than would be the case on an English mast of the same thickness and this, in turn, means that the thickening of the heel of the topmast must be greater than in an English ship.

The mizzen mast was in some ways more like a top-mast than one of the other lower masts. It never needed hounds in its cheeks, even if it had cheeks worth mentioning at all. Of course it must always have had some kind of shoulder to carry the trestle-trees, but in the days of small mizzen topmasts the mizzen trestle-trees would not have required any very elaborate support. What the mizzen did have — in the early part of the 17th century — was a single sheave in the mast itself just below the trestle-trees. Through this went the tie, from aft forward, with halliards on the fore end. There was also a jeer, at least as early as 1625, and this jeer, like those on the fore and main, gradually superseded the tie and halliards. Probably the change began about 1650 and was complete before 1670. I think it would be quite reasonable to omit the sheave in the mizzen mast in any ship after 1655, though there must have been survivals of this method of hoisting the mizzen yard for another ten years or so.

Dutch ships, which kept the tie and halliard method of hoisting their fore and main yards, may have kept it also for the mizzen, a little later than English ships. Certainly Witsen, whose book was printed in 1671, shows a mizzen "knight" or upright timber, with sheaves in it, before the mast and this suggests a tie and halliards. Still, there is plenty of evidence that Witsen was old-fashioned and Dutch models of 1665 have mizzen jeers in the English fashion. The same is the case with French ships of 1670 onwards. One model, which does show the tie and halliard, is the Danish *Norske Löve* (Plate 8). Unfortunately it is difficult to know how far this beautiful ivory model is a portrait of the ship as built in 1634 and how far a model of what a Danish ship was like in 1654, when the model was finished. However, in

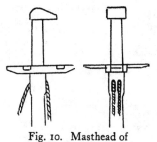

view of the fact that the ship was built by a Scotsman, it is worth noting that she combines the Dutch form of cap on her fore and mainmasts with the English method of taking the ties through double hounds below the trestle-trees (Fig. 10).

Fig. 10. Masthead of the *Norske Löve* model

Of the bowsprit there is little to be said at this stage. The only question is whether its end should be cut off square or bevelled so as to be at right angles to the waterline. This depends mainly on how far out the spritsail topmast is to be stepped. If it is to stand with its heel actually on the bowsprit (Fig. 11), there is no need to cut the bowsprit at an angle; but if the spritsail topmast is to stand clear of the bowsprit with its supporting knee flush with the bowsprit end (Fig. 12), the bowsprit should then be cut at an angle.

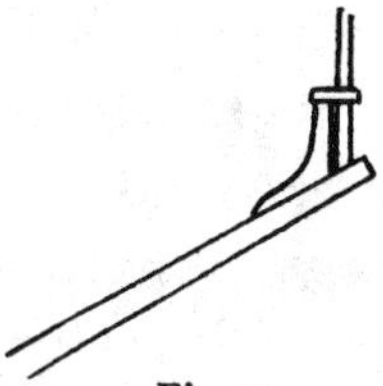

Fig. 11.
Spritsail topmast on the bowsprit-end

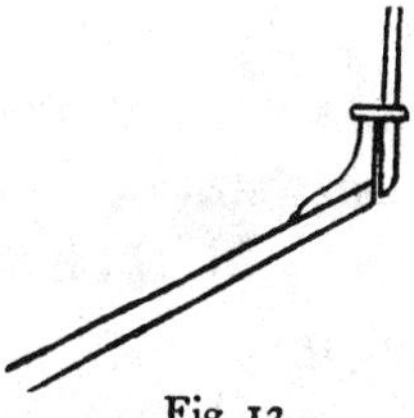

Fig. 12.
Spritsail topmast beyond the bowsprit-end

Generally speaking, English ships, up to about 1670 or 1675, seem to have had their spritsail topmasts on the bowsprit; after that they were stepped further forward with their heels beyond the bowsprit end. Dutch ships kept the spritsail topmast above the bowsprit, up to a later date; it is still there in the ship which illustrates a book of 1702. They did, however, cut the end of the bowsprit at an angle. The French, after their revival as a shipbuilding nation, seem to have started by having the

spritsail topmast beyond the bowsprit and then to have
returned to the method of stepping it actually on the
bowsprit. Altogether there is very little certainty in the
matter. Probably it would be best to step the spritsail
topmast on the bowsprit in ships of any country up to
1670 and to keep it there up to 1700 or later for most
ships other than English.

The three lower masts have to have their tops cut to
take the caps. This is done by cutting a square tenon
rather smaller than the full inscribed square. Sometimes this tenon was hexagonal or even pentagonal, but it
is best and simplest to make it square in a model. The
only question is how deep it should be and this, of course,
depends on the depth of the cap which is to fit on it.
Roughly speaking, the depth of an English style cap was
1/9 of the length of the masthead and that of a foreign
cap, $\frac{1}{5}$. With foreign caps the extreme top of the mast
was cut curved to correspond with the curve of the cap.
This should be left till the cap is actually made and fitted. With English caps the mast sometimes, perhaps
usually, projected two or three inches above the cap. On
a small-scale model this will be a matter of 1/16 in. or
something of that sort.

The mainmast, foremast and bowsprit were usually
"woolded"; that is to say, they were strengthened by being bound round with rope, at intervals. The number
of these wooldings was very variable. The engraving of
the *Sovereign* shows about fifteen on the mainmast,
whereas the *St George* model of 1701 has only six. At
first sight it looks as if the number became less as
the years went on; perhaps there may be something in
the idea, but I would not like to be sure of it. Probably
eight to ten on the mainmast and one or two fewer on

the foremast will be a fair allowance. Dutch ships had
fewer wooldings; five or six will be enough for them.

The wooldings were usually evenly spaced with the
uppermost about half the height of the masthead, or a
little more, below the trestle-trees and the bottom one
two or three feet above the deck. In the *St George* model, the depth of each is rather more than half the diameter of the mast. When there were very few, as in Dutch
ships, the depth of each was greater. In some cases, for
instance, in the plan of the *Prince George,* the upper
wooldings are closer together than those below. The line
used should correspond to about three-inch rope in the
real ship—less, in a small vessel. It is a good thing to put
a little glue of some sort on the mast before winding the

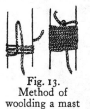

Fig. 13.
Method of
woolding a mast

wooling. Then make a loop at the end of
the line and wind over it with the end sticking out; put the other end through the loop
and pull till it disappears beneath the last
few turns; hammer down the ridge, if it is too
conspicuous, and cut off the ends (Fig. 13).

Close above and below each woolding there was usually a hoop, of a depth somewhere about ⅛ of that of the
woolding itself. Such hoops can be made very success-
fully of brown paper and glue; and when thoroughly
set they can be trimmed up and sandpapered. Hoops
and wooldings can then be painted black.

The bowsprit was not always woolded. If this is done,
there should be one woolding between the stem-head and
the place where the gammoning will come, one a distance corresponding to ten feet or so from the end and
three or four in between. The mizzen should not be
woolded.

CHAPTER II

Trestle-Trees, Cross-Trees, Tops and Caps

AT EACH masthead, and at the bowsprit end as well, in the days of spritsail topmasts, there was a structure consisting of trestle-trees, cross-trees, top and cap; the whole combination being needed to support the topmast and to spread the topmast shrouds. The topmast had its heel between the trestle-trees, which ran fore and aft on each side of the lower mast just above the cheeks. It also passed through the cap, which sat on the extreme top of the lower mast.

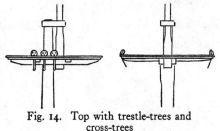

Fig. 14. Top with trestle-trees and cross-trees

The topmast shrouds came to deadeyes at the edge of the top, which was a platform resting on the trestle-trees and the cross-trees (Fig. 14). The length of the trestle-trees and cross-trees naturally depended on the size of the top and that increased very much during the 17th century. The principle on which they were fitted remained the same; the trestle-trees ran fore and aft and had slots in them for the cross-trees, which ran athwartships as their name implies.

Speaking roughly, the length of the trestle-trees should be about equal to that of the masthead. Keltridge, writing in 1675, says they should be six inches longer and the *St George,* of 1701 (according to the model), had hers about one foot longer on the mainmast. Their depth should be about 1/13 of their length and their width about ⅞ or 9/10 of their depth. Another way of reckoning their length is by its relation to the Beam of the ship. Bushnell, in 1664, says the main trestle-trees should be ⅓ of the Beam. Battine's figures of 1684 work out to .3 B. for large ships and .25 for small, but the *St George* gets above the ⅓ with .36 B.

Van Yk (1697) gives the same rule, ⅓ B., for Dutch ships and makes the depth 1/14 of the length and the width ⅘ of the depth. In the "Dictionnaire de Marine," of 1702, a quotation from Witsen (probably from the very rare second edition) makes the main trestle-trees just less than ⅓ B., their depth 1/15 of their length and their thickness ¾ of their depth. In the Berlin model of 1665, the trestle-trees are just about ⅓ B., but in the "*William Rex*," of 1698, they are longer, about .43 B. These figures, by the way, refer to Beam taken in the Dutch manner, inside the planking.

Usually the trestle-trees were tapered towards the ends. The two middle quarters were left the full depth and the two end quarters sloped off upwards so that the ends were about half the depth of the middle. These are the proportions in the *St George*. The Dutch "*William Rex*," of similar date, has the tapering only on about 1/6 of the length, but much steeper, so that the ends are only ⅕ of the full depth. Occasionally the ends were finished off in a curve; sometimes, for instance, in the Berlin model, the after end was left the full depth and the fore end tapered.

Slots have to be cut in the upper sides of the trestle-trees to take the cross-trees. These are exactly the same width as the trestle-trees and half the depth. To get the slots in the right position it is best to put the trestle-trees temporarily in place on the mast with their middle points

just abreast the fore side of the masthead; then the fore
side of the after cross-tree should come half its own
width abaft the masthead and the after side of the fore
crosstree should come far enough forward to leave the
same amount of room for the heel of the topmast fore
and aft as there is athwartships between the trestle-trees.
The result is that the after cross-tree comes a little further from the middle of the trestle-trees than the fore.   I
think this was the normal arrangement in English ships.

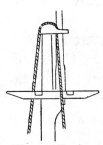

The Dutch often put their after cross-
trees very much further aft, to leave room
for the ties to come down between the
after cross-tree and the mast.   French
ships seem at first to have followed the
same method, but later, both French and
Dutch got over the difficulty in another
way, by putting the after cross-tree right
up against the masthead and bringing the

Fig. 15.   Foreign
masthead and ties

ties down abaft it.   Both the *Royal Louis* and "*William
Rex*," show this arrangement (Fig. 15).

When the trestle-trees have had the places for the
slots marked on them, they can be taken down.   The
cross-trees have to be the same width and half the depth.
Their length is generally a little less than that of the
trestle-trees, but this depends so much on the exact
shape of the top that it is best to get the top made (or a
paper cut to represent it) before the cross-trees are finished.   With this guide the cross-trees can be cut; they
should come as near to the edge of the top as the trestle-
trees do and should then be tapered enough to make
their ends about half the depth of the middle, either by
making their lower side an arc of a circle or by leaving

about ¾ of their length straight and sloping up the ends. The fore and mizzen trestle-trees and cross-trees are made and fitted in the same way. In the *St George*, the fore trestle-trees are about 9/10 of the main and the mizzen, ⅗. Van Yk gives 5/6 and ½ as the proper proportions, but the Berlin model agrees very closely with the figures given for the *St George*. Other models, such as the French *Royal Louis*, of 1692, and the Swedish *Amarant*, of 1654, have the fore trestle-trees about 9/10 of the main and the mizzen just more than ½.

Fitting trestle-trees and cross-trees at the end of the bowsprit is rather a different matter. Here there is no masthead and something has to be provided to take its place. This is done by a knee with one part fixed to the upper side of the bowsprit and the other part vertical. Sometimes the bowsprit was flattened very slightly where the knee was to be secured. The question of how the spritsail topmast is to be carried has been discussed already in the description of the bowsprit. Naturally it governs the position of the knee. If the topmast is to go beyond the bowsprit end, the knee goes out flush with the end of the bowsprit (Fig. 12) ; if it is to be stepped above the bowsprit the knee must be a little inboard (Fig. 11). How much inboard is hard to say, but probably an amount corresponding to two or three feet in the real ship will be about right. The vertical part of the knee should be about ⅖ of the main masthead in length, if the spritsail topmast is to be beyond the end of the bowsprit, and about ½ if it is to be inboard; the other part should be the same length or longer. In width the knee should be about half the main masthead and its upper part should be squared and tapered like a masthead and cut for a cap of proportionate size.

To this knee the trestle-trees are secured with the
cross-trees let into them as usual (Fig. 16).
In size the trestle-trees should be about
one-half of those on the mainmast. Sometimes the construction was more complicated, sometimes — at any rate in models
— it was simpler; the method described
was, I think, the normal practice.

Fig. 16. Spritsail
top and knee

Tops are a difficult subject. Between
1660, say, and 1700, there is not much to worry about; at
least it is easy enough to make something that looks
satisfactory. Before and after these dates the difficulties are of two quite different kinds. For the early years
of the 17th century the question is, how tops were made
and what they looked like. For the beginning of the
18th century it is a matter of knowing the exact date at
which to introduce a perfectly simple modification; the
making of the after side of the tops square.

Taking this last matter first, I must admit I do not
know. I have little doubt that all tops were round (us-

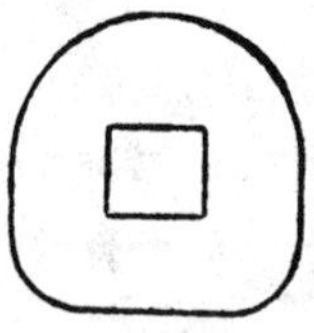

Fig. 17. Probable
shape of top about
1710

ing the term to include an ellipse as well as
a circle) in 1700 and I think that by 1720
they were usually square on their after
sides. I imagine that there was an intermediate stage in which the after side of
the top might be described either as an
ellipse with flattened sides and ends or as
a rectangle with blunted corners (Fig. 17). There are
quite a number of changes in hulls and rigging that
came in at some vague date about 1710 and this is one
of them. There is a drawing of the Dutch *Gertruda*, of
1720, with very definite square tops (Plate 23) and the
same is the case in the model of the *Ary*, of 1725; the

Valkenisse, of 1717, a similar ship, also had square tops, if those belonging to Mr. Collins' model of this ship are contemporary. On the other hand, a model of the *Padmos* and *Blydorp,* of 1723, has the old-style round tops. For English ships we have Baston's prints of about 1721 and in these the *Britannia,* of 1719, shows tops with their after sides square. I have seen such tops on a model of a Scottish East-Indiaman, of 1702, which seems to have its original rigging, but there are so many other suspicious features about this model that I prefer to think that it was rigged rather later than the date which appears on its stern. Personally, I should fit round tops up to about 1705 and square after 1715; in between, I should probably experiment with some sort of hybrid shape.

In any case, the change in shape did not cause any real change in the method of construction and a top of 1730 would be made in much the same way as one of 1670. For the first half of the 17th century the matter is more complicated, because the difference in shape was such that the construction must also have been different. Such a top as is shown or hinted at in the engraving of the *Sovereign,* of 1637, cannot have been made in the same way as those of fifty years later.

If one were to believe this engraving of the *Sovereign,* one would say that her tops must have been extraordinarily small. In this respect the print (Plate 7) must be at fault, for the stern view of the ship which appears in Pett's portrait in the National Portrait Gallery, shows them quite a good size. In this view, the yards seem to have been drawn from a plan or table without allowing for perspective and one can thus get a good idea of the size of the main top by comparing it with the main and main topsail yards. By this standard it seems that her main top was about 13 ft. in diameter at the bottom and 18 ft. at the rim. This would make her trestle-trees rather more than ¼ of her Beam as opposed to the ⅓ of later ships.

On the question of the shape of the tops, the two pictures agree well enough. They were like straight-sided saucers or very shallow flower-pots. The sketches give

Fig. 18. Tops of about 1625

what I believe to be fairly typical tops of the early part of the 17th century (Fig. 18), but I should not like to commit myself as to how they were put together. I am not at all sure whether the planks in their sides ran up and down like those of a barrel or ran horizontally from one upright to another. I am, however, sure that the best way to make such a top is to turn it on a lathe from some very hard wood and to add the uprights afterwards. If there is a detached rail, part of the way round, this will have to be made separately.

Soon after the date of the *Sovereign*, tops began to get shallower. I think Fig. 19 shows a reasonable top for about 1650. After that — perhaps as a result of the experience of the first Anglo-Dutch war — they very soon assumed their typical late 17th century form with

Fig. 19. Top of about 1650

little more than a shallow rim to represent the sides of the former saucer. To make such tops is not at all difficult, though it takes time. The following description is intended for an English top of 1670-90, but it only wants a few obvious modifications to suit it to a foreign pattern or to the straight-after-sided tops of fifty years later.

First, it is necessary to determine the size of the top. When once the trestle-trees have been made this is simple; the full diameter of the lower side of the top should be about 7/6 of the length of the trestle-trees. Most foreign tops were smaller in comparison with their trestle-trees; so small in fact that the trestle-trees, being on either side of the diameter, reached practically to the edge of the top. Some English tops may have been bigger, if Battine's figures are to be trusted; but I think the proportion 7/6 or possibly 6/5 will be pretty near the mark.

In any case, the first step is to draw a circle of the size required, on a piece of wood whose thickness is, if possible, equivalent to about three inches in the real ship. Inside this mark out another circle less in diameter by an amount corresponding to from two feet to five feet, according to the size of the top. Cut out this inner circle and glue the piece left outside to another piece of wood of the same thickness *with the grain running the other way*. When the glue is set, cut both thicknesses together round the outer line.

English tops were sometimes made with a sort of stepped section with the ring part overlapping the floor. This looks very smart, but it means that there is not much depth of wood for the futtock plates to go through and is therefore to be avoided in a small-scale model. In either case it is certainly best to glue the two layers together before trying to cut round the outside of the ring.

Next comes the cutting of the hole in the middle. This was usually square and about ⅖ or ⅓ of the diameter of the top on each side. It might be a little bigger, athwartships, than fore and aft, and it was not neces-

sarily in the middle of the fore and aft diameter of the
top. In English ships it reached from the middle of one
cross-tree to the middle of the other; in Dutch, it just
covered the space between the cross-trees if the ties
came down before the after cross-tree,
or gave reasonable room for them between the cross-tree and the floor of the
top if they came down abaft the cross-
tree. When this hole is marked out the
grain of the floor should run athwartships and that of the ring fore and aft
(Fig. 20).

Fig. 20. Floor and
rim of a top

On the floor of the top there should be glued at regular intervals, a series of radial ribs shaped as shown in
Fig. 21. Van Yk says there should be twice
as many of these ribs as there are feet in the
diameter of the top, but three for every two
feet or even one for every foot, is more reasonable. On a big top these ribs should have a width

Fig. 21
Rib for the
floor of a top

corresponding to about four or five inches and a depth
at their outer ends about the same or rather more. Usually the number of ribs was a multiple of four (12, 16,
20, 24 or 28) so that there could be two in the fore and
aft line and two athwartships. In most cases they projected a few inches, say three or four, beyond the edge
of the top, but sometimes they were finished off flush.

Round the ends of these ribs went an upright rim
about nine inches high or something of that sort. This
can be made of thin metal, but that involves pinning it
to the ends of the ribs and it is very easy to split them in
the process. The same dodge, of brown paper and glue,
that has been mentioned for the mast-hoops, works very
well here too. When once it is thoroughly set it is easy

to sandpaper it down to look like a single strip and a coat of black paint will complete the deception.

By the time the rigging is finished there will have to be a certain number of holes in the tops. Most of these are simply small round holes just big enough for a rope and these can be left till later. The only holes that need be made before the tops are put in place are those for the futtock plates which connected the lower deadeyes of the topmast shrouds to the futtock shrouds below the top. These have to be oblong holes that require the use of a file or a fretsaw and it is best to bore them while the top can be put down on a bench. Naturally the number and arrangement of these holes depends on the number of topsail shrouds. Fuller information on this point will be found under "Standing Rigging," but it may be said here that three to six on the mainmast, three to five on the foremast, and two or three on the mizzen, will probably meet the case.

The foremost hole should come just before the line of the fore side of the masthead and the aftermost about half way from there to the middle of the after side of the top; those between should be spaced in as regularly as the ribs will allow. Occasionally the topmast shrouds in models are found a bit further forward, with the second about where I have said the first should be. This is particularly the case with the mizzen and spritsail tops and in them it is possibly right, but in the fore and main tops I rather doubt it.

The spritsail top does not need such a big hole in its floor as the others; it only requires a slit big enough to take the knee and the heel of the spritsail topmast. The other tops of course varied a certain amount according to date and country. For instance, sometimes the up-

right rim was omitted on the forward third of the top
or more and sometimes it had separate supports instead
of being secured to the ends of the floor ribs. Generally

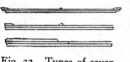
Fig. 22. Types of seven-
teenth-century tops

speaking, though, the tops I have
described would be fairly typical;
other patterns are shown in Fig. 22
and the model-rigger can take his
choice. It may be mentioned that
English mizzen tops, about the end of the 17th century,
often had their after sides flattened to allow for topping
up the mizzen yard.

With regard to caps there is not so much possible
variety except at the very beginning of the 17th century.
There seems very little doubt that the two kinds of cap,
English and foreign, were well established by 1625, if not
before. The method of fitting topmasts so that they
could be "struck" or lowered, is said to have been in-
vented in Holland in 1570; before that they were simply
lashed in place. When the cap was introduced, the
Dutch, perhaps influenced by the practice in Spanish
galleys, used it to form a lead for the ties; whereas the
English, who kept their ties below the trestle-trees, could
be content with a simpler form of cap.

At first both countries probably had the cap open in
front and kept the topmast in place by means of a lashing. At that stage the English form of cap
must have been roughly square; while the
Dutch, which had to provide room for the
ties to run on either side of the mast, would
have to be longer athwartships than fore and
aft. Later on, when the cap was extended
forward to enclose the topmast, the English
type became roughly the shape of a brick

Fig. 23.
English form
of cap

Fig. 24.
Dutch form
of cap

(Fig. 23), while the Dutch was squarer in plan and from the side was like a small letter "b" or "d" laid on its side (Fig. 24).

An English-style cap for one of the lower masts of a big ship should be ½ the masthead in length or a little less. Its width should be 6/11 of its length and its depth 3/7 of its width. Its edges, particularly the up-and-down edges, should be slightly blunted. The middle of the square hole for the tenon on the lower masthead should be about ⅓ of the length from one end and the middle of the round hole for the topmast should be about ¼ of the length from the other end. The size of this hole depends, of course, on that of the topmast. A good rule is to make it half the maximum diameter of the lower mast; it can always be filed out later, if necessary.

Fair average dimensions for a cap of the foreign pattern are:— Length, 9/20 of the masthead; width, ⅔ of the length; depth, ⅔ of the width. The depth at the fore edge should be about half of the maximum. I rather think this part of the cap got heavier with the course of time. To draw out such a cap, make the after part a semicircle in side elevation and produce it into a pro-

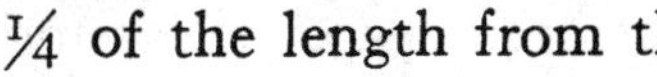

Fig. 25. Types of foreign caps

jecting tongue with more or less of an angle at the point of junction according to date. The drawings in Fig. 25 show a few typical specimens from which a choice can be made. Two grooves for the ties have to be cut round the semicircular part and two holes have to be bored through the after side of the tongue to correspond with the fore ends of these grooves, which should be about ⅛ of the width of the cap from either side. The mizzen and spritsail caps have no grooves or holes. The cap goes on the head of the lower mast with rather more of its semicircular part forward than aft and the round hole for the topmast comes partly in the foreside of the semicircular part and partly in the tongue; the exact place is best found by experiment.

While on the subject of caps it will be as well to mention an unusual feature in those of the model of the *St George*. In them there are sheaves on either side of the fore and main caps for the "top-ropes" which hoisted or lowered the topmasts. Usually the top-ropes went through blocks hanging from eye-bolts beneath the caps; in fact, I have never met another instance of this method of taking them through sheaves in the caps. It seems possible that it was suggested by the Dutch fashion of leading the ties over the caps. The date of the model, 1701, is just when one would expect English and Dutch fashions to be influencing one another to a greater extent than at any other time, because they had then been working continuously together for several years.

When rigging a model it is best to leave the caps loose, so that they can be lifted off as required. It is obvious that they should not be fixed down until the shrouds have been put in place and it will be found, as the process of rigging goes on, that it is often convenient to be able to lift the cap, even quite late in the proceedings. There is no reason why they should ever be fixed down, for there is nothing to pull them upwards and several ropes to pull them down. On the other hand, the trestle-trees and the tops need good fastenings, because there are several things which tend to pull them out of place. I strongly advise fixing the trestle-trees to the masthead with screws and putting other screws through the floor of the top into the trestle-trees near the ends. It may be contrary to what was done in the real ship, but it is easy to conceal the sin and it will save a lot of trouble later on. It is no good following the practice of real ships exactly, if the difference in condition will make things look wrong after all.

One more point needs mentioning. The cap on the knee at the end of the bowsprit should be made so that the spritsail topmast rakes forward rather than aft. When all the rigging is in place there will be a quantity of gear to pull the spritsail topmast aft and nothing to hold it forward. Most models have it pulled aft to a ridiculous extent and few things look worse.

CHAPTER III

Topmasts, Topgallants and Flagstaffs

IN WORKING out the dimensions of the topmasts and topgallants, the first step is to decide on the relation between the mainmast and its topmast. In a general way it can be said that the main topmast of an English ship was ½ of the mainmast, up to about 1650, and that from 1670 to 1720 or later, it was ⅗. The increase was associated with introduction of reefs in the topsails, an improvement which came in somewhere about 1655. Foreign topmasts were usually longer. The *Couronne*, of 1638, had her topmast as much as 7/11 or .63 of the lower mast. It might be thought that she was an exceptional ship whose proportions would not be copied, but Dassié, in 1677, gives ⅔ or .66 as the proper figure and the *Royal Louis* model of 1692, agrees with the *Couronne* in having the proportion .63. The Swedish *Amarant*, of 1654, gives about .66, Witsen, in 1671, says .64 for Dutch ships and Van Yk, in 1697, gets as high as .7. On the other hand the proportion in Spanish ships was .58 both in 1635 and in 1690. The fore topmast should bear the same relation to the foremast as the main topmast does to the mainmast; if anything, it should be relatively a little longer.

The topgallant masts varied in rather an interesting way. In English ships they were about .4 of the topmasts in 1620, and grew, by 1650, to about .5. Then, with the growth of the topmasts, they shrank, relatively speaking, to about .4 again, in 1670. After that the whole upper sail-plan grew and the topgallants became about

.5 of the increased topmasts. In foreign ships the same thing probably happened. At any rate something between .4 and .5 will be about right.

The mizzen topmast is best calculated from the main topmast rather than from its own lower mast. At the beginning of the 17th century the mizzen topmasts of English ships were long. The two mizzen topmasts of the *Bear*, in 1618, were respectively about ⅔ and ½ of the main topmast, and when the single mizzen was well established, in 1640, the mizzen topmast was still about ⅔ or .66 of the main topmast. Then, just as in the case of the topgallants, the mizzen topmast shrank to .6 or even .5 by 1670. Soon, however, it began to grow again and by 1720 it was as much as .7 of the main topmast. Foreign mizzen topmasts were usually shorter; most French and Dutch authorities agree that they should be .5 of the main topmast. Still, there are exceptions; the Berlin model of 1665 has hers about .6 and the proportion in the *"William Rex"* works out to .55.

Taking the length of the spritsail topmast in the same way, it can be said that it should be something between .3 and .4 of the main topmast. Early in the 17th century it might be more, as in the *Bear*, where it was .47. In a general way, though, ⅓ or .33 will not be far from the mark.

With flagstaffs one can please oneself to some extent. Probably the size of the case for the model will have something to do with it. An English plan of 1719 shows the main flagstaff about ⅔ of the main topgallant mast, the jackstaff on the spritsail topmast the same length, the mizzen flagstaff *longer* by about 1/10 and the fore between it and the main. According to Van Yk, the main and fore flagstaffs should be 8/7 of the topgallants

on which they are stepped, the mizzen should be 5/6 of
its topmast and the jackstaff ¾ of the spritsail topmast.
On the other hand, in the *"William Rex"* model, all four
flagstaffs are about ½ of the main topgallant mast.

In thickness, at the point where they go through the
caps, the topmasts should be rather more than ½ of the
diameter of their lower masts at the deck. Something
between .55 and .6 will be suitable. The thickness of
the topgallant masts should bear about the same relation to that of the topmasts. Both topmasts and topgallants should taper so that their thickness below the
hounds is about ¾ of that at the caps.

The heels of the topmasts, and also of the topgallants
and flagstaffs, have to be left square and big enough to
fit loosely between the trestle-trees. Van Yk says the
length of this squared part should be twice the thickness
of the topmast, but in the *St George* model it is as much
as five times that thickness. Probably Van Yk means
twice its own thickness and it must be remembered that
the foreign retention of round mastheads put their tres-

Fig. 26.
Heels of top-
masts, French
and English

tle-trees further apart and made it necessary
to leave a greater thickening on the topmasts
than in English ships. In the French *Royal
Louis* model, the heel of the main topmast is
as much as 5/3 of the thickness at the lower
cap, whereas in the *St George*, it is only
about 6/5 (Fig. 26).

It is difficult to say how far up the topmast the fid-
hole should come. The amount of projection of the heel
below the trestle-trees seems to have varied a good deal.
The *St George* has the topmast as much as twice the
depth of the trestle-trees below them, but plans of 1719
show it less than ¾ of the trestle-trees. Perhaps, if we

say that the fid-hole should be not less than twice and not more than three times the thickness of the topmast at the cap away from the bottom, we shall be not far from the truth.

There have to be sheave-holes in the heels of the top-masts for the top-ropes which were used to hoist or lower them. The arrangement of these sheave-holes will be discussed under the heading of "top-ropes" in the chapter on "Running Rigging of the Topmasts." The usual way of finishing off the heel of a flagstaff or a topgallant mast was to cut its fore side away to something very near a quadrant of a circle, but sometimes it was merely blunted all round. Topmasts were probably shaped in the same way for the greater part of the 17th century, but sometimes they had a short, round projection right at the heel or were nicked round about where the top of this projection would have come. The rounded heel was the general rule in English ships a century later, but it is probably safer for the 17th century to leave the heel square or merely rounded on the fore lower corner unless there is good evidence for the contrary in the source from which one is working.

The mastheads of the topmasts and topgallants were relatively shorter than those of the lower masts. When the lower mastheads were $\frac{1}{8}$ of the length of the masts, those of the topmasts would be $1/10$. Apparently it was usual to square the topmast-heads before this was done to the lower masts, or at least Dutch ships seem to have followed English practice for the topmasts before they did so lower down. This squaring down of the mast-heads does away with much of the need for a thickening of the mast below the trestle-trees, but a slight thicken-

ing, usually octagonal in shape and about twice its own
thickness in depth, seems to have been normal.

In most cases there was a single sheave in the masthead just below the trestle-trees. Further details will
be found under "ties and halliards," in Chapter IX. If
an actual sheave is to be fitted, it must be done at once·
and in any case it will be easier to drill a hole or holes
before the topmast or topgallant mast is in place. Personally, I look on the provision of sheaves as rather a
waste of labour, unless the model is so large as to demand absolute completeness. When once the ties are
rove it is impossible to see whether there is a sheave or
not, especially if there are two holes to represent its top
and bottom and a very slight slot between them.

The trestle-trees and cross-trees on the topmasts and
topgallants were similar in principle to those on the lower masts. Figures for the length of the trestle-trees vary
rather widely. Keltridge (1675) gives the following
rule:— Trestle-trees, five times the diameter of the
masthead, depth, 4/7 of the head, thickness, ½ inch
less. Cross-trees, ½ the diameter of the masthead longer than the trestle-trees, thickness, the same, depth, ½.
A fairly safe rule is to make the topmast trestle-trees ⅖
of those on the lower masts and the topgallant trestle-
trees ½ of those on the topmasts. The mizzen topmast
should have trestle-trees a little longer than those of the
main topgallant and the spritsail topmast trestle-trees
should be the same as those on the fore topgallant. The
depth should be 1/9 or 1/10 of the length and the thickness just less. The cross-trees can be as long as the
length and depth of the trestle-trees added together. In
Dutch ships, according to Van Yk, the fore and main

topmasts should have trestle-trees ½ of those on the lower masts and the topgallant trestle-trees should be ½ of that. Those on the mizzen topmast and spritsail topmast should be a little shorter than the main topgallant trestle-trees. The depth should be 1/13 of the length and the thickness ⅘ of the depth. The cross-trees should be a trifle shorter than the trestle-trees, but the same thickness; their depth should be ¾ of their thickness.

In the first half or even the first three-quarters of the 17th century there were sometimes tops at the heads of the topmasts. The *Sovereign,* as depicted in the engraving, had them even on the topgallants and on the mizzen topmast (Plate 7). The Danish print of about 1625 shows them on the fore, main and main-mizzen topmasts (Plate 5); the Dutch-built Frenchman of the same date has them on the fore and main topmasts only (Plate 6). It was certainly usual for big ships to have tops on the fore and main topmasts up to 1650, but I doubt if they would be found in English ships after 1655. Dutch ships may have kept them a little later; in fact Van Yk, as late as 1695, speaks of upper tops as a possibility, but probably 1665 would be quite late enough to show them without very definite authority. In France, where big ships were very big, there was a tendency to keep topmast tops still later. Dassié, in 1677, says that ships of more than 1000 tons might have them and they are seen in a painting of about this date and in one — but not the other — of a pair of prints of French 3-deckers of 1690. The *Royal Louis* model of 1692 does not show them.

If there are to be upper tops, they can be made and fitted in exactly the same way as those on the lower masts. If not, the cross-trees have to be arranged to

suit the topgallant shrouds; in other words, if there are
to be three shrouds a side, there must be three cross-
trees. It was only in big ships that three topgallant
shrouds were fitted. In such cases the cross-trees have
to be let into the trestle-trees as follows:— The middle
one goes at the middle of the trestle-trees and is then
put hard back against the fore side of the topmast; the

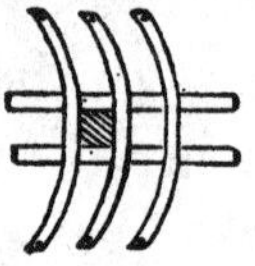

Fig. 27.
Topmast
trestle-trees
and cross-trees

after cross-tree is then put close against the
after side of the topmast and the foremost is
placed a similar distance forward. Usually
the cross-trees were slightly curved aft, so
that the ends of the first came nearly abreast
the middle of the second. This was to bring
the topgallant shrouds further aft. (Fig. 27).

With two cross-trees only it was the middle one that
was omitted. Its place was taken by a mere chock between the trestle-trees. Topgallant trestle-trees and
cross-trees were fitted in the same way, but in their case
the foremost cross-tree was often curved forward instead
of aft. Their only duty was to support the flagstaffs and as
a matter of fact it is very rare to find any sign of shrouds,
but if there had been shrouds there would be
no need to keep them abaft the flagstaff as
was done lower down to allow the sails to be
braced round. In fact it would be better to
have a pair of shrouds leading slightly forward, because that would do away with the
necessity for a stay. Fig. 28 shows typical topgallant

Fig. 28.
Topgallant
trestle-trees
and cross-trees

cross-trees and it should be noted that in this connection
the mizzen topmast and the spritsail topmast can be
looked on as equivalent to topgallant masts.

Caps on the topmasts and topgallants were simply reduced copies of those on the lower masts. Foreign ships

never took their topsail ties over the caps, so there is no need for grooves, but otherwise the shape is exactly the same. At the top of the flagstaffs there must be trucks in the modern fashion. Occasionally the truck came a little way down on the flagstaff and left a pointed end above it (Fig. 29), but more often it was finished off flush in the ordinary way.

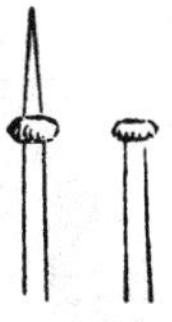

Fig. 29.
Flagstaffs
and trucks

I have not said anything about royal-masts, because there is very little evidence for such fittings at any date covered by this study. There is no doubt that a royal sail or "top-topgallant sail" was a possibility in the first half of the 17th century, but it would be set on the flagstaff without a special mast of its own. The only example that I know of topgallant-mast, royal-mast and flagstaff, as three separate spars, is in the engraving of the *Sovereign* (Plate 7). However, if there are to be royal-masts, there is not much difficulty about them; they are simply reduced copies of the topgallants, a stage higher up.

CHAPTER IV

YARDS AND STUNSAIL BOOMS

IT IS very important to get the yards of a model in proper proportion. Many models have been spoilt in the rigging for want of attention to this point. Nothing looks worse than to see the long topsail yards of 1850 on a hull of 1650, and yet this sort of mistake is often made.

Naturally one should start with the main yard and work the others from that. "The Seaman's Dictionary," written in 1622, says the main yard should be 5/6 (or .83) of the keel. Five years earlier the *Bear*, a ship 110 ft. on the keel, was given new spars; her old main yard was .87 K., her new one .79. For purposes of comparison, especially with foreign ships which were measured in a different way from English, it is easier to take the relation between the main yard and the mainmast. In the case of the *Bear*, the old main yard was 1.06 times the mast, the new was .96. After her time the main yard got a little shorter, but not much. The *Sovereign's* was .92 of the mainmast, and figures all through the 17th century and a bit later agree in giving a value not far from .90. We might take .85 as a minimum and .95 as the maximum. French ships, from 1670 onwards, had their main yards about .90 of the mast; the *Couronne*, in 1638, had had a very long yard, .99 of the mainmast. Dutch yards towards the end of the 17th century were a trifle shorter; the figures are given in terms of the beam and the depth in hold and work out for a ship of

40 ft. beam at a value of .86 for the relation between the yard and the mast.

Having obtained the length of the main yard we can make the fore yard something between .8 and .9 of that length. At the very beginning of the 17th century it might be as little as .75. About 1620 long fore yards, even more than .9 of the main, seem to have been tried, perhaps to balance the newly introduced mizzen topsails. With the abolition of the second mizzen the length of the fore yard fell to little more than .8 of the main and remained there till about 1675, when it rose to .85. After that it stayed between .85 and .9.

The topsail yards of 1600 were about .5 of their lower yards and this relation persisted until the introduction of reefs in the topsails (about 1655 or soon after) made it necessary to lengthen the topsail yard-arms. At first the increase was very small; .55 would be quite enough up to 1680 and .6 up to 1710. Then the topsail yards seem to have grown suddenly, for the plans of 1719 make them more than .7 of their lower yards. Topgallant yards were very small at first; .4 of the topsail yards would do for 1620. By 1640 they had reached .5 and this relation held good till the beginning of the 18th century, when they grew (just before 1720) to about .58 of the topsail yards.

The mizzen yard was about the same length as the fore yard, sometimes a little longer, sometimes shorter. In the *Bear*, the two mizzens were .8 and .6 of the main yard. The crojack yard and mizzen topsail yard were usually roughly equal to the main topsail and topgallant yards; but when the main topsail suddenly grew, the crojack yard remained at about .6 of the main yard. The same thing applies in the case of the spritsail and spritsail topsail yards; normally their lengths were very much the same as those of the crojack and mizzen topsail. There was, however, a tendency in the middle of the 17th century to have very long spritsail yards. The *Sovereign,* in 1640, had a spritsail yard .6 of her main yard and the 70-gun ships of 1677 had the same. Keltridge, in 1675, gives some ships spritsail yards as much as .7 of the main yard, but this must have been exceptional.

In French ships the same process of growth of the upper yards can be traced. The *Couronne,* in 1638, had her topsail yards just, but only just, longer than .5 of the lower yards. Dassié's figures for 1677 work out to .54, while the *Royal Louis* model of 1692 and a manuscript of 1690, agree in the value .62 or .63. For the fore yard a length of .9 of the main will be about correct for French ships. The topgallant yards should be .5 of the topsail yards. The mizzen yard should be the same as the fore yard; the crojack and spritsail yards should be respectively a trifle shorter and a trifle longer than the main topsail yard, while their topsail yards should be the same as the main topgallant yard or very nearly so. Dutch ships had their fore yards a little shorter; Witsen, in 1671, gives .88 and Van Yk, in 1697, .86. The topsail yards grew in them, as in the ships of other nations, from .52 in Witsen to .57 in Van Yk and .63 in the *"William Rex"* model rigged in 1698. Spritsail yards were a good deal longer than main topsail yards; Witsen gives .65 and Van Yk .62.

The thickness of the yards was normally ¼ in. for every foot of length. Battine, in 1684, suggests ⅝ in. for each yard of length but his own figures work out to ⅔ in. or ¾ in. to a yard. I think ⅔ in. per yard or

1/54 of the length might be looked on as the minimum and ¾ in. per yard or 1/48 of the length as the maximum for English ships. The French also used the ¼ in. per foot rule and so did the Dutch, but in the latter case the fact that their foot contained 11 inches, made the absolute value 1/44 of the total length. In all cases the rule was to have the ends ⅓ of the middle. The taper was worked as an arc of a circle, that is to say, it was very slight in the middle and became steeper towards the ends. Keltridge gives an easy way of getting this effect and his diagram is copied in Fig. 30. The mizzen yard and crojack yard were thinner, about ½ in. to a yard of length or a trifle less; the mizzen yard was also less tapered at its fore end; its thickness there was ½ its maximum (Fig. 31).

Fig. 30. Proportions for yards of square sails (thickness exaggerated)

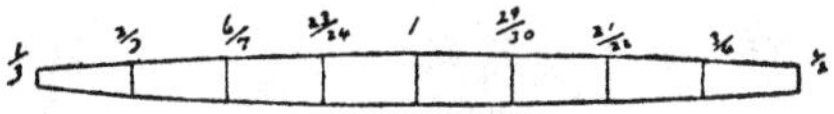

Fig. 31. Proportions for mizzen yard (thickness exaggerated)

The yard-arms of the fore and main were each roughly 1/25 of the total length of the yard. Those of the spritsail and crojack yards were often relatively longer, about 1/20. The other square yards were proportioned in the same way as the fore and main yards until it became necessary to lengthen the topsail yard-arms to allow of reefing. As the topsails were much wider at the foot than at the head they were quite a bit wider at the reef-bands than they were on the yard. Obviously, when the sail was reefed, the wider portion had to be accommodated on the yard and for this purpose the yard-arms had to be lengthened. Increasing the total length of the yards helped both directly and indirectly;

it allowed the topsails to be squarer and at the same
time it made it possible to give them longer yard-arms.
The question of reefs will be dealt with fully under
"Sails," in Chapter XII; at the moment it will be enough
to say that a single reef in the fore and main topsails
probably came in very soon after 1655, that by 1680
there were two reefs in the fore and main topsails and
one in the mizzen topsail, and that another reef in each
seems to have been added between 1715 and 1720. The
growth of the yard-arms no doubt kept pace with the
increase in the number of reefs. By 1720 the topsail
yard-arms were about 1/12 of the yard — roughly twice
as long, relatively speaking, as those of the lower yards.

Now we come to two questions to which I do not pretend to know the answers. When did cleats at the yard-
arms come into use? When did the yards, or at any
rate the lower yards, begin to have a piece left octagonal
in the middle? For cleats my earliest evidence is in the
two almost contemporary models *"William Rex"* and
St George, 1698 and 1701. Certainly "The Seaman's
Dictionary" of 1622 mentions the word *cleats,* but it
describes them as pieces of wood to keep ropes from
slipping *off* the yards, whereas the cleats to which I am
referring had an exactly opposite duty, being intended
to prevent the lifts, braces, etc., from
working too far on to the yards (Fig.
32). The Danish *Norske Löve* model
and the Dutch models of 1665 have no
yard-arm cleats, but even so this leaves
a long gap before 1698 and it is quite
possible that English ships had them before Dutch. One
can say that they were in use by 1700, but how much
earlier to fit them is a matter of guess-work. Personally

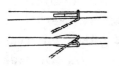

Fig. 32. Cleats at
yard-arm

I should guess at about 1680, but I might well be 15 years wrong either way.

The octagonal piece in the middle of the lower yards appears in the *St George* and in other English models of the early part of the 18th century. It does not appear in Dutch or French models; in fact Van Yk, writing about 1695, is very emphatic that the yards should be round throughout. Keltridge, in giving directions for shaping English yards, in 1675, says nothing about an octagonal piece, so it seems probable that it was an introduction of later date than that.

Cleats towards the middle of the yards, to hold the ties or jeer-blocks and the parrel-ropes in place, were probably in use earlier. There is no suggestion of them in the engraving of the *Sovereign* of 1637, but the *Norske Löve* model, made in 1654, has them and so have the Dutch models of 1665. At first they were confined to the fore and main yards, but by the end of the century the topsail yards had them also. In the *St George* there are cleats on the fore and main, the spritsail and the fore and main topsail yards; they are not fitted on the cro-jack, spritsail topsail or mizzen topsail yards and would probably be omitted on the topgallant yards if the model had any. The French *Royal Louis* has them everywhere except on the spritsail, spritsail topsail and topgallant yards.

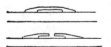

Fig. 33. Cleats at middle of yard

These cleats might appear in two forms; they might consist of a single bow attached to the yard at each end or they might take the form of two separate horns with a slight gap between their points (Fig. 33). As far as I can judge the bow was the earlier shape, but it is possible that the bow was foreign and the horns English in origin. The *Royal Louis* has bows, the *St George* has horns and so has the Dutch *"William Rex,"* but the earlier Dutch and Danish models have bows.

The over-all length of these cleats, either singly or as a pair, should be from ⅛ to 1/10 of the whole length of the yard. The open space inside should be about half the full length. The depth of the opening depends on the thickness of the ropes that have to go inside it, but a fairly good rule is to make it ⅛ of the thickness of the yard. For the up-and-down thickness ¼ of the diameter of the yard will be about right.

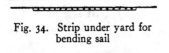

Fig. 34. Strip under yard for bending sail

A fitting sometimes added to the lower yards is shown in Fig. 34. In the ordinary way the sails were bent to the yards by means of robands passing right round the yards. At the middle of the yard there was a danger that the robands might get worn through by rubbing against the mast or the lower rigging. Sometimes, therefore, the sail in this part of the yard was attached to a long thin strip of wood with holes in it secured underneath the yard. This, like the cleats for the ties, might be in one piece or in two. A German book of 1700 describes it as a single strip, but in models it appears in two parts with a gap corresponding to the opening of the cleats before the yard. In the *St George* model the strop of the quarter-block for the topsail sheet goes over the fore cleat and just inside the strip under the yard (Fig. 35). In her case, with a 100 ft. main yard (on the scale of the model),

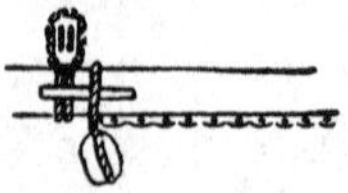

Fig. 35.
Cleat, block and strip in the *St George* model

the two strips are 6 ft. apart and each is 12 ft. long; the holes in them are 1 ft. apart. In the *"William Rex"* the

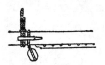

Fig. 36.
Cleat, block and strip in the *"William Rex"* model

strips are rather shorter and further apart; in her case the quarter-block strops go inside the cleats as well (Fig. 36). I doubt if this was a very usual fitting and I should not put it on a model unless I was copying from some definite authority.

If the model is to have stunsail booms, their boom-irons have to be fitted on the lower yards. The history of stunsails is somewhat obscure. There is no doubt that they were known and used from the middle of the 16th century and very likely before. For instance, the "Treatise on Rigging," of about 1625, mentions them as "set on either side of your fore and main sails." It is, however, very rare — to say the least — to find any mention of them or of their gear in official documents before 1660. Probably they were something in the nature of an unofficial "lash up." Even the *St George* model, as late as 1701, has no stunsail booms or fittings for them, though she has blocks for topsail stunsails on both fore and main.

The official "Establishment" of stores, of 1686, gives English ships main and main topsail stunsails and the same is the case in the semi-official lists of Keltridge and Battine in 1675 and 1685. The earliest official reference that I know of is 1655, in a list of the stores of the ships returning from Jamaica. I think one ought to provide for main stunsail booms after 1660, at any rate, and that it would be justifiable to add them on the fore yard in 1690 or thereabouts. Foreign ships seem to have carried fore stunsails sooner than English, or at least to have recognised their carrying earlier, since Dutch models of 1665 show stunsail booms on both lower yards. Witsen (1671) mentions them on the main only, but he is often somewhat old-fashioned. In France, Dassié (1677) suggests, though he does not state definitely, that there were stunsails forward as well as amidships.

Dutch ships carried their stunsail booms abaft the yards; English, and in all probability most other ships, had theirs before the yards. Otherwise the method of fitting was much the same everywhere. The booms were at first about 3/10 or ⅖ of the length of the yards on which they were carried. Battine (1685) gives the shorter value for English ships; Van Yk (1697) gives the longer for Dutch. In England the booms soon grew longer and in the model of the *Royal George*, of 1715, they are practically half as long as the lower yards. In diameter they were about 1/50 of their length at the butt and tapered outwards to about half this thickness.

They were connected to the yards by means of two pairs of "boom-irons" which formed rings through which they could be slid in and out. The inner boom-iron should be fitted about ⅓ of the way in along the yard. It is best to make it as a simple strap bent into a figure of eight (Fig. 37). Unless the model is on a large

Fig. 37.
Inner stun-
sail-boom iron

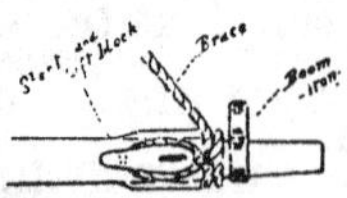

scale it is difficult to make any sort of a hinged fitting, even if we knew that such a thing was in use and how it was designed. In foreign ships and, I believe, in English ships in the 17th century the outer boom-iron was also a figure of eight and was fitted on the yard-arm itself outside the braces and lifts (Fig. 38). Quite early in the 18th century, and perhaps

Fig. 38. Dutch outer
stunsail-boom iron

earlier, the outer boom-iron of English ships changed

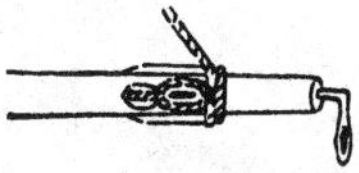

Fig. 39. English outer stunsail-boom iron

its shape and became a sort of prolongation of the yard-arm with the ring turned at right angles to the shank (Fig. 39). Models show it simply driven into the end of the yard, but it is possible that it was really made with jaws to fit on the yard as was the case later.

The lower booms, which spread the clews of the lower stunsails, are seldom shown on models. Unless the stunsails are actually set, there is no need for them. To set stunsails involves setting the other sails as well and a model seldom looks well with the foresail and mainsail set. To tell the truth I consider that a model is better without sails at all; some people think otherwise, but they will probably admit that the foresail and mainsail are better clewed up. In actual practice the lower booms were hooked to the channels and their length, according to Battine, was about ½ to ⅗ of that of the lower yards.

CHAPTER V

Fittings on the Hull

A STUDY of rigging necessarily includes a discussion of certain fittings on the hull. If one is rigging or re-rigging a contemporary model one will find a good deal settled already; but even then it is more than likely that it will be necessary to make additions quite apart from repairs and replacements. To find a model with enough cleats and eye-bolts is rare indeed. If, on the other hand, the actual model has to be designed and built, such things as channels, bitts, knights, cleats and belaying pins have to be provided, and at the risk of trespassing on the ground of the model-maker, as distinct from the rigger, I think it will be best to consider the disposal and design of these in some detail.

I. The Channels

ANYONE who is thinking of rigging a model is no doubt aware that the shrouds of the lower masts had deadeyes at their ends and that these deadeyes were connected by laniards to other deadeyes which were held down by metal fittings of some sort and were kept some little distance away from the ship's side by projecting platforms called "chain-wales" or "channels."

The first thing to be considered with regard to these channels is their height in relation to the tiers of guns. This is a point on which it is possible to be really definite for once, at least as regards English 3-deckers. All through the 17th century English 3-deckers, with the possible exception of the *Prince Royal*, of 1610, had their fore and main channels just below the ports of the middle-deck guns. The *Prince Royal* seems to have been built with the channels only just below the upper-deck guns and to have had them moved down when she was repaired or rebuilt in 1621. Pictures showing her as she was in 1613 have the channels up and those showing her in 1623 have them down. Below the middle-deck guns they remained till 1702, when it was ordered that two ships then being rebuilt, the *St Andrew* (later called *Royal Anne*) and *Royal Katherine,* should have their channels raised to a position above the middle-deck ports. Four years later the change was extended to all new 3-deckers. One ship of 100 guns, 1 90 and 3 80's had been built in the interval and these probably had their channels at the old level.

The Dutch only built 3-deckers between 1682 and 1721. When they did, they placed the fore and main channels above the middle-deck guns and the English order of 1702 was, in fact, based on observation of Dutch ships. The first French 3-deckers of their own building very probably had their channels even higher; at any rate a drawing of the *Royal Louis,* of 1668, shows them above the upper-deck guns. If this fashion was ever general it did not last long, for drawings and models of 1680, onwards, agree in having the channels between the upper-deck and middle-deck ports (Plate 16). For other countries the information is scanty, but the probability is that such of them as built 3-deckers put the channels below the middle-deck guns up to about 1680 and above them after that.

In 2-deckers it is safe to say that English ships had their channels just beneath the upper-deck guns from 1620 to 1740. At the very beginning of the 17th century it is possible that they had them higher, particularly in the case of the fore channels. Usually there were a pair of wales fairly close together and the channels were fixed on the upper wale with the chain-plates reaching down to the lower. In Dutch ships the matter was complicated by the fact that they had their wales more widely spaced; thus, if the lower wale of a pair came clear above the lower-deck ports amidships, the upper tended to rise into the line of the upper-deck ports before the after end of the main channels was reached. Soon after 1650 it

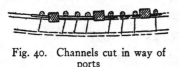

Fig. 40. Channels cut in way of ports

became necessary, if the main channels were to be kept on the line of this wale, to cut pieces out of them opposite the upper-deck ports and to fit them in two, three or even four sections (Fig. 40). Many models and drawings of about 1665 show this arrangement (Plate 11), but even then it was on the point of being superseded. Drawings of ships built in Holland for France, in 1665-7, show the channels shifted up to the next wale, which ran above the upper-deck guns, and this remained their standard position in men-of-war. Curiously enough Indiamen do not seem to have followed suit, but to have kept their channels below the upper-deck ports. To do this they must have reduced the sheer of the wales or put them closer together — probably both. At any rate models and drawings of Dutch East-Indiamen of 1720-25 still show the channels in the old position and not cut into sections (Plate 23).

Right at the beginning of the 17th century Dutch ships probably had their channels high up as the English did. Barentsoen's print of 1694 shows this fashion

(Plate 1). The date of the change can be guessed from the fact that of two pictures of French ships built in Holland in 1626, one has the channels above the upper-deck guns and the other below. When the French began again to build ships for themselves, they very likely led the way in raising the channels in 2-deckers as they did in 3-deckers. Other countries were apt to follow Dutch fashions, but in a general way it seems that they managed to keep the channels below the upper-deck guns. The ship in the Danish print of about 1625, the *Norske Löve* and another Danish model of about 1680-90, all have their channels in this position. The Swedish *Amarant,* of 1654, is an early example of cutting the channels; her main channels have had to be cut for two of the upper-deck ports. Russian prints of about 1700 (Plate 18) show the channels still below the upper-deck guns. By the way, Charnock's "Spanish 2nd-Rate of 1670" is of no value as evidence of Spanish practice, because she has been proved to be really a Dutch-built ship of 1665.

The mizzen channels were usually a deck higher than those of the other masts. Sometimes they were higher still. For example, the *Sovereign,* which has her main channels below the middle-deck ports, has the mizzen channels on a wale which bisects the upper-deck ports (Plate 7). The Danish 2-decker of some 10 years earlier (Plate 5) has her mizzen channels as high as the side of the ship allows. In some cases where the fore and main channels were exceptionally high — such as one of the Dutch-built Frenchmen of 1626 — the mizzen channels were on the same wale; in others — for instance the French 3-decker of 1668—the mizzen channels were higher still. As a rule it is best to put them on the next wale above those of the main, or at all events a deck higher. Quite often the mizzen channels were very modest affairs. The *Sovereign* has nothing more than a slight thickening of the wale, if that. The Berlin model has merely a timber of roughly square section. The only need was to get the lower deadeyes far enough out to keep the shrouds clear of the side, and if the channels were well up and the side was still "tumbling home," a very slight projection of the channels was enough. The same rule is the best guide to the projection of the fore and main channels; the shrouds must clear the side with something to spare, but too much projection is bad, because it exaggerates the unfair pull on the chain-plates.

Having settled the positions of the channels, the next thing is to distribute the deadeyes along them. As far as possible the deadeyes must be arranged so as to give the ports above the channels a clear field of fire and a chance to open freely. With channels cut in sections this happens automatically, but with continuous channels it is a matter which has to be watched. There will also be one or two tackles to be allowed for and their ring-bolts must also be kept clear of the ports. The fore end of the channels should come abreast of the middle line of the mast or a trifle further forward and the centre of the foremost deadeye should be level with the after side of the mast. That is for a mast somewhere about upright; if the mast rakes aft a lot, the foremost deadeye can be rather further aft.

The distance from the foremost deadeye to the aftermost, along the channels, should be about $\frac{2}{5}$ of the vertical height of the trestle-trees above the channels. With the channels high up and cut in sections the proportion may rise as high as $\frac{1}{2}$ and at the foremast it may be as little as $\frac{1}{3}$. The mizzen will have its deadeyes spread over a length equal to about ½ that at the main, as a maximum, and ½ that at the fore, as a minimum. The question whether there is a port to be avoided will naturally have to be considered.

The number of shrouds of course varied with the size of the ship. Other things being equal it was greater at the beginning of the 17th century than at the end. In 1618, the *Bear,* which was about the size of the 60-gun ships of fifty years later, had 10 shrouds a side on the mainmast, 8 on the fore and 5 on the main mizzen as against their 8, 7, 4. The *Constant Reformation,* a slightly smaller ship built in 1619, had 10, 8, 6. The *Prince Royal* seems to have had 11 shrouds on the main, the *Sovereign* had 12, 11, 7. After her time the number fell and became more or less standardised at 10, 9, 6 for 100-gun ships, 9, 8, 5 for 90's, 8, 7, 4 for big 2-deckers and 6, 5, 3 or 5, 4, 3 for smaller ships. In 1719 the three classes of 3-deckers, 100's, 90's and 80's, had respectively 10, 9, 7; 9, 8, 6 and 9, 8, 5.

Foreign ships kept to very much the same standards. The big Danish and French 2-deckers of 1626, have 11, 9, 6 and 10, 8, 5. Hollar shows 10 main shrouds in a large 2-decker of 1647; Zeeman, a few years later, gives a 60-gun man-of-war 11 main shrouds and an East Indiaman as many as 13. By 1670 the standard allowance for the largest Dutch ships was 10, 9, 6 or 9, 8, 5. At the end of the century the model of the *"William Rex,"* a large 2-decker, has only 8, 7, 5, but the 3-deckers of the same period seem to have had 10, 9, 6. This is also the number in the French *Royal Louis* of similar date; smaller French 3-deckers of 1680-90 had 9, 8, 6, but a late 17th century drawing of a 100-gun ship (Plate 16) has as many as 11, 10, 6.

The deadeyes have to be stropped with metal with a certain amount of loop left beneath them (Fig. 41). The

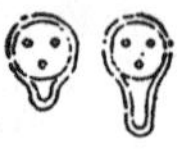

Fig. 41.
Deadeyes
and Strops

length of the loop depends largely on the nature of the fitting beneath it; when there are true "chains," the loop is long enough to go well below the lower side of the channels and to look like the first link of the chain; when there are simple "chain-plates" in one piece, the loop is usually shorter and only projects below the channels just enough to leave room for the chain-plate to hook into it.

This matter of chains or plates is not easy. As far as I can judge, ships of all countries used plates for the first forty years of the 17th century. After that chains seem to have been universal for some fifteen years. Dutch ships and most other foreigners stuck to chains, but English ships reverted to plates soon after 1655 and kept them for nearly a century. Exceptions to this rough summary are found in a French picture of about 1680 and a Danish model of the same period, both of which show plates instead of chains.

It will be easiest to describe the standardised fittings of the end of the 17th century before dealing with those of its earlier years. The chain-plates of English ships were shaped as in Fig. 42. They were bent into an arc of a circle and had a sudden reverse angle where they came to the hull. At the top they were narrowed down and made into hooks which passed through the loops in the strops of the deadeyes just below the channels. At the bottom they widened into disks with holes in them for bolts passing through the wales.

Fig. 42.
English
Chain-
plates, end
of 17th
century

Dutch ships had longer loops to their deadeyes; these

loops formed links lying parallel to the hull and there

were short links pointing upwards from the bolts in the wales. Between the two went longer links lying at right angles to the side (Fig. 43).

Fig. 43.
Dutch Chains,
end of 17th
century

In foreign ships there were often short backing links going from the bolts in the wales to other bolts in the planking just below (Fig. 44). Dutch ships had this fitting by about 1660, but English ships do not seem to have had anything of the sort till after 1700, or rather till after they raised their channels in 1702. When they did, they had longer chain-plates with two bolts through them (Fig. 45). The whole matter of chains and chain-plates is difficult. The sketches must serve to show some of the possibilities and the rest must be left to individual judgment.

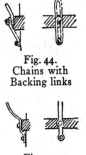

Fig. 44.
Chains with
Backing links

Fig. 45.
English chain-
plates about 1710

There are several possible ways of stropping deadeyes. In my opinion the method of twisting the wire together beneath the deadeye (Fig. 46) is the worst. The disadvantage of this method is that there are two ends to be dealt with; one can make a fairly tidy job of one end, but the other is left unaccounted for and has either to be left as a hook, which is likely to open up, or to be twisted round what is already an undesirably lumpy "stalk." A good way in large models is to drill a couple of holes in the top of the deadeye and to turn the two ends in there; a drop of solder will hide the deception (Fig. 47). Another good way is to

Fig. 46.
Bad method
of stropping
Deadeyes

Fig. 47.
Good method
of stropping
Deadeyes

take the two ends below the deadeye and to make them into two hooks one outside the other (Fig. 48); then solder them together and finish up with file and drill.

Deadeyes in the period 1650-1720 (and afterwards) were set in slots on the outer edge of the channels and covering strips were nailed over them. Models often have holes

Best method
Fig. 48.
of stropping
Deadeyes

drilled in the channels near the edge to give the same effect. At an earlier period the deadeyes seem to have been right on the plain edge without slots. The print of the *Sovereign* shows no connection at all between the chain-plates and the channels; the plates are bolted to the lower wales and merely rest against the channels (Fig. 49). In the Danish print of rather earlier date there are clearly bolts in the channels as well (Fig. 50). Apparently her chain-plates extend well above the channels and then have the deadeyes hooked in, but it is possible that what the artist meant was the arrangement

Fig. 49.
Chain-plates
in the
Sovereign of
1637

Fig. 50.
Chain-plates
in a
Danish ship
about 1625

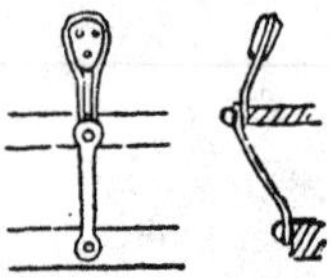

shown in Fig. 51 where the loops on the deadeyes are long and narrow and the bolt passes through both the loop in the strop of the deadeye and the hole in the chain-plate and thus makes the connection. This was how I interpreted it in my *"Mayflower"* model. It may be

Fig. 51. Possible
arrangement of
deadeyes and
chain-plates

wrong, but it makes quite a neat fitting, particularly if the deadeyes are just slotted into the channels.

It has been mentioned that the mizzen channels were

sometimes quite rudimentary, if they existed at all. In the same way the chains or chain-plates were often simpler at the mizzen than elsewhere. For instance, the Berlin Dutch model, of 1665, has no chains at all, but merely has bolts through the strops of the deadeyes into a baulk of timber not much bigger than the wale (Fig. 52). In the *Sovereign,* which has no mizzen channels, the chain-plates are shapped to fit round the wale and are bolted to the side just beneath it (Fig. 53).

Fig. 52.
Mizzen
Channels and
Deadeyes in
Dutch model
of 1665

Fig. 53.
Mizzen
Chain-plates
of the
Sovereign

As far as possible the chains or chain-plates should run in lines radiating from the masthead. That is to say, the fore-most should be upright and the others should gradually rake more and more forward so as to point in the same line as the shrouds to which they belong (Fig. 54). The positions of the ports below the channels may make it impossible to do this perfectly and it may even be necessary to fit one or two chain-plates shorter than the others with their fastenings above the ports. The diameter of the deadeyes should be half that of the mast; the thickness of the chains or chain-plates can be judged by eye.

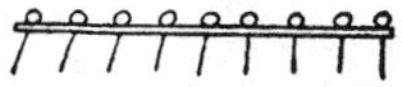

Fig. 54.   Chain-plates
with increasing rake

There will have to be two or three ring-bolts in each of the fore and main channels for tackles. These tackles will be discussed in the chapter on "Standing Rigging." Normally an English ship of 1670-1720 would require three ring-bolts in each fore and main channel and a foreigner two. The positions of these rings have to depend to some extent on the ports above and below the

channels, but if possible there should be one between
the first and second deadeyes, one between the 2nd and
3rd or 3rd and 4th deadeyes from aft and one (in English ships) between these two. They should be on a line
just inside that of the deadeyes and should have holes
drilled in the channels for them. About 1720, one or
more of the rings were sometimes fitted in the ship's
side above a port when it was impossible to put them on
the channels without fouling one of the guns. Apart
from the actual ring they can be made in one piece with
an eye at the bottom for a bolt into the hull and another
eye at the top, lying in and out ways, to take the ring.

Besides the lower shrouds, the topmast and topgallant backstays have to be provided with connections to
the hull. If the model is of earlier date than about 1640,
this necessity does not arise, because the backstays, if
there were any, were simple pendants and whips and
their falls started and finished on the rail or the timber-
heads. "Standing backstays" are indeed mentioned in
1618, but there is no reference to them in the "Treatise
on Rigging," of about 1625, and the print of the *Sovereign* does not show them. When they became general
they were usually set up with deadeyes and laniards in
English ships and with blocks and tackles in foreigners.
The number of backstays will be discussed fully under
"Standing Rigging," so there is no need to go into details of evidence at this stage. It will be enough to say
that fastenings have to be provided in English ships for
one standing topmast backstay a side on the fore and
main between 1640 and 1650, for two between 1650 and
1665, and for three after that date.

With one or two pairs of backstays there is little doubt
that they led to the ship's side a little abaft the lower

rigging. Their deadeyes were attached directly to the
wales, either to the same wale as the channels or, less
often, to the next above it. When the third backstay
was introduced, the arrangement remained the same for
a little while, but after a bit, first one and then two of
the backstays were shifted forward to give more lateral
support to the topmasts. In plans of 1719, two of the
backstays are brought to the channels, while the third
goes a little abaft them. In the *St George* model, of 1701,
only one backstay goes to the channels. How early this
process began I do not know; it was clearly before 1700
and I should imagine it was after 1680 — possibly ten
years after. In the same way the second change was after
1701 and, I think, after 1704, but before 1715. Perhaps the
raising of the channels had something to do with it.

When there were two pairs of backstays on the channels their deadeyes were arranged as follows:— The
aftermost pair were placed between the second and third
or the third and fourth deadeyes from aft. In the bigger
ships there were three deadeyes abaft them on the main
and two on the fore; in the 80's it was two in each case.
The other pair went two or three gaps further forward.
The deadeyes were about half the size of those for the
lower shrouds and their chain-plates were shorter, even
when there was no port beneath them. The third pair
were placed on "stools," which were simply short separate
channels carried above the upper-deck guns and just
above or a trifle abaft the after ends of
the real channels (Fig. 55). These
stools, in 1720 and thereabouts, had
two deadeyes on them, the foremost for
the topmast backstay and the other for
that of the topgallant.

Fig. 55. Stools for
Topmast Backstays

A little earlier, when there was only one pair of dead-eyes in the channels, they were placed in the first gap abaft the middle. The other two pairs went to the stools, which were set on the uppermost wale. This is the ar-rangement in the *St George,* but it is quite possible that before her time these aftermost backstays were taken to deadeyes fixed to a wale without stools. At any rate it is probable that stools were unknown in the days of three backstays abaft the lower rigging and that then and earlier, the deadeyes were attached directly to a wale or even to the side between the wales.

Standing backstays for the topgallants were a late fitting. They are not mentioned in 1670 and lists of 1675-85 give them for the main topgallant only in the first three Rates. Up to the time when the second pair of topmast backstays moved to the channels the top-gallant backstays probably had deadeyes on a wale; when the stools no longer had to accommodate two pairs of topmast backstays their after deadeyes were used by the topgallant backstays.

The mizzen topmast began to have standing back-stays soon after 1670. Lists of 1675 allow them for the first two Rates and in 1685 the 3rd-Rates are included. In 1719 they had stools just abaft the after end of the mizzen channels and as high up as possible; in 1701 there were no stools and the deadeyes had long strops and were bolted to the side in a similar position.

Dutch ships set up their topmast backstays with two fiddle-blocks and a tackle. The lower block was usually hooked into a ring-bolt fitted at the after end of the fore or main channels just inboard of the line of the dead-eyes. Sometimes the rings were on the wales instead, abaft the channels or above their after ends. One top-mast backstay each side for the fore and main would probably be correct after 1650 or earlier. The mizzen topmast seems to have begun to have backstays about 1665. Towards the end of the century big ships had two backstays to the fore and main topmasts. The *"William Rex"* model has her main topmast backstays on an extension of the channels, but those of the fore topmast go to the side abaft and *below* the channels, while the mizzen topmast backstays go to the wale above the after end of the channels. As far as I know the Dutch did not adopt the practice of having one pair of backstays about the middle of the channels, but kept them always further aft. They seem to have taken to topgallant backstays, on both the fore and main, about 1665. These came down to the side close abaft the topmast backstays and were set up by a laniard passing through a ring-bolt in the side and a ring spliced into the end of the backstay.

One would expect the French to follow Dutch fashions, but it seems that their ships in the last quarter of the 17th century were more like the English in this respect. Certainly they seem to have used deadeyes rather than blocks and to have had one or even two of their topmast backstays well forward in the channels. I should not be surprised to find that they led the way in this change. Danish ships of the same date used blocks in the Dutch manner, but the *Norske Löve,* of the middle of the century, is remarkable not only in having deadeyes for her backstays, but in having two pairs to the main topmast, both attached to the channels, one on either side of the last deadeye for the main shrouds (Plate 8).

II. *The Knights and Bitts*

THE question whether knights have to be fitted or not depends on the method of hoisting the lower yards. A knight was a vertical timber with sheaves in it, standing close to the foot of the mast and used for the halliards of the lower yard and for the end of the top-rope which hoisted the topmast. In the chapter on "Running Rigging of the Mainsail and Foresail," the matter of how the yards were hoisted will be discussed at length; at present it will be enough to consider how to make and fit knights if they are needed.

One very important point is whether the knight should be on an open deck or under cover. Obviously it makes things very much easier if the knight is in the open and I strongly advise that this should be done whenever it is reasonably permissible. Unfortunately there is no doubt that the knights were often between decks. Van Yk, writing in 1697, about Dutch shipbuilding, says that the knights in men-of-war were on the lower deck of a 2-decker and the section in Allard's book of 1705 shows the main knight in an almost incredible position on the lower deck of a 3-decker. A French section, of 1691, shows the knights on the middle-deck of a 3-decker with both upper deck and forecastle above the fore knight; but the *Royal Louis* model, of similar date, has her fore knight on the forecastle and the main knight on the upper deck with only the half deck over it. At an earlier period (about 1650) the Swedish *Amarant* has the fore knight on the upper deck and the main on the lower, while the Danish *Norske Löve* has her fore knight on the forecastle and the main probably on the upper deck.

The position of the knights is naturally associated

with that of the capstans. To follow the matter further would lead into all sorts of side-issues only remotely connected with rigging. There is little doubt that the knights of Dutch ships of the 17th century were more often than not between decks and the same would probably hold good for English ships in the first part of the century, when they were using such fittings.

It is impossible to give any general rule for fitting knights. The important thing to remember is that they must be well secured to something firm. If possible they should be fixed to two decks at least; otherwise there is a danger that they may pull the deck out of shape when the rigging shrinks. If this cannot be done, it may be possible to secure the knight firmly to one deck and to take a wire from that deck to the next or even to the keel. Again it may be possible to nick the knight to fit round the beams of a deck where no actual fastening can be managed.

According to Witsen, the main knight should measure one inch athwartship for every eight feet in the

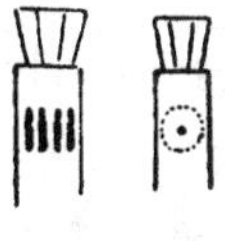

Fig. 56.
Main or Fore
Knights

ship's length from stem to sternpost. Put more simply, it should be 1/88 of the length. Fore and aft, it should be a little less. It should be shaped as shown in Fig. 56 and should have four sheaves in it and an eyebolt on one side. The fore knight should bear the same relation to the main as that between the two masts. At the end of the 17th century the knights stood about as far abaft the masts as the diameter of the masts themselves. In earlier days they were further aft and very often one was a little to one side of the centre line and the other on the opposite side. The mizzen knight was much smaller and had only two sheaves; it stood on the open deck *before the mast* (Fig. 57).

After the lower halliards and the top-ropes, the topsail sheets have to be given a lead and a
place for making fast. They went to the bitts,
which were a pair of timbers rather like the
knights but smaller, which stood just before
the lower masts, one on each side. At first
they were probably simple uprights with a
single sheave in each (Fig. 58), but later —
somewhere about 1660 in English ships and
later in foreigners — they were connected by a
cross-piece as in figure 59. About the same
time, when English ships took to double jeers
instead of ties and halliards, a second pair of

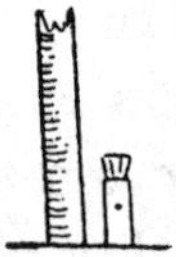

Fig. 57.
Mizzen
Knight

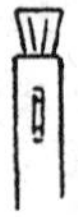

Fig. 58.
Single
Bitt

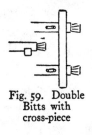

Fig. 59. Double
Bitts with
cross-piece

bitts, with a cross-piece, took the place of
the knight abaft the mast and provided
for the hauling parts of the jeers. At this
period and later it was usual to carve the
tops of the bitts into the shape of heads, a
custom which lasted in English ships till
the early years of the 18th century.

The sheet-bitts and jeer-bitts were sometimes nearly
as inaccessible as the knights. The model of the *Prince*,
of 1670, has the fore bitts beneath the forecastle and the
Dutch section of the end of the century shows the main
bitts on the middle deck of a 3-decker. By 1700, and
probably before that, English ships had
raised their fore bitts to the forecastle.
About the same time it became usual in
English ships to carry the uprights of
the main jeer-bitts up higher than the
sheet-bitts and to fit a second, longer

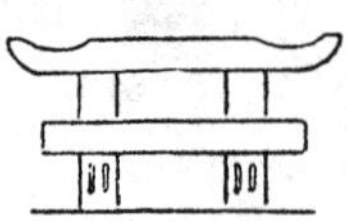

Fig. 60. Bitts
with Gallows
for Spars

cross-piece on top of them to carry the after ends of the spare spars which were stowed in the waist (Fig. 60).

III.   Cleats, Kevels and Belaying-pins

THE bitts, however much use is made of them, provide for the "belaying" or making fast of a very small proportion of the running rigging. Nine ropes out of ten have to be belayed somewhere and somehow on or near the bulwarks and rails. For this purpose there were three devices, different in details, but the same in principle, cleats, kevels and belaying-pins. With each of these the rope was secured by taking it several times in figure-of-eight fashion round two projecting arms. In a model it is best to add a half-hitch to make sure. There were also what the Dutch called simply "small knights"; these were upright timbers with sheaves in them secured

at various places to the inside of the bulwarks. At one time the Dutch went in largely for such fittings. Van Yk, in 1697, gives a list of sixteen on each side and four central.

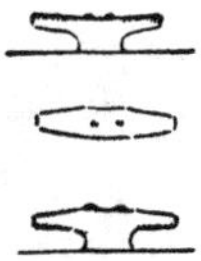

Fig. 61.
Cleats

Cleats were single pieces of wood shaped as shown in Fig. 61 and nailed or bolted to a flat surface such as the inside of the bulwarks.

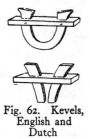

Sometimes there were cleats on the masts and occasionally they were lashed to the collar of the main-stay or even to the shrouds. Kevels were made as shown in Fig. 62 and were used for heavier duties such as belaying the lower sheets and

Fig. 62.   Kevels,
English and
Dutch

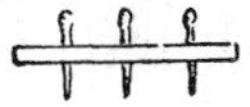

braces. Belaying-pins were simply stuck through the rails or through strips of timber fitted for the purpose (Figure 63). In a general way they did the lightest work.

Fig. 63.
Belaying Pins

It would be impossible — to me at any rate — to give a complete list of the type and position of the fastening for every rope. The best I can do is to show the fasten-

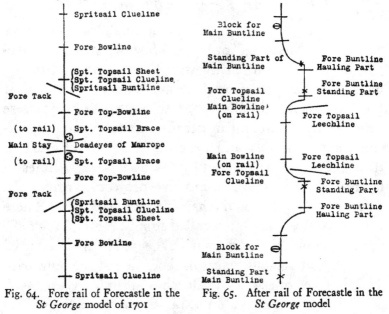

Fig. 64. Fore rail of Forecastle in the *St George* model of 1701

Fig. 65. After rail of Forecastle in the *St George* model

ings that I have noted on some models which I believe to be trustworthy, with the proviso that even the best models never seem to be satisfactorily equipped in this respect and that to put a rope back on the wrong pin is one of the easiest mistakes for a restorer to make. Such as they are, the drawings in Figs. 64-68 illustrate models of different countries in the period 1665-1715. It is probable that in the early part of the 17th century a great part of the running rigging was merely hitched to the rails, to the timber heads beneath them, or to the shrouds.

For purposes of comparison I give Van Yk's list of "small knights." It is as follows:— One each for the mizzen halliards and the three topsail halliards; two each for the main and fore lifts, bowlines, buntlines and

leechlines; two for the mizzen topsail sheets; two each
for the main and fore topsail braces, bowlines and buntlines; and two for the fore braces

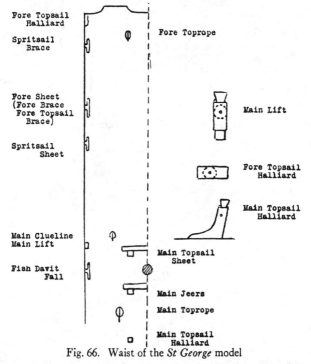

Fore Topsail
Halliard

Spritsail
Brace

Fore Toprope

Fore Sheet
(Fore Brace
Fore Topsail
Brace)

Main Lift

Spritsail
Sheet

Fore Topsail
Halliard

Main Topsail
Halliard

Main Clueline
Main Lift

Main Topsail
Sheet

Fish Davit
Fall

Main Jeers

Main Toprope

Main Topsail
Halliard

Fig. 66. Waist of the *St George* model

There are other things in the hull that are directly
concerned with rigging. For instance, the lower sheets
and tacks require ring-bolts, sheaves and fair-leads,
while the gammoning needs a hole in the cutwater.
These things will be dealt with as they arise in the course
of the description of standing and running rigging and
it seems unnecessary to go into them here as well. I
hope that anyone who attempts to rig his first model
with this book as a guide will read right through the
book before starting work. Those who have rigged
models before will know what to look for and in which
section to find it.

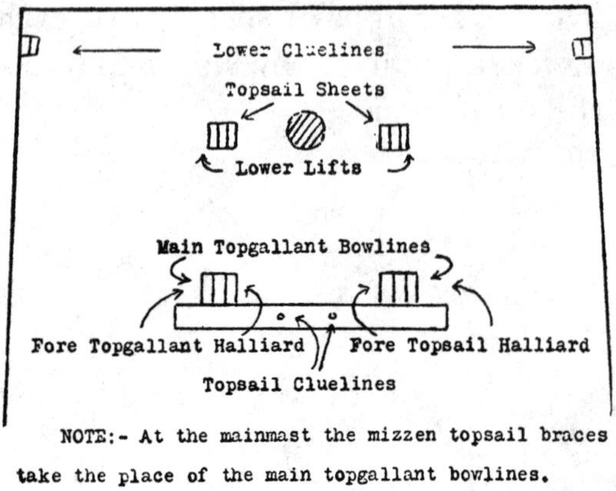
Lower Cluelines
Topsail Sheets
Lower Lifts
Main Topgallant Bowlines
Fore Topgallant Halliard
Fore Topsail Halliard
Topsail Cluelines
NOTE:- At the mainmast the mizzen topsail braces take the place of the main topgallant bowlines.

Fig. 67. Forecastle of Dutch model of 1665

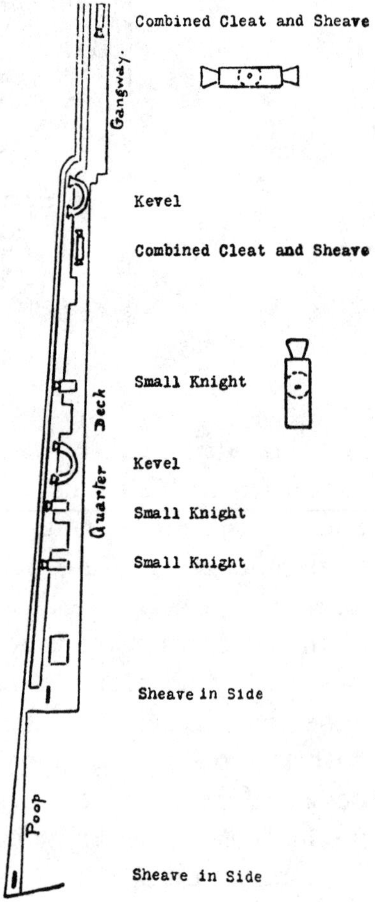
Combined Cleat and Sheave
Gangway.
Kevel
Combined Cleat and Sheave
Small Knight
Quarter Deck
Kevel
Small Knight
Small Knight
Sheave in Side
Poop
Sheave in Side

Fig. 68. Quarter Deck of English model of about 1715

CHAPTER VI

STANDING RIGGING

THE exact line between "standing" and "running" rigging is hard to draw. Some things, such as the shrouds and stays, are obviously standing rigging, and others, such as the tacks and sheets, are equally obviously running rigging. The difficulty comes with such things as the tackles on the one hand and the robands and foot-ropes on the other. Some of the tackles had a definite share in supporting the masts and are therefore rightly included under standing rigging, although they might be shifted and used for other purposes; but others—particularly those amidships over the main hatch—were essentially moveable and had nothing to do with holding up the masts. On the other hand robands and foot-ropes were permanent stationary fittings, and yet it would be very unusual to find them classed with the standing rigging. From the point of view of the model-maker the distinction is unimportant; all he needs to know is the best order for fitting the rigging. Looked at in this way such rigging as is connected with the masts only may be considered as standing rigging, while that which is directly concerned with the yards and sails may be called running rigging and left till later.

As an introduction to a detailed treatment of standing rigging it may be explained that the masts were held sideways and backwards by the shrouds and forwards by the stays. Certain tackles were fitted inside the shrouds and when in that position helped the shrouds

in their work.   Other tackles were carried between the
mainmast and foremast for lifting purposes.   The shrouds
of the lower masts led to the "channels," which were
platforms projecting from the side of the ship.   Each
shroud had a "deadeye" at its lower end and these deadeyes were connected to similar deadeyes on the channels
by means of "laniards" passing through the holes.   The
stays led forwards and downwards; the forestay went to
the bowsprit, the mainstay to the stem-head, the mizzen-
stay to the foot of the mainmast; they were "set up" in
very much the same way as the shrouds.   The topmast
shrouds came down towards the edge of the top.   Their
lower deadeyes were connected to the "futtock shrouds,"
which in turn were secured to the lower shrouds a little
way below the top.   The fore-topmast stay went to the
bowsprit rather further out than the forestay; the main-
topmast stay went to the fore top; the mizzen-topmast
stay went to the main top or to the main shrouds a little
below it.

Shrouds, stays and tackle-pendants were often (perhaps I should say "usually") "cable-laid."   Ordinary
rope is laid "right-handed," that is to say, its strands
run downwards from right to left as do the threads of
an ordinary screw.   Three-stranded rope of this kind is
called "hawser-laid"; four-stranded is "shroud-laid"—
from the model-maker's point of view the difference is
negligible.   "Cable-laid" rope is strictly nine-stranded
and consists of three hawser-laid ropes laid up together
left-handed.   For models it is enough to be sure of some
kind of left-handed rope, but this is not always easy to
get.   As a matter of fact — I am writing as an English-
man — I have found it very difficult to get and very ex-
pensive.   Fortunately it is not difficult to make one's

own cable-laid rope. My own rope-machine is a crude enough affair, but it works. The essentials are as follows:— On a fixed upright surface such as a wall there must be three hooks which can be made to revolve simultaneously in one direction at the same speed. On a travelling carriage there is another hook which can be revolved at the same speed as the other three. All that happens is that three right-handed lines are attached to the three hooks at one end and are then attached side by side at the same tension to the single hook at the other end. The three hooks are then revolved so as to twist up the three separate strands right-handed and the extra twist thus put into them is taken out again at the other end by revolving the travelling hook and laying the three strands round one another left-handed. It is necessary to keep the strands apart by means of a "top" or spool with three nicks in it. As the rope is laid up, the top is gradually forced along towards the three hooks and at the same time the travelling carriage is pulled in the same direction. The hardness of the rope is governed by the speed at which the top is allowed to travel.

This sounds like a three-man job; one to turn at each end and one to look after the top; but as a matter of fact it is quite safe to take a good many turns at one end and then the same number at the other, while the top can be controlled by a weight dragging on the floor or something of that

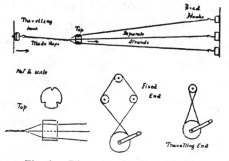

Fig. 69. Diagrams of a Rope-Machine

sort. I will not go further into details, because it will be far more satisfactory for the intending rope-maker to devise his own machine if he has to. The sketches in Fig. 69 will help to explain the method of working.

To save time later on I may as well give a few rules for the thickness of standing rigging. The Main Stay should have a circumference equal to half the greatest diameter of the mainmast. For all practical purposes it is near enough to say that its diameter should be 1/6 of that of the mast. The Fore Stay should be about ⅘ of the Main Stay; the Main Shrouds and Maintopmast Stay, ½; the Fore Shrouds, Foretopmast Stay and Mizzen Stay, ⅖; the Maintopmast and Mizzen Shrouds, ¼; the Foretopmast Shrouds and the Stays of the two Topgallants and the Mizzen Topmast, ⅕; the Shrouds of these three last, 1/6 or less.

The Bowsprit

THE rigging of a model, like that of the real ship, should begin with the bowsprit. The standing rigging of the bowsprit until the end of the 17th century was simplicity itself, because it consisted of the gammoning and nothing else. The gammoning is a heavy lashing by which the bowsprit is held down to the beakhead. Its thickness should be about ⅖ or ⅜ of that of the Main Stay, but it should be ordinary right-handed rope. The question of where to put it is not easily decided even in a contemporary model, unless the model has been rigged before. The most perfect models have often no provision for a gammoning and sometimes have not even a hole for the bowsprit. If there is a slit ready for the gammoning it should be used unless it is obviously due to ignorant rigging at a date much too late for the hull.

If there is no slit one must be made and then it is necessary to decide two points. Are there to be two gammonings or one, and how far down the knee of the head is the slit or slits to be cut?

The matter of two gammonings or one, probably had some relation to the size of the ship or the length of the bowsprit. The *Prince Royal*, of 1610, had two, but the Danish print of a few years later and a French drawing of similar date agree in showing only one. On the whole I think two gammonings were usual in big English ships from the beginning of the 17th century till about 1690; after that, or at any rate between 1700 and 1720, I should expect to find only one. In Dutch ships a single gammoning was more usual; in large French ships, towards the end of the 17th century, there were often two. Altogether there is very little certainty in the matter.

The place for the slit or slits is more definitely a question of date. At the very beginning of the 17th century

Fig. 70.
Gammoning
about 1610

the gammoning seems to have gone right round the knee of the head without a slit at all; this is what is seen in the *Prince Royal* (Fig. 70). A little later, as shown in a drawing of the *Antelope* (Fig. 71), the slits were cut just below the cheeks of the head and this remained the normal position for a long time. When there were two cheeks, the usual thing was to take the gammoning round them both and below the lowest pair, but sometimes only the one gammoning went as low as this. For example, the Dutch *Ary*, of 1725, has two gammonings and in her

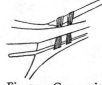

Fig. 71. Gammoning
about 1630

case the outer gammoning goes below the lower cheeks and the inner encloses the upper cheeks only.

The position of the gammoning in a horizontal direction changed very little, but the change in the shape of the head made it seem to work further forward as time went on. For instance, in the *Prince Royal* even the outer gammoning is only ¼ way out from the stem-head to the end of the beak; in the *Antelope* (as drawn in 1648) it is about ⅓ of the way out, in the *Victory*, of 1667, it is about half way and this half-way position was about the standard for the single gammoning of 1700 and later. With the short heads and deep figure-heads then in vogue this meant that the gammoning came almost hard up to the after side of the figurehead.

The slit should be just deep enough to take the gammoning comfortably and wide enough to allow of about eight to ten turns for a single gammoning and perhaps six or seven for each of a pair. It should be fairly close up to the cheeks — just far enough away to allow of an easy turn — and it should run parallel to the lower side of the cheeks.

To prevent the gammoning from slipping aft, down the bowsprit, there have to be small cleats. Five would be the usual number, one central and two on each side, and they should be cut and fitted so as to let the gammoning run straight. In thickness they should be just equal to the rope and in length they should be rather more than the total width of the gammoning. Usually the gammoning went vertically and the fore side of the cleats came just above the after side of the slit; but sometimes, particularly in early ships, the cleats were a little further aft, so that the gammoning raked aft a bit.

When the slit in the beakhead and the cleats on the

bowsprit are ready, the actual gammoning can be fitted.

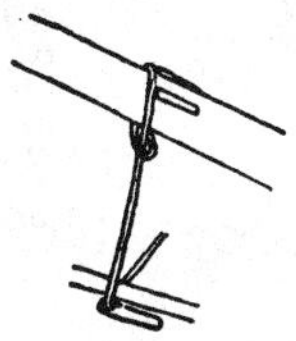

Start by making a small eye-splice on one end and pass the other end under the bowsprit from port to starboard, over the bowsprit from starboard to port and through the eye. Draw up tight and pass the end through the slit from port to starboard (Fig. 72). The slope of the slit and of the

Fig. 72. First turn of Gammoning

bowsprit will make it obvious that the turns have to start from aft on the bowsprit and from forward in the slit, so that the gammoning crosses itself every time halfway down on each side (Fig. 73). Go on till the full number of turns

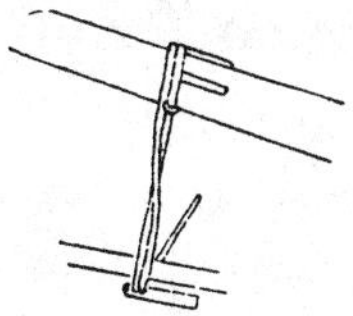

Fig. 73. Second turn of Gammoning

has been taken through the slit and then take one more over the bowsprit. At this stage the gammoning should be tight but not strained. The final tightening is done

as follows:— Bring the end down as if about to take another turn, pass it between the two sides of the gammoning from forward aft and take a half-hitch round the port half of the gammoning just below half way down (Fig. 74). Then take the end outside the starboard half from forward aft and go on round out-

Fig. 74. Tautening up the Gammoning

side everything pulling the two sides closely together. To finish off, put the last two turns round slackly, pass the end through them both downwards and pull tight (Fig. 75). The number of these horizontal turns should be about the same as the number of turns round the bowsprit.

Fig. 75. Finishing off the Gammoning

This is not strictly the way in which the gammoning

was secured in a real ship. There, each turn was "nip-pered" or seized to the turn before it and the end was eventually seized to one of the earlier turns. On a mod-el of very large scale this might be copied, but on any-thing small it will be best to accept a modification which looks very like the real thing.

Towards the end of the 17th century the bobstay was introduced. It is hard to understand why such an ob-vious fitting was so late in appearing. Several of the stays, not to mention a great part of the running rig-ging, combined to pull the bowsprit upwards and all it had to hold it down was the gammoning, which was too far inboard to have much leaverage. Whatever the rea-son, it is certain that the bobstay was unknown before the last quarter of the 17th century and I should hesi-tate very much before fitting one in a ship of before 1685.

I rather fancy the bobstay was a French invention; at any rate the earliest evidence for it is all French. It appears in two French prints of 1690 or 1691 and in the *Royal Louis* model of 1692. This last is, perhaps, a little doubtful, but there is other evidence. A manu-script which is believed to have belonged to Colbert shows a bobstay and Colbert died in 1683. In the book "Le Musée de Marine du Louvre" there is a "Vaisseau dessiné par Puget — 1650" with a bobstay (Plate 16); the date 1650 is impossible, for several reasons, but the heavy decoration of the hull suits the ascription to Puget and he died in 1694. In England, the contemporary rigging of the *St George,* of 1701, includes a bobstay and the same is the case in the Dutch *"William Rex,"* of 1698. Its first appearance in print is, I believe, in a German book of 1700.

In the English and Dutch models the bobstay is

fitted thus:— A deadeye is seized into a collar which is spliced round the bowsprit just before the collar of the forestay. This collar is quite short and the deadeye is close under the bowsprit. A much longer collar is spliced

through a hole in the cutwater close to the edge and about half way from the fore side of the gammoning to the fore side of the figurehead. Another dead-eye is seized in the bight of this collar which is also seized close up to the cut-

Fig. 76. English or Dutch Bobstay about 1700

water. The two dead eyes are then connected by a laniard in exactly the same way as will be described for the lower shrouds with the exception that the laniard starts and finishes at the fixed deadeye instead of the other. (Fig. 76). The German book describes the exact opposite; the long collar goes on the bowsprit and the short one on the cutwater (Fig. 77). This is also the

Fig. 77. German Bobstay about 1700

case in the drawing in the "Colbert book" and in one of the French prints, but the Puget drawing and the other print show another meth-od with a block under the bowsprit, another on the cutwater, and a 2 or 3-part tackle with its end leading inboard from the upper block (Fig. 78). This was the typical French 18th century fitting.

Fig. 78. French Bobstay about 1700

Bowsprit shrouds came in a little later than the bob-stay. In 1706 the English Navy Board issued an order that they were to be fitted in future, because they were

one of the unauthorized extras on which the spare gear
was expended as soon as ships were out of dockyard
hands.   From this one would suppose that they must
have been in use from 1700 at least, though it is not
usual to find them in plans or models before 1720.   They
were single ropes with hooks at one end and deadeyes
at the other.   The hooks went into eyebolts on the lower
wales and the deadeyes were set up to other deadeyes
on the bowsprit, secured by collars or by a single collar
close before that for the bobstay.

The Foremast and Mainmast

IN rigging the foremast and mainmast the first thing
to do is to fit the tackle pendants.   Ships of any size had
two on each side; they were made of the same rope as
the shrouds and were fitted in the same way.
A single rope was doubled in the middle and
a round seizing was put on it leaving a loop
just big enough to go over the masthead. (Fig.
79).   The rope should be long enough to let
the ends hang about half way down to the
deck with a bit to spare.   The starboard pair
goes on first.   Small ships, particularly of

Fig. 79.
A pair of
Shrouds
seized
together

Fig. 80.   Cut-splice

Fig. 81. Possible sub-
stitute for a Cut-splice

early date, may perhaps have had
only one on each side; in that case
there must be eye-splices to go over
the masthead or a "cut-splice," which
was practically a double eye-splice
(Fig. 80).   The latter is the more
likely.   In a very small model it
might be permissible to dispense with

splices and to use a single rope arranged as shown in
Fig. 81; there should never be knots of any kind at the

masthead. Before putting these tackle pendants in place "bolsters" should be fitted on the trestle-trees. These

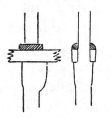

were simply quarter-round pieces of wood meant to ease the angle and to prevent the pendants and shrouds from getting cut on the edge of the trestle-trees (Fig. 82).

Fig. 82. Masthead showing Bolsters

After the tackle pendants come the shrouds. They are fitted in exactly the same way and go on starboard and port alternately, starting with the foremost pair on the starboard side. They should be left long enough to reach a litle below the channels. If there is an even number of shrouds on each side, well and good; if not, the last shroud on each side must be put on with an eye-splice. They all come down between the cross-trees (Fig. 83).

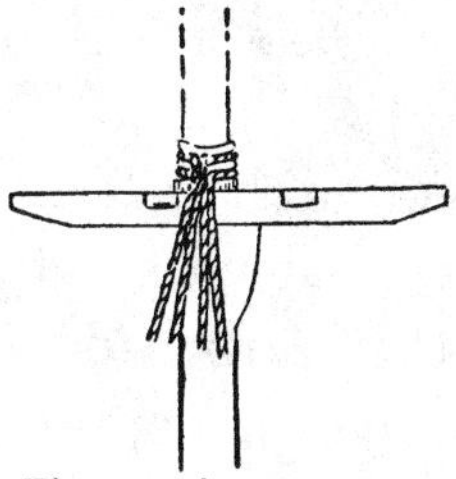

Fig. 83. Arrangement of Shrouds at Masthead

A deadeye has to be "turned in" at the bottom of each shroud. Before doing this it is as well to get the mast fixed at its proper rake by means of a temporary stay and backstay made fast anywhere convenient. The diameter of the deadeyes should be about half that of the mast to which they belong. They should bulge in the middle and go quite thin round the edge; modern machine-made deadeyes for models are usually much too flat-faced (Fig. 84). They should be turned in at such a position on the shrouds that there is a drift between them and the corresponding deadeyes on the channels equal to about twice their diameter or a little more. This will probably have to be adjusted later,

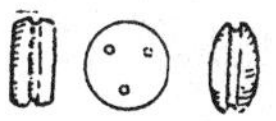

Fig. 84. Deadeyes, bad and good.

but it is as well to get it nearly right to begin with.

When a deadeye is turned in there is a difference in the treatment of "cable-laid" and "hawser-laid" rope. In either case the end goes under the deadeye and inside the standing part, that is to say, nearer the midship line.

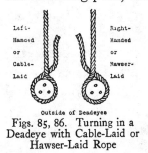

Figs. 85, 86. Turning in a Deadeye with Cable-Laid or Hawser-Laid Rope

With cable-laid or left-handed rope the end is passed under the deadeye from right to left as one looks at it from outboard; it then crosses the standing part and comes up on the right hand side of it. With right-handed rope the end goes from left to right and comes up on the left hand side of the shroud. The result of this is that with cable-laid shrouds the ends lie forward on the starboard side and aft on the port; with ordinary rope the opposite is the case. Figs. 85 and 86 will help to make this clearer. Where the end crosses the standing part, a "throat seizing" is made and the end is further secured by two round seizings, one about four feet (on the scale) above the deadeye and one half way. Above the upper of these two seizings the end is whipped and cut off. The whipping can be done with the end of the seizing or can be omitted altogether in a small model. Fig. 87 shows the

Fig. 87. Turning in of a Deadeye completed

turning in of the deadeye completed, but it is really best to leave the end long till a much later stage in the rigging. Shrouds are more likely to stretch than to shrink, but it is best not to risk finding the shroud too short later on.

Now comes the "setting up" of the shrouds by means of their laniards. These should be of ordinary right-handed rope and should be just less than half the shrouds in thickness. They have a knot on one end — strictly speaking it should be a "Matthew Walker," but a "fig-ure-of-eight" will do well enough for any ordinary-sized model. The deadeye is adjusted with the

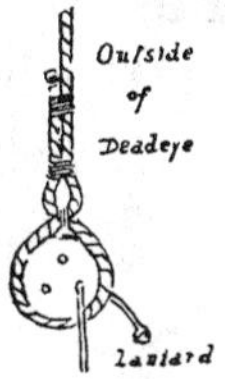

Fig. 88.
Position of
Laniard in
relation to
end of Shroud

apex of the triangle formed by its three holes pointing upwards and the laniard is passed outwards through the hole furthest from the end of the shroud (Fig. 88). It is then taken inwards through the corresponding hole in the lower deadeye, outwards through the middle or uppermost hole in the upper dead-eye and so on through the three remaining holes. It is now drawn taut, taken up be-hind the upper deadeye, passed over the standing part of the shroud, through between the throat seizing and the deadeye and led under itself to make a half-hitch (Fig. 89).

Finally the end is wound several times round both parts and finished off in any way that looks neat. It ought to be stopped to the shroud, but this is perhaps too much to expect. A half-hitch and the end passed be-

Fig. 89.
Securing a
Laniard

tween the two parts of the shroud and cut off makes a very good job, or the end can be passed under the last two turns as was done with the gammoning. Whatever method is employed the laniard should not be cut off short at present, because it will almost certainly have to be readjusted as the rigging progresses.

The shrouds should be set up alternately starboard and port to ensure keeping the mast straight and the foremost shrouds should be done first. When they are all set up their deadeyes should run in a straight line parallel to those on the channels.

The stays present more difficulty than the shrouds, both in knowing what to do and in doing it. First there is the question of fitting or omitting "spring" or "preventer" stays, which were lighter ropes running just above the ordinary stays and intended to help them in their work and to provide a safeguard against their loss in action. With one very notable exception I know of no evidence for spring stays before the last decade of the 17th century. The *St George*, of 1701, has them and they appear in a print (Plate 20) which seems, from the decoration of the hull to be at least as early. The *"William Rex"* (1698) has none, but they are mentioned in Aubin's "Dictionnaire de Marine," of 1702, and the "Admiral-ship of Holland," in the 1705 edition of Allard, has a spring mainstay. In the same way they do not appear in the French prints of 1691 or in the *Royal Louis,* of 1692, but they do appear in the ship ascribed to Puget, whatever her date may be. From this evidence one would suppose that they came in about 1695, but now comes the exception — they are shown very clearly in at least three of Zeeman's Dutch etchings and these date from about 1650-70. Two of them come from the first set of his "Various Ships and Views of Amsterdam" and the fact that the first shows "Two new Frigates equipped for War against the Parliament of England" (Plate 10) seems to date this series within a few years of the First Dutch War of 1652-4.

Personally, I should not fit spring stays in any model of earlier date than 1690, but if anyone wishes to fit them — particularly in a Dutch ship — at any time after 1655, it would be difficult to prove him wrong. On the other hand it would probably be quite justifiable to omit them up to 1720 or later. Baston's prints of about 1720 do not show them, nor do the plans of the 1719 establishment; but the model of the *Royal George,* of 1715, in Hanover has them (Frontispiece). In the same way the drawing of the Dutch *Gertruda,* of 1720 (Plate 23), shows spring stays, while the models of the *Ary* and *Padmos,* similar ships of a few years later, do not. No doubt the explanation is that some people looked on them as permanent fittings and others as additions made before going into action.

The attachment of the stays to the mastheads is easy to explain but not so easy to do. An eye is spliced in one end and the other end goes through this to form what would be a running noose if it were not for a "mouse" or lump which is worked on the stay to prevent the noose from closing up (Fig. 90). The first thing to do is to make the eye — big enough for the stay itself to go through comfortably, but no more. Then pass the eye up between the cross-trees on one side of the mast, round abaft the masthead and the tops of the shrouds and down between the cross-trees on the other side. Then mark the place for the mouse. With the stay in position the fore side of the mouse, where the eye will go, should be about under the fore edge of the top — perhaps a little before it.

Fig. 90. Use of a Mouse on the Stay

The mouse was not made by knotting the stay in either sense of the word "knot." It was not a "figure-of-eight" or a "crown and wall" or anything of that sort. It was not even a "Turk's head" made on the stay, but a special piece of rope-work used for this purpose only. Its making or "raising" will be found described in detail by Darcy Lever, but the method employed in a real ship will not work very well in a small model. The follow-

ing is a good way of getting the right effect:— Pad
out the stay to roughly the shape
of the mouse by wrapping wool round
it and put a lashing of thin thread
very loosely round the stay above and
below the padding (Fig. 91). Take
a long piece of thin line on a needle and starting by
sticking it through the stay with a knot, at the end of

Fig. 91. First stage in
raising a Mouse

the padding furthest from the
eye, go backwards and forwards
between the two lashings till the
whole circumference of the padding is loosely covered with lon-
gitudinal lines (Fig. 92). Then,

Fig. 92. Second stage in
raising a Mouse

beginning at the other end, so as to have an odd number of longitudinals, go round and round the padding
under and over the longitudinals
as if darning (Fig. 93). Finish
up by taking a few turns round
the stay and passing the end once
or twice through the strands of the
stay itself.

Fig. 93. Third stage in
raising a Mouse

This method of fitting the stay with a small eye and
a mouse was the invariable rule at the end of the 17th
century, but I am not sure that it was always employed
in earlier days. A good many pictures of the first half of
the century suggest a simple long eye-splice and this
even appears in the silver-wire rigging of the Danish
Norske Löve model, made in 1654 but representing a
ship of 1634. On the other hand the ship in Furttenbach's "Architectura Navalis," of 1629, certainly has the
eye and mouse fitting (Plate 4) and I think the same is
the case in Vroom's painting of the *Prince Royal*, of 1610.

The forestay, as has been said already, went to the bowsprit. For the early part of the 17th century, the point on the bowsprit to which it should lead can be found fairly accurately by looking on the foremast, the bowsprit and the forestay as forming an isosceles triangle with the forestay as the base. Later on the side of the triangle represented by the bowsprit became shorter; in English ships of 1700 and thereabouts it was about 5/6 of the side represented by the foremast; while foreign ships, with their shorter bowsprits, might have the proportion ¾ or even less.

There were three possible ways of setting up the forestay; blocks, deadeyes or hearts. Between 1650 and 1720 it seems safe to say that foreign ships (French, Dutch and Danish) nearly always used blocks, while English ships used deadeyes up to about 1690 and hearts afterwards. Before 1650 there is less certainty; most pictures, whether of English or foreign ships, suggest blocks, but Furttenbach's ship, drawn from a model probably of Dutch origin, shows deadeyes very clearly and English books of similar date speak of deadeyes, at any rate, for the mainstay.

Whatever method is employed, the lower fitting—block, deadeye or heart is secured to the bowsprit by means of a spliced collar and a round seizing. The upper one is turned in on the stay itself in the same manner as the deadeyes of the shrouds; some early pictures show the end wound round the standing part instead of being brought up beside it, but this is a small point. Deadeyes may perhaps have five holes instead of three; blocks should probably be 3-sheaved. With deadeyes the laniard will start with a knot in the usual way; with blocks it will be eye-spliced round the bight of the stay beneath the upper block; with hearts it will be spliced

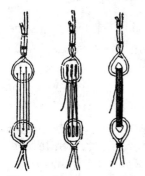

through the upper heart itself. When hauled taut its ends can be secured round the stay or round the collar at the seizing, or it can be finished off with turns round the middle of the tackle in the same way as the gammoning. This last seems to have been the most usual finish when blocks were used. The three different types of attachment are shown in Fig. 94.

Fig. 94. Stays set up with Deadeyes, Blocks or Hearts

The main part of the mainstay is exactly like the fore-stay except for its greater size. Its lower collar has to be very much longer, since it has to extend from a point on the stem to somewhere very near the foremast and often abaft it. It should be a spliced collar about ¾ of the thickness of the stay. In English ships it ran as a general rule through a hole in the knee which filled the angle between the stem and the

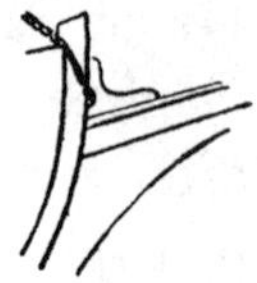

Fig. 95. Lower end of Collar of Mainstay

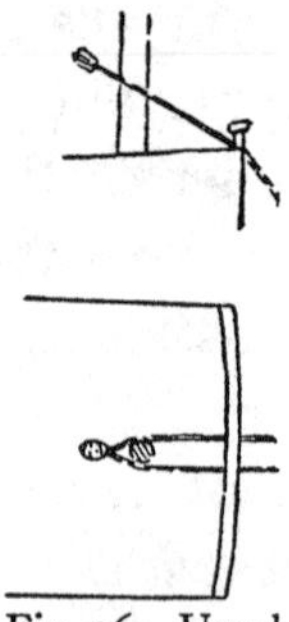

beakhead or through a nick cut in the after side of that knee (Fig. 95). Foreign builders seem to have preferred a hole in the stem itself a trifle higher up. For the first half of the 17th century the collar was long enough to allow the dead-eye or block, which was secured by a throat seizing, to come just abaft the fore-mast. The two parts of the collar ran on either side of the foremast and over the beakhead bulkhead but under its rail (Fig. 96). When the bowsprit was central, they naturally went down on either side of it.

Fig. 96. Usual lead of Collar of Mainstay

Sometimes, particularly in Dutch ships, there were holes in the forecastle deck and in the beakhead bulkhead to give the collar a fairer lead and sometimes the collar was crossed between the stem and the bulkhead (Fig. 97).

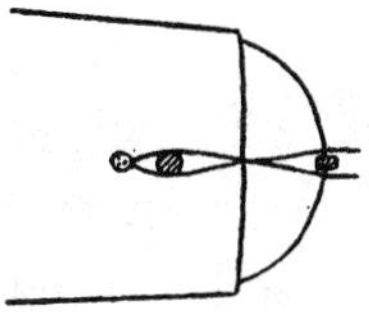

When hearts were introduced, it was usual to have the collar a little shorter, so that the lower heart was only just on the forecastle and the upper one just before the foremast. This involved bring-

Fig. 97. Alternative lead of Collar of Mainstay

ing the stay past the foremast on one side — usually the starboard (Fig. 98). Probably this was done to some extent with deadeyes, for the series of drawings made by Deane, in 1670, show the setting up of the mainstay sometimes before or beside and sometimes abaft the foremast.

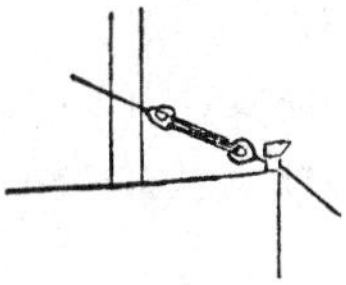

Fig. 98. Mainstay set up before Foremast

Spring stays, when present, should be fitted in very much the same way as the real stays. At the top they are led round the mastheads above the stays in exactly the same way. The fore spring stay went to the bowsprit about two feet further out than the forestay. The main spring stay usually went to the foremast just above the line of the mainstay. English ships set them up with deadeyes; foreigners, with blocks. One French drawing shows a long collar on the main spring stay running forward to the stem like that of the mainstay. This was not usual, but it is quite possible. The French *Royal Louis* model shows an unusual method of fitting the collar of the mainstay. It is not really a collar at all but a long span with its two ends secured separately to the bowsprit just inside the gammoning. It is quite pos-

sible that the collar sometimes went round the bowsprit
without going down to any more permanent anchorage,
but I must say I doubt this double-ended attachment.
I also rather doubt the method of setting up the mainstay (not the spring stay) to the foot of the foremast;
pictures often seem to suggest this and I have seen it in
modern models, but I think it is probably based on mistakes in drawing.

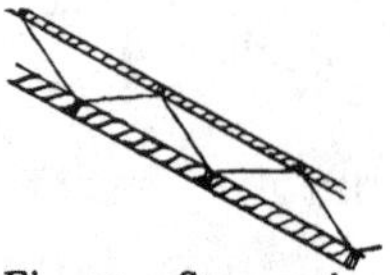

Sometimes the stay and its spring
stay were "snaked" together. This
means that a thin line was seized to
the stay and the spring stay alternately (Fig. 99) the seizings on each
being about four feet apart. The *St*

Fig. 99. Stay and
Preventer Stay
Snaked together

George model has this snaking and it appears in the drawing attributed to Puget;
but other early representations of spring
stays show no snaking. Its purpose was to
keep the stay or the preventer stay from
falling on deck if one of them were cut.

Fig. 100.
Runner and
Tackle

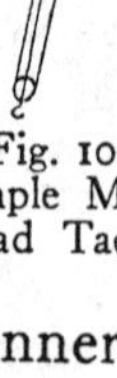

When the shrouds and stays have been set
up it is time to fit the tackles on to their
pendants. These tackles varied a good deal.
The English "Treatise on Rigging," of about
1625, describes them as consisting of a runner and a 4-part fall with a double block at
the end of the runner and a single block in
the channels (Fig. 100) and says there were
two or four to each mast according to the
size of the ship. This remained the usual
way of fitting one pair of tackles on each
mast in English ships; the other pair had no
runners, but had double blocks on the pendants (Fig.

Fig. 101.
Simple Mast-
head Tackle

101). Early in the 17th century these simpler tackles were called "swifters," a name which was soon transferred to the aftermost pair of shrouds. The description of swifters in the "Treatise on Rigging" reads as if they were merely shrouds with a special name, but the "Seaman's Dictionary," of similar date, is quite definite in its description of swifters as 4-part tackles hanging from pendants.

Early in the 18th century the arrangement in English ships was as follows:— The tackle with a runner came forward on the foremast and aft on the main and the actual runner was before its tackle on the foremast and abaft it on the main. In the *St George* model the ring-bolts are disposed in the channels as shown in Fig. 102; in plans of some 15-20 years later the arrangement is slightly different but the same in principle (Fig. 103). Information with regard to the practice of the middle part of the 17th

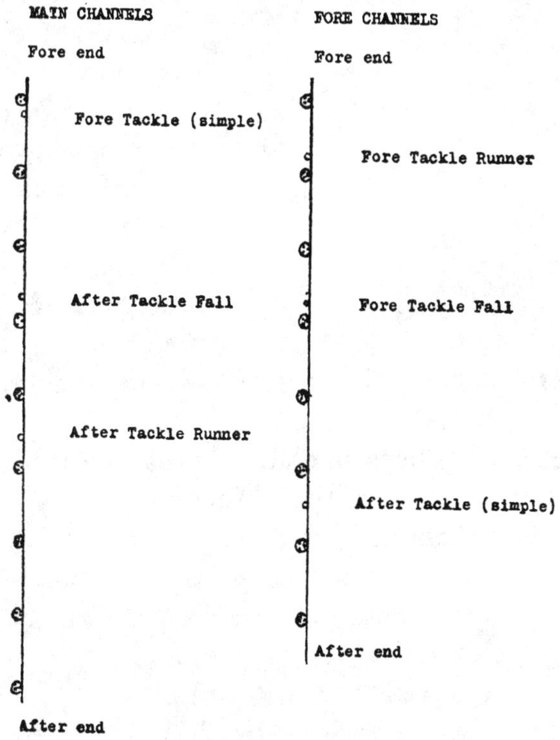

MAIN CHANNELS

Fore end

Fore Tackle (simple)

After Tackle Fall

After Tackle Runner

After end

FORE CHANNELS

Fore end

Fore Tackle Runner

Fore Tackle Fall

After Tackle (simple)

After end

Fig. 102. Positions of Tackles on Mainmast and Foremast of the *St George* model of 1701

century is scanty; I know of no really satisfactory draw-ings and the available lists of rigging and blocks leave the matter still un-certain. On the whole I think it would be safe to fit tackles in the same way back to 1660. Before that one might intro-duce more va-riation; one might have two runner tackles on each side, as is indicated in the engraving of the *Sovereign*,

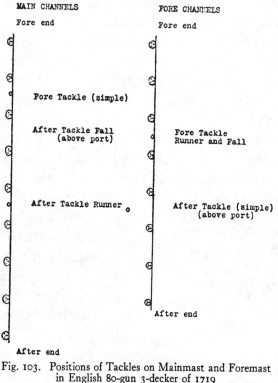

MAIN CHANNELS
Fore end

Fore Tackle (simple)

After Tackle Fall
(above port)

After Tackle Runner

After end

FORE CHANNELS
Fore end

Fore Tackle
Runner and Fall

After Tackle (simple)
(above port)

After end

Fig. 103.   Positions of Tackles on Mainmast and Foremast
in English 80-gun 3-decker of 1719

or one might perhaps have two simpler "swifter" tackles with no runners.

As to thickness: it has been said already that the pend-ants should be the same as the shrouds. The runners should be about ⅔ of the pend-ants and the falls rather more than ½ the runners.   All the blocks should be stropped with rather long eyes and those on the pend-ants should be secured with a throat and a round seizing (Fig. 104).   The *St George* has her runners spliced through the eyes on their

Fig. 104.
Upper
Tackle-block
secured to
Pendant

blocks and hooks spliced in at the other end. The blocks in the channels have hooks on the eyes of their strops and the fall is spliced through the strop above the block (Fig. 105).

Foreign ships do not seem to have used the runner type of tackles. They usually had fiddle-blocks on one pair of pendants and ordinary double blocks on the other. In the channels there were single blocks beneath the fiddle-blocks and double blocks beneath the others. The fall started from below in the former case and from above in the latter; thus the fiddle-blocks had 4-part tackles (Fig. 106) and the double blocks 5-part (Fig. 107). Sometimes the fiddle-blocks came forward on both masts, sometimes aft. Probably the correct way is to have the 5-part tackle aft on the fore-mast and forward on the main.

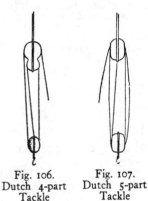

Fig. 105.
Lower
Tackle-block
with Hook
and Fall

Fig. 106.
Dutch 4-part
Tackle

Fig. 107.
Dutch 5-part
Tackle

While on the subject of tackles it will be as well to dispose of those which were carried in the neighborhood of the main stay. In the early part of the 17th century there were two tackles here in English ships, the "garnet" and the "winding tackle." The garnet had a pendant from the mainmast head and a single block at the end of it. This pendant was seized to the mainstay in such a position that the block came just over the main hatch. The runner had a hook at one end and a fiddle-block at the other. The fall started from a block with a hook beneath it and ran in four parts. When in use the runner was attached to the

weight to be lifted and the lower fall-block hooked to
a convenient eye-bolt in the deck (Fig. 108). When not
in use the whole tackle was carried along the mainstay
with its two hooks
fixed to the collar of
the stay or to a
strop on the fore-
castle rail (Fig.
109).

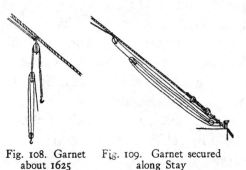

Fig. 108. Garnet   Fig. 109. Garnet secured
about 1625   along Stay

The winding
tackle had also a
pendant from the
mainmast head, but
it was not seized to the mainstay. Instead it had a guy
to the foremast, sometimes to the masthead, but more
often to the forecastle at the foot
of the mast (Fig. 110). The upper block might be double or
treble and the lower single or
double. Manwayring, in 1623,
describes the upper as "a great
double block with three shivers
in it"—this probably means a

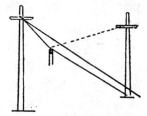

Fig. 110. Winding Tackle
about 1625

fiddle-block with two sheaves in the upper part—and
the lower simply as "another double block." Such an
arrangement would give a 6-part tackle, but what is
found in the *Sovereign* is a 4-part tackle with an ordinary fiddle-block at the top.

It is possible that by the time of the *Sovereign* (1637)
the old form of garnet had gone out of use and that its
name had been transferred to something very like the
old winding tackle. Certainly this was the case by the
middle of the century; every authority from Bond in

1642 to Sutherland in 1711, shows or describes the garnet as consisting of a free pendant, a fore-guy and a fall. Sutherland gives a winding tackle as well and shows it as similar to the garnet but heavier and with its fore-guy taken to the masthead. He explains that it was only rigged when it was wanted to hoist guns in or out.

The pendant of the garnet should be about as thick as the main shrouds, the guy should be ⅔ or ⅝ of this and the fall ½. The fiddle-block has a long eye to its strop and both the pendant and the guy have long eyes spliced in them. The pendant goes up between the cross-trees on the starboard side, inside the stay-collar but outside the trestle-trees; it is taken round the masthead above the shrouds and

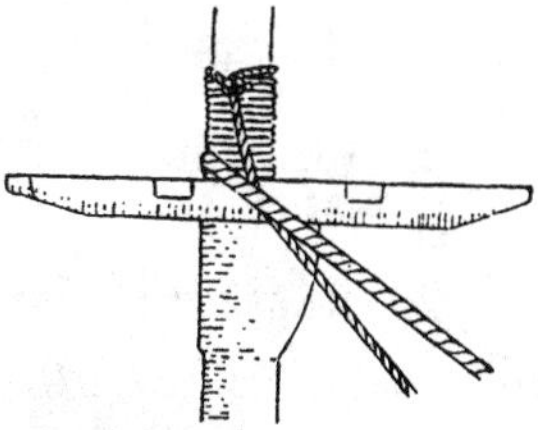

Fig. 111. Masthead showing attachment of Pendant of Garnet

clinched round itself (Fig. 111). Possibly it was sometimes led through an eye in its own end; this certainly makes a neat job on a model. Then, first the strop of the block and then the eye of the guy are taken over and through the eye of the pendant (Fig. 112). In another method, which comes to very much the same thing in the end, the strop of the block is put through the eye of the guy and over the eye of the pendant and the guy is then rove through the eye of the pendant beneath the strop of the block (Fig. 113). The lower block is stropped with a hook and attached to a ring-bolt in the deck; the fall can be hitched round

Fig. 112. Connection of Pendant, Block and Guy of Garnet

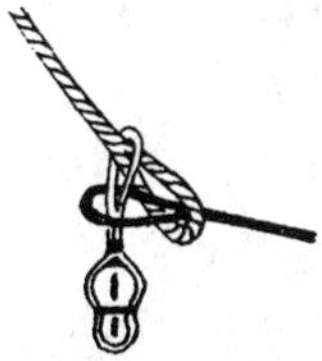

Fig. 113. Alternative method of connecting Pendant, Block and Guy

the strop or taken to a leading-block hooked to another ring-bolt and hitched there. The fore-guy goes to the foot of the foremast or to the after rail of the forecastle.

Foreign ships varied so much in the arrangement of their hoisting tackles that I can do little more than mention some of the methods employed. The most usual fitting in French ships between 1680 and 1700 seems to have been a fiddle-block on a pendant from the mainmast head with a 2-part guy to the foremast head (Fig. 114). The *Royal Louis*

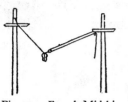

Fig. 114. French Midship Tackle about 1700

model has two of these, though with multiple-sheaved blocks instead of fiddle-blocks, and that was the normal French 18th century practice. Sometimes the pendant tackle seems to have been replaced or supplemented by a tackle attached directly to the stay. In Dutch ships there is the same variation, but I fancy the method of slinging the tackle from the stay is the older form. In the latter part of the 17th century there was usually a single fiddle-block tackle hung from the mainmast head and guyed to the foremast head with a single guy. The *"William Rex"* model shows a variation of this with a second tackle seized to the pendant of the first (Fig. 115). By about 1720 — at any rate in East Indiamen — the French practice of

Fig. 115. Midship Tackles in *"William Rex"* model

having two pendant tackles with double fore-guys was being followed, but even then there was sometimes a block seized to the stay for a third tackle.

The Mizzen-mast

BEFORE going any further with the rigging of the fore-mast and mainmast it will be as well to deal with the mizzen. First, it is necessary to decide whether there are to be tackles or not. Apparently English ships had mizzen tackles of the pendant, runner and fall type up to about 1655. Bond's book, of 1642, mentions them and Hayward, in 1655, gives them to all the bigger old ships but not to any of the ships built after 1650. They appear again in Deane's manu-script of 1670 in the form of "burton tackles" with two single blocks and a 3-part fall (Fig. 116). By 1700, though still called "burtons," they had fiddle-blocks on the pendants and 4-part falls (Fig. 117). They were then car-ried well abaft the shrouds and attached to ring-bolts high up on the side outboard. Pre-

Fig. 116.
Mizzen
Burtons
about 1660

sumably they acted as shifting backstays and the lee tackle was slacked off when the mizzen was set. I am not sure if the true burtons of 1670-85 were carried in the same position, but should expect to find it so.

Fig. 117.
Mizzen
Burtons
about 1700

Mizzen shrouds were similar to those of the fore and main except that there were fewer of them and that they were not much more than half as thick as those on the mainmast. The mizzen stay was rigged in exactly the same way as the other stays and was set up by means of a pair of dead-eyes to a collar on the mainmast a few feet above the deck. Foreign ships usually had fiddle-block and single block tackles, but took them to the mizzen channels between the first two shrouds instead of leading them aft. Their stays were rigged in the same way as those of English ships, but were set up with blocks more often than with deadeyes.

Futtock-shrouds and Catharpins

THE lower deadeyes of the topmast shrouds were placed close to the edges of the tops. Naturally, as soon as topsails began to be relatively large sails, it became impossible for the tops to stand the strain which would come on them if the deadeyes were fixed to them and to them only. Accordingly the deadeyes were connected to the lower shrouds by means of ropes called "puttocks" (later called "futtock-shrouds"), which passed through holes in the rim of the top. The idea of taking them to necklaces on the lower masts came very much later. At the end of the 16th century the puttocks were still merely ropes and wore out very quickly where they passed through the tops. To get over this difficulty the deadeyes were given "puttock-plates" of metal and the puttocks or futtock-shrouds were attached to these below the tops. This was the general rule by 1620 or very soon after.

I am not at all sure whether the puttock-plates should be distinct from the strops of the deadeyes or not. At the end of the 18th century the whole thing was in one piece, but it is possible that at an earlier date the puttock-plates were made in the same way as the lower chain-plates with hooks for the deadeyes. The way they are mentioned in store-lists rather suggests this and the *Norske Löve* model, which I look on as a very good authority on such points, has this arrangement. I know of no other model which shows it; but I think, if I were making a large-scale model of a ship of the first half of

the 17th century, I should be inclined to follow the
Norske Löve. In a small-scale model or in anything
later, I should make the whole fitting in one piece. It is
simply a matter of lengthening the strop of the deadeye, otherwise it can be made in the same way as those
for the lower rigging. As a rough rule it may be said
that the puttock-plate should reach below the top about
as much as the diameter of its deadeye or perhaps a little
more. If necessary the wires can be given a twist or two
a little way below the deadeyes; the rim of the top will
hide this part of the fitting if it looks clumsy.

At their lower ends the futtock-shrouds were taken
round the futtock-staff, a bar seized horizontally outside the lower shrouds about as far below the top as the
masthead extended above it. At a later date the futtock-staff ended short of the foremost and aftermost
shrouds, but during the greater part of the period covered
by this book it went across the whole number and was
seized to each of them. Somewhere about 1690 it
became the rule to leave the foremost shroud clear,
though the futtock-staff still extended over the aftermost; this is the state of affairs in the *St George,* of
1701, and later English models, in the Dutch *"William
Rex,"* of 1698, and *Padmos,* of 1723, and in the French
Royal Louis, of 1692.

The futtock-staff had a double duty; it provided a
point of attachment for the futtock-shrouds and also
for the "catharpins," which were tackles (or at any rate
collections of ropes) running across from the shrouds of
one side to those of the other and helping to keep them
taut and to hold them in against the pull of the futtock-
shrouds. It is best to set up the catharpins before the
futtock-shrouds. If this is not done, it will be found

that an attempt to pull the lower shrouds together by means of the catharpins causes the part of the shrouds above the futtock-staves to go slack.

The way in which the catharpins were rigged varied greatly. The English method of about 1625 is described very clearly in the "Treatise on Rigging." Two ordinary 3-holed deadeyes were each stropped to a single block. The "legs" of the catharpins passed through the holes in the deadeyes, making six parts to each, and each leg was secured to a shroud. The "fall" started from one block, ran through the two blocks and was made fast between the block and the deadeye on the opposite side from its standing part. Fig. 118 shows this form of catharpins. The legs were probably each given a half-hitch round one of the shrouds and the futtock-staff at the same time. Possibly

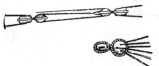

Fig. 118. English Catherpins about 1625

there was not always a futtock-staff at all; in that case the legs would be hitched to the shrouds only. According to "The Seaman's Dictionary," of much the same date, these upper catharpins (the lower catharpins will be mentioned later) "are ever made fast and do not run in blocks." This may mean that the two deadeyes were connected by some sort of lashing without blocks, but it is more likely to mean nothing more than that the fall was made fast aloft and the legs attached separately to the shrouds.

How long this type of fitting lasted it is hard to say. As late as 1670 and 1675, Deane and Keltridge mention "legs" and "falls" for the catharpins, and Battine, ten years later, gives two thicknesses of rope which correspond to those in the earlier lists, but at the same time both Keltridge and Battine give a number of blocks for catharpins equal to the number of shrouds and say nothing about deadeyes. This looks as if they were dealing with the lower catharpins, which will be discussed in due course, though it will be seen that there is no need

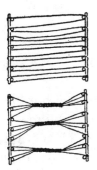

for separate legs and falls in their case. At all events, a new form of catharpins was in vogue by 1700. This consisted of a simple lashing round the shrouds and futtock staves from one side to the other (Fig. 119), tightened up by having its parts frapped together in three bundles. Purely as a guess I should start fitting this new form after 1690.

Fig. 119. English Catharpins about 1700

Dutch ships apparently did without these upper catharpins until the very end of the 17th century. The first evidence for their use seems to be in the *"William Rex"* model, which was rigged in 1698. True, the *Prins Willem* model has them and she belongs to 1650, but unfortunately she has them in a comparatively modern form and there are too many suspicious points about her rigging to allow of its being taken as real evidence.

In the *"William Rex,"* deadeyes are used for the catharpins in exactly the opposite way to the English fashion. There the deadeyes were used as leads for the legs to individual shrouds, while the setting up was done by means of the blocks stropped to them. In the Dutch ship the two deadeyes are connected by a laniard which does the setting up and the legs are connected in some obscure way to the deadeyes. I am not very clear how this was done, but it is probable that they were seized in pairs through the strop of the deadeye (Fig. 120). There were not often catharpins on the mizzen, but the *William Rex*" has them in a modified form shown in Fig. 121.

Fig. 120. Possible method of rigging Dutch Catharpins

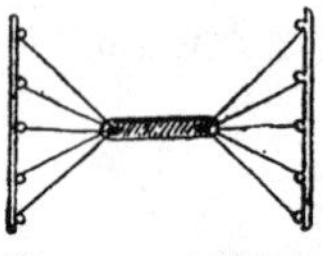

Fig. 121. Mizzen Catharpins in "*William Rex*" model

The *Blydorp* model of 1723 has neither deadeyes nor blocks. Its catharpins are similar in principle to those of the *St George,* but are gathered into two bundles only, and these two bundles are further set up by means of two fore-and-aft lashings (Fig. 122). At the fore there are six shrouds apart from the foremast independent shroud; at the main there are seven and the middle shroud is left out in the lead of the catharpins. The mizzen is without catharpins, as was usual.

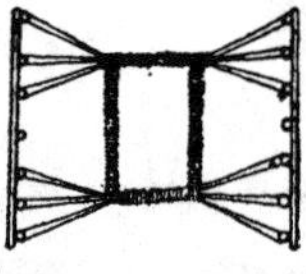

Fig. 122. Dutch Catharpins about 1720

As to the practice of other countries I have not much information. The Swedish *Amarant* model of 1653, has catharpins like those of the "*William Rex,*" but they may be due to restoration. The *Norske Löve,* of 1654, has none, as was to be expected, and another Danish model, which may be as late as 1690, is also without them. In French ships, too, it seems to have been usual to dispense with catharpins up to 1700 at least.

The lower catharpins appear to have been peculiar to English ships, or perhaps it would be more correct to say that it is a peculiarity of English models to show them. "The Seaman's Dictionary," of 1623, describes them as "small ropes which run in little blocks . . . from one side of the shrouds to the other near the deck,"

but the "Treatise on Rigging" does not mention them
and the print of the *Sovereign* does not show them.   In
point of fact pictures never or hardly ever do show them.
I think the explanation is that they were really an emer-
gency fitting, used to set up the shrouds quickly if necessary, but not left permanently rove.

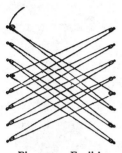

On each shroud about half way between the rail and the futtock-staff
there was a small block and through
these blocks ran a continuous line as
shown in Fig. 123.   Its end may have
been made fast, but was more probably brought down to the deck.   The
St George, of 1701, and the *Royal
George*, of 1715, show this fitting in

Fig. 123.   English
Lower Catharpins

model form, but plans and pictures do not even show
the blocks for it.   As far as I know it is not shown in
foreign models.   The *"William Rex"* has blocks in the
right place, but nearly all of them are used simply as
leading blocks for the running rigging.   There is little
doubt, however, that the device was used in Dutch ships,
because it is mentioned in books; but it is probable that
it was looked on as a temporary piece of gear, not suitable for representation in a model or a picture.   Personally I should fit it in an English model and omit it in a
foreigner, but I think that it would be quite justifiable
to fit or omit it in either.   If fitted, the lower catharpins
should be only just taut, not set up hard enough to pull
the shrouds out of line.

Having at length finished with catharpins we can get
back to the futtock-shrouds.   The number of these
should be the same as that of the topmast shrouds; as
a rough rule we may take this to be half as many as the

lower shrouds, 4½ counting as five and so on. There is not very much to say about them. In their usual form they were the same thickness as the topmast shrouds, half as thick as the lower shrouds or a little more, and

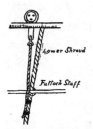

had eye-splices at one end with hooks in them. The hooks went through the puttock-plates and each futtock-shroud was then given a half-hitch round the futtock-staff and one of the lower shrouds and seized to the shroud as well (Fig. 124). Sometimes, more particularly in Dutch ships, the futtock-shrouds were double.

Fig. 124. Method of securing Futtock Shrouds

In this case the hooks were not needed; the shroud simply went through the hole in the puttock-plate and its two parts came down side by side. They were seized together once or twice on the way and then parted and secured in the usual way to two adjacent shrouds (Fig. 125).

It would be possible at this stage to start "rattling down" or fitting the ratlines across the shrouds, but it is far better to leave this until at least the topmast shrouds and stays are set up. It is quite likely that the pull of

Fig. 125. Double Futtock Shrouds

the topmast rigging will make it necessary to readjust some of the lower shrouds and this will throw the ratlines out of line if they are already fitted.

The Topmasts

TOPMAST rigging will not require so long a description as that of the lower masts. In the first place it was simpler and in the second, most of it was the same in principle as that already described.

As in the case of the lower rigging the tackle pendants go first, if there are any; they are the same thickness as the shrouds. It is safe to say that there should be one each side on the fore and main in English ships throughout the period covered by this book and that the mizzen topmast also should have one on each side in large ships up to about 1650. The Dutch do not seem to have had tackles on their topmasts until the last quarter of the 17th century; at least models of 1665 and books of 1670-80 do not include them, whereas Van Yk's book of 1697 and the *"William Rex"* model of 1698 have them on the main and fore but not on the mizzen topmast. Probably French practice was similar to Dutch; I think 1680 would be quite early enough for topmast tackles in a French ship. The Danish *Norske Löve* model of 1654 has tackles on the fore and main topmasts, but it must be remembered that the original ship was built by a Scotsman and that Danish shipbuilding in the first half of the 17th century was largely influenced by English methods. I am not sure whether the two pendants should have independent eye-splices or whether they should be cut-spliced into one another. This would be correct for a later date, but that does not necessarily make it right for the 17th century. However, it will take a very sharp eye to detect the difference when once the shrouds and backstays are in place as well.

There is nothing to say about topmast shrouds. They are fitted in exactly the same way as those of the lower masts. It is as well not to set them up too tight; the only result will be to pull up the lower deadeyes and puttock-plates and to upset the lower shrouds.

Next come the backstays. They are of the same thickness as the shrouds and are fitted on the masthead over the shrouds in the same way. I think the odd backstays should be eye-spliced, but I am not sure. If there are an odd number of shrouds and also of backstays it is a good dodge to combine the last shroud and the first backstay.

English ships in the first forty years of the 17th century had only "running backstays," which were really pendants and whips. The pendants came down as far as the level of the main top or fore top and had blocks spliced into them. The fall started from a timber-head or from the rail just abaft the lower rigging and returned to nearly the same place (Fig. 126). There was one backstay of this kind on each side at the fore and main but none at the mizzen. It is possible that part of the elaborate tackles that run from the topmast heads to the lower stays, in early 17th century prints (Plates 1, 5, 6, 7), is intended for backstays, but personally I prefer to interpret the whole thing as topsail halliards and it will be so described in Chapter IX.

Fig. 126.
English Running Backstay about 1625

Standing backstays are mentioned as far back as 1618, but I very much doubt if they were at all usual before 1640. Bond's book of 1642 gives them to the main topmast as well as the running backstays, but gives none to the fore topmast. Hayward, writing in 1655, gives all the older ships both running and standing backstays, but the running variety disappear in the ships built after 1650 and two pairs of standing backstays are indicated in their place. By 1670, in Deane's plans, all but the smallest ships have three pairs of backstays at the main, while the 3-deckers have three at the fore as well. By

1675, according to Keltridge's lists, the bigger 2-deckers had also three pairs of backstays at both fore and main. The mizzen topmast began to have standing backstays between 1670 and 1675, but had only one a side. The Dutch seem to have had single main and fore topmast backstays after about 1650 and mizzen topmast back-stays from about 1665. After about 1690 they had two a side for the fore and main.

When the backstays have deadeyes, as in English ships, they are set up exactly like shrouds. When they have blocks in the Dutch fashion it is a matter of two fiddle-blocks and a 5-part fall (Fig. 127). The blocks were usually stropped and the ends of the backstays were secured with a throat and a round seizing as shown. The blocks can be a little further apart than deadeyes would be, but it is a mistake to have the tackle too long. The third backstay, when there was one, seems to have been led over and abaft the after topmast cross-trees; the others came down between the cross-trees in the same way as the shrouds.

Fig. 127.
Dutch
Backstay
Tackle

Topmast stays are fitted at their upper ends in precisely the same way as the lower stays. The fore topmast stay leads to the bowsprit, the main topmast stay to the fore top and the mizzen topmast stay to the main top or the main rigging. The fore topmast stay was usually set up with a rather complicated tackle. Various forms are shown in Fig. 128 and need no explanation. Miller's diagram leaves us somewhat in the dark, as it is impossible to say for certain which is the hauling part.

I imagine that it is really much the same as that shown in the *Sovereign* and that there should be another block at X. Apparently there was a short period about 1670-80 when the fore topmast stay was set up with deadeyes in the usual man-

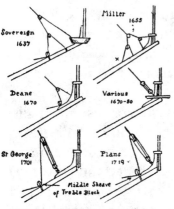

Fig. 128. Methods of setting up Fore Topmast Stay in English Ships

ner. Drawings of 1673 (Plate 14) show this and Keltridge's lists of 1675 give two deadeyes and no blocks. On the other hand Battine, in 1685, gives one long double block and one single; this probably means a tackle like that in the *St George* but without the end coming aft. By the way, the end in the other forms of tackle was more often hitched to

the collar of the fore-stay, or perhaps the gammoning, than brought right in-board.

Foreign methods are shown in Fig. 129. It is quite likely that the lead shown in the Danish model is what Miller was trying to indicate for English ships in 1655. After the early 17th cen-tury period of "crows-feet," the Dutch took to a simple whip and

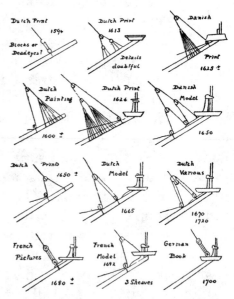

Fig. 129. Methods of setting up Fore Top-mast Stay in foreign Ships

kept to the same general method with a gradually increasing complexity in the tackle, though there is evidence that occasionally they were content with a pair
of deadeyes or more probably a pair of double blocks.
Two double blocks were evidently usual in French ships
of 1675-85, but after that there was a tendency towards
the old whip form again.

The usual lead for the main topmast
stay was through a block lashed to the
foremast head just above the top or to
the collar of the fore stay then down
abaft the mast (Fig. 130). There was
a fiddle-block at its end and a single
block hooked to an eye-bolt in the deck
with a 4-part tackle. Sometimes the
stay was set up in the top — with two
deadeyes, as described in the English

Fig. 130. Lead of
Main Topmast Stay

"Treatise on Rigging," of 1625, or with two double
blocks, according to the German "Geöffnete Seehafen,"

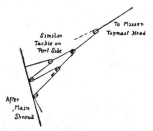

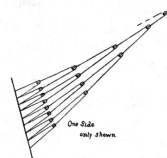

Fig. 131. English Mizzen Topmast Stay about 1620

Fig. 132. Mizzen Topmast Stay
in the *Sovereign* of 1637

of 1700. Sometimes it led under the fore top through a
pendant block, as in the *Royal Louis* model; but on the
whole I think the lead into and through the top, with a

tackle to the deck abaft the mast, was by far the most usual arrangement in either English or foreign ships.

At the beginning of the 17th century the mizzen topmast stay led to the aftermost pair of main shrouds. The "Treatise on Rigging" describes it as shown in Fig. 131. The print of the *Sovereign* shows the same thing in a far more complicated form (Fig. 132). The date when this was given up in favour of a lead to the mainmast head can be gathered for English ships by the fact that Hayward's lists of 1655 give the old form for the ships of 1645 or earlier and a simple stay without pendants, runners or parts for the ships of 1650 and

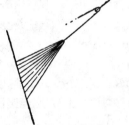

later. Still, there is no doubt that the old fitting lingered on for a long time. It appears with elaborate crowsfeet in pictures which are at least as late as 1665 (Fig. 133), while drawings of 1673 certainly show the mizzen stay going some-

Fig. 133. English Mizzen Topmast Stay about 1665

where well below the top (Plates 14 and 15). Not only this, but it appears (probably for the last time) in the *St George* model of 1701 (Fig. 134). Probably, therefore, it would be fair to say that one can please oneself which form of mizzen topmast stay to fit for any date in the last half of the 17th century. If the rigger is seeking effect he will adopt the lead to the main shrouds; if simplicity of work is more

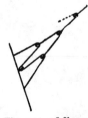

Fig. 134. Mizzen Topmast Stay of *St George* model of 1701

important, he will take the stay to the main top. There it should probably be set up with deadeyes, though it is possible that sometimes it ran through a block and had

a tackle to the deck in the same way as the main topmast stay.

Foreign ships were very like English in this respect. The Dutch print
of 1594 and the Danish of 1625 or
earlier, show the stay as a pendant
with a runner set up to the main
shrouds on either side by means of
crowsfeet (Plates 1 and 5). The
Franco-Dutch ship of 1626 has something nearly as complicated as the
Sovereign (Fig. 135). Zeeman's etchings show a slightly different form

Fig. 135. Mizzen Top-
mast Stay of Dutch-
built French Ship
of 1626

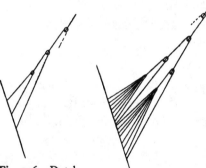

Fig. 136. Dutch
Mizzen Topmast
Stay about 1660

Fig. 137. Mizzen Topmast
Stay of *Norske Löve* model

from anything that I
have seen in English
ships (Fig. 136). The
Norske Löve has al-
most the same ar-
rangement as the
"Navire royale" of
1626 (Fig. 137). Wit-
sen (1671) shows an
elaborate double crow-
foot, but his ship is

distinctly old-fashioned in her appearance and a print of 1678 has the lead to
the main top. After 1660, I think it
would be correct, in most cases, in Dutch
ships, to take the mizzen topmast stay
through a block on the mainmast head
close above the top and to give it a tackle
leading down to the deck. French ships
kept the lead to the main shrouds later.

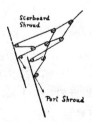

Fig. 138. Mizzen
Topmast Stay of
Royal Louis model

They certainly had it as a general rule in 1680-90 and the *Royal Louis,* of 1692, has it in a particularly complicated form (Fig. 138).

The Topgallant-masts

WHEN there are topgallants to go above them, the topmast shrouds have futtock-staves, but there are no catharpins. Normally there is nothing to worry about in the topgallant rigging save shrouds, stays and backstays. Occasionally there may have been tackles as well; Hayward gives them for the bigger ships of 1640 and before. If they are fitted, they should presumably be fairly simple tackles and certainly only one each side. The shrouds should be fitted in the same way as those of the topmasts. Most ships had two shrouds a side, but 1st-Rates had three. When, as sometimes happened, there were tops at the heads of the topmasts, the method of fitting topgallant shrouds and futtock-shrouds was probably identical with that for the topmast rigging. When there were no tops, the futtock-shrouds ran through holes in the ends of the cross-trees. I fancy it was usual to splice the futtock-shrouds into the strops of the deadeyes without hooks, or even, in early days, to splice the deadeyes into the futtock-shrouds without any metal fittings. No doubt hooks were sometimes used and models often show the strops of the deadeyes finished off as hooks which go through eye-splices in the futtock-shrouds. Probably the best way in small models is to splice the deadeyes in; if this is too difficult they can be seized in and the seizing hidden in the hole in the cross-trees.

If there is to be a topgallant backstay and there are also three shrouds, it is a good idea to combine the

backstay with the aftermost shroud. If there is not an
odd shroud, the backstays can be eye-spliced singly, cut-
spliced together, or even seized together like a pair of
shrouds. In the first half of the 17th century the topgallant backstays were pendants and whips like those of
the topmasts. After about 1645, English ships seem to
have given up topgallant backstays and to have done
without them till about 1670-5, when they returned
as standing backstays set up with deadeyes, at first on
the main topgallant only. Dutch ships began to use
standing backstays on both topgallants a few years
sooner, 1665 or thereabouts, and set them up with two
rings and a lashing. Further details will be found in
Chapter V.

The topgallant stays had no mouses but were merely
given a long spliced eye at the top. The fore topgallant
stay usually led to the head of the spritsail topmast. It
seems a ridiculous lead, because there was nothing to
keep the spritsail topmast forward except its own stiff-
ness, but there is no doubt about it. The engraving of
the *Sovereign* shows an even more absurd lead, to a very
elaborate series of crowsfeet on the spritsail topmast
shrouds (Plate 7). In her case the lead to the spritsail
topmast head is reserved for the fore royal stay. Many
people look on the idea that this ship carried royals as
absurd, but quite enough evidence of royals before 1640
has been found to prove that they must sometimes have
been carried. However, it will probably be best to avoid
them in a model, unless it is based on some authority
which gives them beyond dispute.

A block should be lashed to the head of the spritsail
topmast and the fore topgallant stay should lead through
it. Sometimes, for instance in the French *Royal Louis,*

it then passed through another block attached to the
knee of the spritsail topmast and went through the top
and aft along the bowsprit; more often it was made fast
in the top to one of the trestle-trees. Occasionally there
was a block on the end of the stay and it was set up with
a whip starting from one trestle-tree and finishing on
the other.

In the same way the main topgallant stay went
through a block abaft the fore topmast head and ran
down to the fore top. It might simply be made fast
there or it might have a whip or even a 3-part tackle on
its end. Occasionally, but not often, it seems to have
been set up at the fore topmast head by means of a pair
of blocks or deadeyes.

The Spritsail Topmast

THE standing rigging of the spritsail topmast consisted of shrouds and a backstay. There were usually
three shrouds a side; in small ships there might be two
only. The shrouds were set up in the usual way to the
puttocks by means of a pair of deadeyes.

According to the "Treatise on Rigging"
there were iron cross-trees beneath the
knee on the bowsprit and the puttocks
came to them. As far as I can understand
this it must have been something like Fig.
139. The puttocks were probably of rope,
spliced round the deadeyes and seized at
the iron cross-trees. I doubt if this arrangement lasted
very long even if it were ever the general rule. By 1650,
and probably earlier, the puttocks went to bolts under
the bowsprit. Probably the puttock-plates were long
enough to do the whole job and the deadeyes were hooked

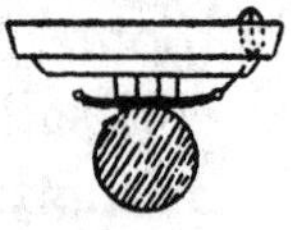

Fig. 139.
English Sprit-
sail Topmast
Puttocks about
1625

into them.   In a small model it will be best to make the
strop of the deadeye and the puttock-plate
all in one piece.   Possibly there were sometimes actual futtock-shrouds leading from
short puttock-plates to eye-bolts under the
bowsprit.   It makes quite a nice-looking job
if these are made with two or three parts of
thin line and then served over (Fig. 140),
but whether such an arrangement is correct
is, I think, rather doubtful.

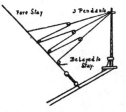

Fig. 140.
Possible
method of
rigging
Spritsail
Topmast
Futtock
Shrouds

The spritsail topmast backstay was one of
the places where the early 17th century rigger let himself
go.   Even in the "Treatise on Rigging" it is complicated

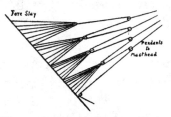

Fig. 141.   English Spritsail
Topmast Backstay about
1625

Fig. 142.   Spritsail Topmast Backstay of *Sovereign* of 1637

enough (Fig. 141), but in the print of the *Sovereign* it is
still more so (Fig. 142), though the same in principle.

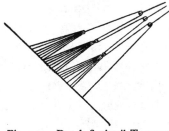

Fig. 143.   Dutch Spritsail Topmast
Backstay of 1626

Fig. 144.   Danish Spritsail Topmast
Backstay about 1625

Other early variations can be seen in Figs. 143 and 144 from the Dutch and Danish prints of 1626 and similar date. As the century went on some of the crowsfeet disappeared, but the tackle remained pretty complicated.

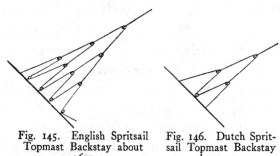

Fig. 145 shows it as it appears in an English drawing of 1673 (Plate 14), while Fig. 146 is from a Dutch print as late as

Fig. 145. English Spritsail Topmast Backstay about 1670

Fig. 146. Dutch Spritsail Topmast Backstay about 1700

1702. According to Keltridge, in 1675, the spritsail topmast "craneline" or backstay required eight blocks, while Battine ten years later gives ten for big ships and eight or six for small. Anyone can easily devise a tackle to use the number of blocks required.

So far the spritsail topmast backstay had led to the

Fig. 147. Dutch Spritsail Topmast Backstay about 1680

forestay. When the fore topmast staysail became well established there was a tendency to shift the backstay to the fore topmast stay to give the new sail room to draw. Dutch drawings of about 1680 show backstays to both the forestay and the fore topmast stay; the former appears to have been set up with deadeyes in some obscure way (Fig. 147). This would seem to make it even more of a fixture than before, but it is possible that there was a block at the spritsail topmast head and that the whole thing could be slacked off at that end.

By the time of the *"William Rex"* and *St George,* the lead to the fore topmast stay was probably by far the more usual. Fig. 148 shows the tackle as given in the *St George;* it is simply the old apparatus shifted further forward. Some of Baston's prints,

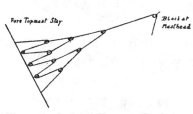

Fig. 148. Spritsail Topmast Backstay of *St George* model of 1701

as late as 1720, still have the old lead to the forestay, so it must have lingered on, but it must have been merely a nuisance and as a matter of fact, English plans of 1719 show no spritsail topmast backstay at all. The best course, in my opinion, will be to take the backstay to the forestay up to about 1680, to the fore topmast stay from then to about 1710, and to omit it altogether after that date. This is, of course, only a rough rule; if any particular print or picture is being reproduced in model form, it should be followed in this as in other details, unless there is very good reason to the contrary.

The Ratlines

Now comes the long job of "rattling down." There is no doubt about its being a long job and a monotonous one, but it does pay for a little care and perseverance; nicely rattled shrouds will not exactly cover a multitude of sins, but they will certainly draw attention away from them. I rather doubt if 17th century ratlines were eye-spliced and seized at each end as they were at the end of the 18th century. Even the most perfect and largest-scale models show them hitched at the ends as they are on the intermediate shrouds and I think the modern model-maker is quite justified in following the example

of his 17th century predecessors. Rattling down thus
becomes simply an interminable process of making clove-
hitches. At the ends it may be possible to pass the end
of the ratline through the shroud before cutting it off, or
an extra half-hitch may be added for safety. In any
case a drop of glue will be useful to make sure that the
ratlines do not come undone as the rigging proceeds.

In spacing the ratlines it is best to start from the futtock-staff. The distance beween ratlines is a little uncertain. Books of about 1800 say 12 or 13 inches. Mr.
Davis, writing mainly of the period 1860-80, says 14 or
15 inches. Against this English plans of 1719 and the
French *Royal Louis* model of 1692, agree at 16 inches,
while the *St George* model has its ratlines still further
apart. Probably 15 or 16 inches will be about right. A
greater spacing looks bad, while less means more work
and particularly dull work at that.

In English ships the ratlines on the fore and main
usually stopped short of the aftermost shroud; on the
mizzen and the topmasts they ran across the whole rigging. Foreign ships do not seem to have followed the
English example in this respect; their ratlines are always
shown running right across. Topgallant shrouds were
seldom rattled, but those of the mizzen topmast and the
spritsail topmast were. The lower futtock-shrouds were,
of course, rattled. It may be necessary to vary the spacing of the ratlines here to get them regularly distributed
between the futtock-staff and the edge of the top.

One more piece of standing rigging remains — the
crowfeet from the tops to the stays. These were intended to prevent the topsails from getting caught under
the tops. They are easy enough to fit. One only requires a "euphroe," which was a long piece of wood with

a lot of holes in it, a pair of blocks, and a number of

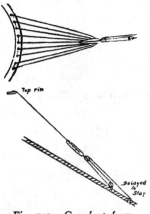

holes in the rim of the top. The whole thing was rigged as shown in Fig. 149. As a model-maker's trick it will probably be found best to reverse the natural order of things, to make the tackle fast first and to set up with the crowfoot line. If it is done the other way it is difficult to get all the parts of the crowfoot taut at the same time.

Fig. 149. Crowfoot from Top-rim to Stay

These crowfeet were not used at the beginning of the 17th century. It was only as tops got bigger, and topsails also, that they appeared. I doubt if they were in use before 1660. When there are upper tops as well, it will perhaps be best to fit crowfeet there too, but the ordinary topmast cross-trees did not have them.

CHAPTER VII

THE rigging belonging to a square sail is of two kinds. There are the ropes which control the yard and are only indirectly concerned with the sail and there are those which are actually connected to the sail itself. In the first class come the Ties, Halliards and Jeers for hoisting or lowering the yard, the Parrel for holding it to the mast, the Lifts for keeping it horizontal or for lifting it at either end, and finally the Braces for moving one end or the other forward or aft. There may be also Foot-ropes beneath the yards and Yard-tackles for hoisting the boats in and out. In the second class are the Tacks, Sheets and Bowlines for setting the sail and the Clewlines, Leechlines (or Martnets) and Buntlines for hauling the sail up to the yard when it is to be stowed. It must be noticed that the order in which these pieces of gear are discussed is not necessarily the order for fitting them. That matter will be mentioned as occasion arises.

Ties, Halliards and Jeers

YARDS might be hoisted by two very different methods. They might have ties and halliards or they might have jeers. As a matter of fact they might have both at once, but that complication can be left for the present. In the tie and halliard method there was no block on the yard; the ties, as their name suggests, were simply ropes for transmitting to the yard the pull given by the halliards. For this purpose they went upwards from the yard, through some kind of block or fair-lead somewhere about the masthead and then came down abaft the mast; the mechanical advantage was obtained by having a multiple block at the after end of the ties and by reeving the halliards through this and through a series of sheaves in a heavy timber called the "knight," which stood upright abaft the mast (Fig. 150). With jeers, things were almost exactly reversed; there were blocks on the yard and at the masthead and only a single part of the tackle came down to the deck (Fig. 151).

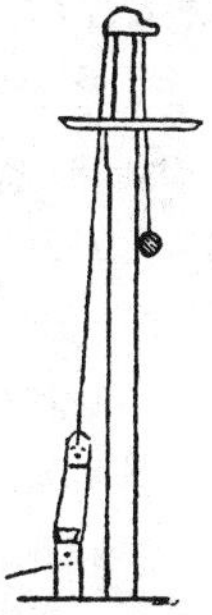

Fig. 150.
Lower Yard hoisted by Ties and Halliards

Fig. 151.
Lower Yard hoisted by Jeers

There is little doubt that English ships were the first to take to using jeers to the exclusion of ties and halliards. This has been mentioned already in the discussion of the shape of mastheads in Chapter I. It is not a matter of knowing when to begin fitting jeers, because jeers of some sort were in use from the beginning of the 17th century; the point is to know when to abandon ties and halliards and to fit the elaborate jeers which are needed if they have to do the whole work of hoisting the yard.

As in the case of almost every change, there can be little doubt that there was a long period of overlap, when one ship used one method and another used its opposite. This is well shown in the tables which Hayward published in 1655, under the title "The Sizes and Lengths of Riggings for all the States Ships and Frigats." In these, all the older ships down to the *Resolution* (ex *Prince Royal*), rebuilt in 1641, have ties and halliards

and all save the smallest ships have jeers as well. Among
the ships built after 1649, the bigger ships, such as the
Speaker, have jeers only, the 4th-Rates and 6th-Rates
have ties and halliards only, and the 5th-Rates have
both. Deane's table of 1670 mentions both methods for
the foremast, but has the lengths and thicknesses completed for the jeers only; on the mainmast ties and halliards are not mentioned at all. In a manuscript of 1675,
Keltridge ignores ties and halliards altogether. Speaking roughly one might say that ties and halliards ought
to be fitted in English ships down to 1650 and might
reasonably be fitted for another twenty years.

Foreign ships kept ties and halliards very much longer.
I should hesitate to do without them in any foreign
model before 1720 and it would be quite justifiable to
fit them a good deal later than that. A German book
of 1700 does describe one form of jeers as an alternative
way of hoisting the lower yards, but says it is mainly
used by the English, while a Dutch book of 1717 still
finds it necessary to urge the use of jeers instead of ties
and halliards, as a desirable reform. A Spanish manuscript of 1750, or later, describes two forms of ties and
halliards and no jeers, and even as late as 1783, the
French "Encyclopédie Méthodique" speaks of ties and
halliards for the lower yards as a fitting still in use in
some ships.

The ties should be about the same thickness as the
shrouds. One end is secured to the middle of the yard as shown in Fig. 152;
the other end is then taken through
one of the hounds, in an English ship,
or — in a foreign ship — either over the

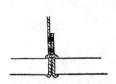

Fig. 152. Method of
securing Ties to Yard cap or through a block hanging beneath

the cap. It then goes through a hole in the upper part of a big square block with three sheaves in it and back by the same route on the other side of the mast to the middle of the yard where it is secured in the same way as the first end. To get the length right, try the yard up and down. The ties must be long enough to let the yard be lowered to the rail and short enough to leave some drift between the halliard block and the knight when the yard is fully hoisted.

It is difficult to be precise as to when foreign ships took to leading their ties through blocks instead of over the caps. The German book of 1700 mentions the former lead only, while a Dutch book of 1705 gives the two alternatives without comment. On the other hand the models of the French *Royal Louis*, of 1692, and the Dutch *"William Rex,"* of 1698, both show the old method. At a guess I should say that the change began about 1695 and was complete by about 1710. The pendant blocks on the new system were seized

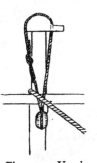

Fig. 153. Usual method of hanging Tie-blocks from Cap

in the bight of a rope about as thick as the ties. The two ends were then passed up inside the stay and outside the trestle-trees; the fore end went up and over the cap and was joined to the other end on the after side of the masthead by means of a pair of seizings on both ends (Fig. 153). It is possible that the blocks were sometimes hung by means of simpler pendants as shown in Fig. 154, but the other method was probably the more usual; it

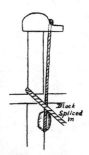

Fig. 154. Possible method of hanging Tie-blocks from Cap

was the universal practice in French ships towards the middle of the 18th century.

The halliards should be about ⅔ as thick as the ties. They start from an eye-bolt in the side of the knight and lead in turn through a sheave in the halliard block from aft forward and through a sheave in the knight from forward aft; after passing through the third sheave of the knight they are belayed to the knight itself (Fig. 155). As long as the knight stands on an open deck this is simple enough, but in many cases the fore and main knights are out of sight below the forecastle and the half deck or even below the upper deck. In this case the parts of the halliards have to pass through a scuttle or through separate holes in the deck or gratings. If this difficulty is foreseen before the model is built, the best way is to reeve the halliards before the deck is fixed down and to tighten up the tackle at the other end by means of the ties.

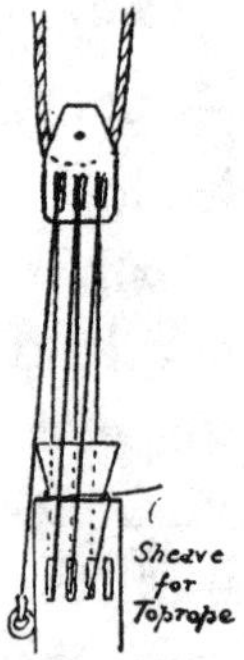

Fig. 155.
Lead of
Lower
Halliards

The top-rope, which goes through a fourth sheave in the knight, must be treated in the same way. If it is a case of rigging a model whose decks are already in place, the matter becomes far more difficult. Each case must be treated on its own merits; it may be possible to do something with a bent wire or it may not. At the worst it ought to be possible to pass the halliards down through the deck, round a beam and up again, so that the part that is visible looks as if it is properly rove.

Jeers naturally varied in complexity according to the share that they took in hoisting the yards. In their simplest form they are rigged as follows:— A block is attached to the middle of the yard, as shown in Fig.

156, its strop having two legs with eyes in them and the eyes being seized together round the yard. Another block of the same size hangs just below the trestle-tree on one side. It may be spliced into the end of a pendant and the other end secured round the masthead above the shrouds, as shown in Fig. 157, or it may have a very long strop which acts as a pend-

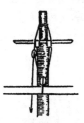

Fig. 156.
Method of
securing
Jeer-block
to Yard

ant and that strop may be lashed to the masthead (Fig. 158); in either case the pendant or strop goes down inside the stay and outside the trestle-tree. The actual fall of the jeer starts from the masthead where it is secured above the pendant either by being seized round itself in the same

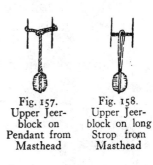

Fig. 157.
Upper Jeer-
block on
Pendant from
Masthead

Fig. 158.
Upper Jeer-
block on long
Strop from
Masthead

way as the pendant or by being rove through an eye in its own end. It is then taken inside the stay, through the block on the yard, through the pendant block and down to the deck beside the mast (Fig. 159). It may either be belayed there or taken through a third block hooked to a ring-bolt and then belayed to the bitts or otherwise secured. The whole question of what to do with the ends of ropes depends so much on the scale, the finish and the condition of the model that it is impossible to give any hard and fast rules.

Fig. 159. English
Jeers about 1625

This is a jeer such as would be fitted in an English ship of the early part of the 17th century and might sometimes be found in a foreign ship also. As a variation, there might be two blocks at the masthead and

two ends coming down to the deck (Fig. 160) and in
that case it seems probable that one end would be secured

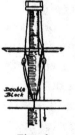

to the ship's side and the other used for hauling; there might even be a tackle on the
free end. A further development of this idea
is shown in a Spanish manuscript of about
1750, in my possession. In this case there is
an elaborate tackle on either end of the jeers;
in fact, in spite of the block on the yard, one
is bound to look on this more as a variation
of the tie and halliard than of the jeer.

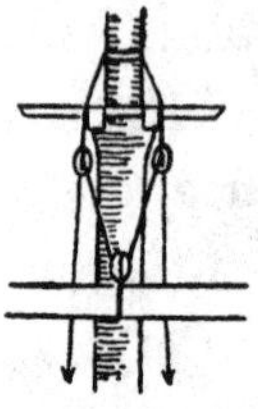

Fig. 160.
Possible
form of
Jeers about
1640

A more complicated form of jeer is described in the
German book of 1700. This makes use of the two pendant blocks described in the later forms of foreign ties and
halliards and has also a *double* block on the yard. The
single rope starts from the masthead, goes through one
sheave of the block on the yard, up to the nearest pendant block, back through the second sheave of the double
block, through the pendant block beside
its standing part and then down to the
knight and through one of its sheaves.
It is said to be an English device and it
seems likely that it, or something very like
it, was employed in England
just when jeers began to sup-
plant ties and halliards and
before the later form of double
jeers came into general use.

Fig. 161.
German
Jeers about
1700

Fig. 161 shows the jeer as described and
Fig. 162 what I think may have been done
in English ships at one time.

With double jeers, which I think must
have been normal in English ships very soon

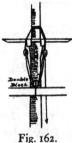

Fig. 162.
Possible
English Jeers
about 1660

after 1670, there were two double or treble pendant blocks and two similar blocks on the yard. Two of the possible variations are shown in the model of the *St George*, of 1701, probably the earliest English model with contemporary rigging still well preserved. On the foremast, the upper blocks are treble and the lower double; the rope starts from the yard, rove through an eye in its own end and placed just inside the block, goes in turn through the upper and lower blocks and leads down from the third sheave in the pendant block. On the mainmast, both blocks are treble and the rope starts from the masthead in the usual way. Fig. 163 shows these two leads. In each case the fall comes down to the bitts abaft the mast and is belayed there. Both blocks have long strops put on double;

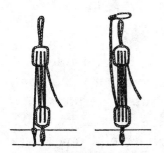

Fig. 163. Fore and Main Jeers of the *St George* model of 1701

on the yard the two loops are seized together underneath, while at the masthead they are long enough to act as pendants and are secured side by side by a lashing round the masthead above the shrouds. This arrangement can be seen in the photographs of the *St George's* fore and main tops (Plate 19) and is also drawn in Fig. 164. Some years earlier, about 1680, there had been two treble and two double blocks for the jeers of both the foresail and mainsail in 3-deckers, four double blocks in

Fig. 164. Upper Jeer-blocks of the *St George* model

the biggest 2-deckers, two double and two single in the 4th-Rates and 5th-Rates, and two single and one double in the smallest vessels.

Foreign double jeers, when they did at last come into use, must have been very much the same as English, except that in their case the upper blocks would be slung from the caps in the same way as the tie-blocks had been instead of being attached to the masthead just above the shrouds. In thickness, the jeers must have varied according to the number of parts in the tackle; for the complex jeers of the end of the 17th century a thickness equal to ⅞ of the shrouds will be about right.

Parrels

A PARREL for one of the lower yards is fully described in the "Treatise on Rigging," written about 1625. Some-

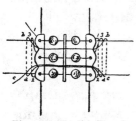

Fig. 165. English Parrel about 1625

what modernised in expression the description is as follows:— The parrel is formed of a rope, trucks (or balls) and ribs. The rope goes three times loosely round the mast and has the trucks and ribs threaded on it, there being one hole in each truck and three in each rib. It is fastened to the yard in three parts on either side, making six parts in all, and then goes in two notches in the ribs for six parts more. My interpretation of this description is shown in Fig. 165. For the sake of clearness I have only drawn three ribs and two rows of trucks, though there would really be far more. I imagine that each place where the rope led from the last rib towards the yard was considered a "part"; there are thus three parts (1, 2, 3) on either side and then three more (a, b, c). Possibly the parrel rope started by being attached to the yard and ended in the same way, but it is more likely—in view of what was done later—that the end "c," after going round the yard, passed through a block or a thimble on the end "i" and was then connected to a tackle leading down to the foot of the mast.

The only other way of fitting a parrel, that I can give from contemporary evidence, is the Dutch method of

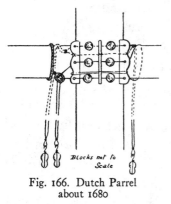

Fig. 166. Dutch Parrel about 1680

the end of the 17th century (Fig. 166). There are two separate parrel-ropes, each spliced to make an endless rope. The first runs through the two lower lots of holes in the ribs and round the yard on one side; on the other it passes through a double thimble secured by a strop to the yard and finally has a fiddle-block in its bight.

The second passes through the uppermost lot of holes and along the upper notch; its two parts are seized together just outside the outer ribs and there is a fiddle-block on either side.

Though my sketch and description are based on excellent authority, I am bound to admit that there seems to be something wrong. With no sail bent things look reasonable enough, but as soon as a sail is fitted it becomes necessary to bring the two bights of the second parrel-rope down to the deck *before* the sail or to pass them between the yard and the bolt-rope before leading down. The first course is ridiculous and the second would obviously throw a very severe strain on the bolt-rope and the robands. I can only suppose that there ought to be a pair of eyes or thimbles beneath the yard and that the parrel-rope passed through them

before leading down abaft the sail. Fig. 167 shows what
I mean. This Dutch parrel has a pair of smaller holes
in each rib and these are used for a permanent lacing to hold the parrel together and
for fixing the upper parrel-rope in its place in
the upper notch.

Fig. 167.
Probable
lead of Truss-
tackles
from Dutch
Parrel

For other parrels — say for English ships
of 1650-80 — I have no authority whatever.
All I can suggest is that they should be fitted
in some way that will work, that is to say
that will allow of being set up or slacked
off. Fig. 168 shows a method which
seems to satisfy this condition and
which looks well both aloft and in
its lead down to the deck. If it is
preferred to have two tackles, the
eye-splice at "a" can be omitted and
this end can also be taken down to
a fiddle-block. Another method ap-

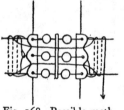

Fig. 168. Possible meth-
od of rigging Parrel

pears in Fig. 169. In this the parrel, in the sense of the collection of
ribs and trucks, is held together by
a line that has nothing to do with
the yard; while the truss-rope,
which passes round the yard runs
only in the notches on the outside
of the ribs. A similar arrangement
appears on the oldest English rigged

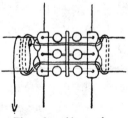

Fig. 169. Alternative
method of rigging Parrel

models, but in their case the truss-rope is secured to the
yard at each end and there is no tackle on it. For small-
scale models this is probably the best method to follow;
for larger models, where the absence of a truss-tackle
would be noticeable, one can adopt one of the others and

have one, two or even three tackles leading down to the deck. As a matter of fact in the Dutch models the lower (single) blocks of the truss-tackles are secured to the collar of the main-stay or mizzen-stay, but no doubt there were cases where ring-bolts beside the foot of the mast were used instead.

Lifts

In comparison with the gear for hoisting the yards the lifts were simple and constant. In most cases there was a single block either just below the top or hanging from the cap and another fixed at the yard-arm. The lift started from the upper block or near it and went through the lower and upper blocks and thence to the deck. The main points to be considered are the shape of the blocks, the method of their attachment and the question of the date at which the upper blocks shifted to the cap.

Taking the last point first: 1690 will not be far wrong. Perhaps the change came a few years earlier in French ships and perhaps the Dutch kept to the old fashion a little longer than the French and English; still, there is little doubt that the new method was in universal use by 1700.

Whatever the position of the upper block, that of the lower was always the same, it was connected or combined with the topsail-sheet block at the yard-arm. In English ships there were two separate blocks, one much larger than the other; the topsail-sheet block was stropped in the ordinary way with an eye big enough to fit over the yard-arm and the strop of the lift block went through that of the topsail-sheet block. Later on, probably about the middle of the 18th century, the two

blocks were included in a single long strop. The drawing
in Fig. 170 shows the usual 17th century arrangement
and also the peculiar shape of the topsail-sheet block,
intended to prevent the sheet from getting nipped between the block and the yard. How early this refine-

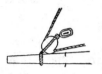

Fig. 170. English
Topsail-sheet and
Lower Lift blocks

ment came in I do not know. Lists of
stores in 1661 mention "topsail sheet
blocks" separately and I personally
should show it after 1660 and should
certainly not show it before 1640, but this
is mainly guess-work. As to size, the
length of the topsail-sheet block should
be about equal to the maximum diameter of the yard and
that of the lift block should be ⅔ of this or a little less.

In foreign rigging, the topsail-sheet and lift blocks
were combined in the form of a pear-shaped block with
its two sheaves at right angles to one another (Fig. 171).
The strop passed *through* the block just short of the
smaller sheave. The total length of
such a block should be about 7/4 of
the maximum diameter of the yard,
more rather than less. With a block
of this kind the strop must have
rather a long eye with a good length
seized together between the block
and the yard-arm; otherwise the

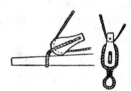

Fig. 171. Foreign com-
bined Topsail-sheet and
Lower Lift block

whole block will stand too much upright to give the lift
a fair lead when the yard is hoisted.

Sometimes, early in the 17th century, foreign ships
seem to have used ordinary fiddle-blocks with the two
sheaves in the same plane. Such blocks are shown in
the Danish print of about 1625 (Plate 5) and in a Dutch
print of about 1613, meant to represent the English

Prince Royal but probably a fancy picture based on Dutch practice (Plate 2). Possibly there was a time when both English and foreign ships used two separate blocks on the yard, one inside the other. The wording of the English "Treatise on Rigging," suggests this and some foreign pictures hint at it also. In any case, by 1630 or so, the two characteristic 17th century methods were well established.

As regards the pendant blocks there was a similar difference between English and foreign rigging. In England, they were ordinary single blocks spliced into the

ends of the pendants. Abroad, they were flat elongated blocks with a sheave in the middle and with a hole at each end at right angles to the sheave; the pendant was spliced into one hole and the standing part of the lift into the other (Fig. 172). In the early part of the 17th century English lifts started by

Fig. 172. Foreign Pendant-block for Lower Lifts

being seized to the two parts of the stay; this is the arrangement described in the "Treatise on Rigging," of 1625, and is apparently what was done in the *Sovereign* of 1637 (Plate 7); but by 1660, and probably earlier, the standing part was spliced into the strop of the pendant block or rather into the pendant itself where it was spliced round the block. In any case the pendant came from the masthead above

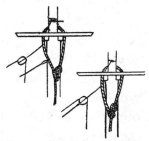

Fig. 173. English Lower Lifts about 1625 and 1660

the shrouds and went inside the stay. It was long enough to let the block almost touch the futtock-shrouds when it was pulled out sideways. Fig. 173 shows the two methods just described.

When the upper blocks moved to the caps, there was less uniformity about their shape and the way they were fitted. At first the Dutch kept their old form of blocks and had them on pendants as before; the only change was that the pendants were now attached to eye-bolts in the cap and that the lifts ran above the top instead of below. The pendants varied in length; sometimes they were long enough to let the blocks stand well clear of the topmast rigging, in which case the end of the lift came down to the deck clear of the top (Fig. 174); sometimes they were much shorter, the blocks were inside the

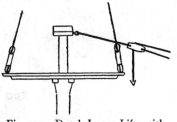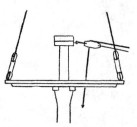

Fig. 174. Dutch Lower Lifts with long Pendants

Fig. 175. Dutch Lower Lifts with short Pendants

rigging and the fall went through the top (Fig. 175). The eye-bolts were fitted in the sides of the cap about abreast of the middle of the masthead.

In English ships the two upper blocks were spliced into the two ends of a single rope which was hitched round the cap just abaft the topmast. The amount of slack necessary for this made it impossible to get the blocks right up against the cap, but they were very much closer than Dutch blocks would have been. Round the parts of this rope, on the upper side of the cap, near the two edges, went two seizings and the standing parts of the lifts were spliced round just inside these seizings.

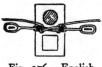

Fig. 176. English Cap with Lower Lifts and Pendants

This arrangement is shown in Fig. 176 and in the photograph of the *St George's* main top (Plate 19); it seems to have been the normal practice up to 1720 at least; eye-bolts in the sides of the caps for the lifts were a later fitting.

Early in the 18th century the lifts sometimes went in three parts instead of two. English rigging plans of 1719 shows this, but none of Baston's prints show it and it does not appear to have been general. There was a fiddle-block at the cap, secured in the usual way, and the standing part of the lift was spliced into the strop of the yard-arm block (Fig. 177). Something very similar is shown in the French *Royal Louis* model, where the fiddle-block is fixed to an eye-bolt in the masthead below the cap and the standing part of the lift is secured to the strop of the

Fig. 177. English 3-part Lower Lifts about 1715

big yard-arm block by being rove through an eye in its own end round the two parts of the strop between the block and the yard-arm. With the fiddle-block shifted to the cap and with the standing part secured to the yard just inside the block, similar 3-part lifts were common in foreign ships in the 18th century, though the English 2-part lift was also used. Fig. 178 shows the arrangement in the *Royal Louis* and Fig. 179 the similar

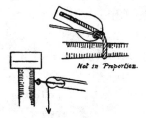

Fig. 178. French 3-part Lower Lifts about 1700

Not in Proportion.

Fig. 179. French 3-part Lower Lifts about 1750

arrangement of later years. Lifts, by the way, should be about ⅜ of the lower shrouds in thickness. Their pendants should of course be thicker, say ½ the shrouds or more.

Braces

DURING the 17th century and the early part of the 18th there was very little variation in the lead of the fore and main braces. Naturally there were differences in detail, but in general principles the braces were the same all the time and in all countries. There were always long pendants from the yard-arms with single blocks on them and the main and fore braces always ran to the ship's quarters and to the main stay. The pendants should be about half as thick as the shrouds, the braces themselves about ¾ of the pendants. Eyes should be spliced in the ends of the pendants and fitted over the yard-arms inside the topsail-sheet and lift blocks. The length of the pendants varied, but as a rough rule it may be said that their blocks should reach more than ⅓ and less than ½ of the way in towards the middle of the yard; those of the foresail should be relatively shorter than those of the main. Their blocks should be about ⅔ of the maximum thickness of the yard in length. Normally they should be spliced into the ends of the pendants. Not

Fig. 180. Dutch Brace-pendants and Blocks

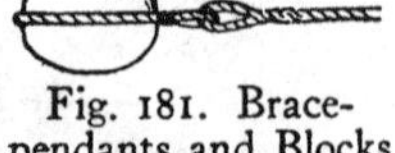

Fig. 181. Brace-pendants and Blocks in *St George* model

always, for Dutch models of the 17th century nearly always have their brace-blocks stropped with small eyes and the pendants rove through the eyes and finished off with a wall and crown or some such knot (Fig. 180). The English *St George* model of 1701, has a further refinement, the blocks are stropped and the pendants spliced through the eyes (Fig. 181). Personally I rather suspect this to be a piece of model-maker's fancy work, but it is possible that it was the fashion for a little time.

The standing parts of the fore braces were attached to the main stay. As time went on the point of attachment moved gradually up the stay. In English ships, at the beginning of the 17th century, it was about ⅖ of the way from the foremast to the mainmast along the stay and even as late as 1670 it was less than half way. Soon after this it must have passed the half-way mark and by 1720 the braces were attached about 4/7 of the way from the foremast to the main. Foreign ships seem to have gone through the same process; if anything their braces led the way in the gradual rise. I think it would be right to put Dutch braces rather more than half way up the stay in 1670, but 4/7 or 5/9 in 1720 would be right for Dutch ships as for English.

The braces might be attached to the stay in one of two ways. There might be an eye-splice in the brace itself and a seizing on to the stay, or there might be a short rope with an eye in each end clove-hitched to the stay to form two short pendants and the brace fixed to this

Fig. 182. Standing parts of Fore Braces

with a sheet-bend and a seizing (Fig. 182). Probably the first method was more usual in Dutch ships and the second in English. When the braces were seized directly to the stay one was just above the other, but whether there was any rule as to which went uppermost I do not know.

From the stay the braces went to the pendant blocks on the yard and then back to blocks attached to the stay nearer the foremast than their standing parts. How much nearer was a very variable matter; there had to be a compromise between the risk of getting the tackle twisted if its parts were too close together and the certainty of loss of power if they were too far apart; naturally opinions differed on such a question. Perhaps an angle of about 10° between the two parts would be a reasonable average.

As with the standing parts there were two ways of attaching the leading blocks to the stay. They might be stropped and seized to the stay one above the other or they might be spliced into the two ends of a short span which was clove-hitched to the stay. Again, I rather think the former method was more usual in Dutch ships and the latter in

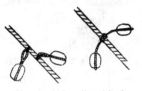

Fig. 183. Leading blocks for Fore Braces

English, though this is the sort of thing that might well be decided by individual fancy. Fig. 183 shows the two methods and Fig. 184 gives a general view of the lead of the fore brace.

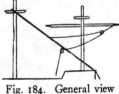

Fig. 184. General view of Fore Brace

What to do with the end of the rope after passing it through the leading block is, as usual, a problem. Even the best contemporary models give little help; for instance the *St George* model has her fore sheet, her fore brace and her fore-topsail brace all belayed on one cleat. There must, of course, have been another leading block attached to the deck or the bulwarks and a cleat somewhere near it. The French *Royal Louis* model, which is better off for cleats and such fittings than the majority of models, has a leading block on deck just beside the gratings about the middle of the waist and a cleat just before it. The objection to this is that the lee fore brace would foul the main staysail; for this reason it seems more likely that the leading block would be well out towards the side of the ship, if not actually on the bulwarks. In a model I think the best thing to do with the fore braces is to take them straight to a pair of cleats on the bulwarks well forward near the forecastle bulkhead.

The main brace started from somewhere just below the rail as far aft as possible, went through the pendant block and returned to a place close to its standing part. According to the "Treatise on Rigging," of 1625, the standing part was secured to the aftermost timber and the hauling part belayed to the next timber. Presumably there must have been a leading block and it seems reasonable to interpret the description as meaning that the leading block was attached to the second timber from aft. With a few modifications in details this was and remained the standard arrangement. Usually the standing part was secured to a ring-bolt in the ship's side about level with the uppermost deck aft by means of a throat seizing and a round seizing (Fig. 185). At

Fig. 185.
Standing part
of Main Brace

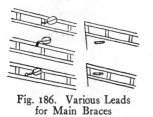

Fig. 186. Various Leads
for Main Braces

the same time the leading block might be seized to the rail or to a ring-bolt on top of the bulwarks instead of to a timber, or it might be done away with and replaced by a sheave in the bulwarks or in a block of wood fitted between the rail and the bulwarks right aft. Fig. 186 shows some of the possibilities. In any case the hauling part was belayed on a cleat a little way forward, sometimes far enough forward to come on to the next step in the after decks.

In one model, the Berlin Dutchman of 1665 (Plate 11), the main brace is fitted in a way which gives a double mechanical advantage. From the ring-bolt in the side through the pendant block there goes a runner with a block on its end. The leading block is secured to another ring-bolt on top of the bulwarks right aft and has a rope spliced into its strop; this rope goes through the runner block and back to the leading block (Fig. 187). I have not seen such an arrangement in any other model or drawing of this period.

Fig. 187. Dutch Main Brace of 1665

Foot-ropes

THE history of foot-ropes or "horses" is a little obscure. One would rather expect that they would have been introduced first on the topsail yards where reefs were first used. This was apparently not the case. They seem to have been used on the main yard first, long before there were reef-points on the mainsail. That being so, it is strange that they were not used until well into the 17th century. It is impossible to say when they did first appear, but I believe it to be a fact that the first evidence for them is in Bond's "The Boatswain's Art," of 1642. Certainly they are not mentioned in the English books of 1620-40, such as Manwayring and Boteler.

As far as English ships are concerned, the evidence (or some of it) is as follows:— Bond (1642) and Deane (1670) give "horses" on the main yard only; Keltridge (1675) adds the fore yard and Battine (1685) gives horses to the main, fore, main-topsail, fore-topsail and spritsail yards. In 1701, as shown by the *St George* model, there were foot-ropes on the mizzen-topsail and spritsail-topsail yards as well; this model has no top-gallants, but it is probable that, if she had, they would also have foot-ropes.

In France, Dassié, in 1677, speaks of foot-ropes on the main and fore yards only, while the *Royal Louis* model of 1692 has them everywhere except on the crojack yard. In Holland, the evidence rather suggests that foot-ropes were used on the topsail yards first. Models of 1665 and prints of 1678 both show foot-ropes on the topsail yards and not elsewhere. By 1700, and probably by 1690, there were footropes on the lower and topsail yards in ships of every nation. As to the topgallants I am not so sure. The *Royal Louis* has them, as has been said, and they are shown in English plans of 1719, but Sutherland, writing in 1711, does not give them in his list or show them in his plate; he omits them also on the mizzen-topsail and spritsail-topsail yards.

The thickest foot-ropes should be equivalent to about five inch rope and the thinest should be about half this. There should be two foot-ropes on each yard, eye-spliced round the yard-arms and put on inside both the brace-pendants and the topsail-sheet and lift blocks. Dutch ships usually had the inner ends of the foot-ropes made fast to the parrels on either side. The German book of 1700 describes this also, but says that the lower yards had deadeyes on their foot-ropes and that the two dead-eyes were connected by a laniard in the usual way. This is what is shown in the *St George* model; the smaller foot-ropes have eye-splices in them and are seized to the parrel-ropes; but those of the fore and main yards, where the parrel-ropes had to be moveable, are fitted with deadeyes as shown in Fig. 188.   There is a lashing be-

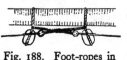

Fig. 188. Foot-ropes in the *St George* model

tween the strops of the two quarter-blocks for the topsail sheets and
this and the parts of the laniard
of the foot-rope are all seized together.

From the agreement between what appears here and
the description in the German book there can be little
doubt that this arrangement was in vogue about 1700.
Against this we must put the fact that lists of 1675, 1685
and 1711 all give four deadeyes for the horses on each
yard.   This must obviously mean that there was a deadeye on each horse and another pair on the yard.   Such
a method of fitting the horses or foot-ropes is seen in the
French *Royal Louis* model (Fig.
189) and described in Dassiés
book of 1677.   The inner deadeyes are secured to the yard inside the cleats.

Fig. 189.   Foot-ropes in the *Royal Louis* model

If the foot-ropes are to go through "stirrups" from the
yard, they must be rove through before the deadeyes are
fitted.   I am not at all sure that stirrups were generally
fitted at this period.   The *St George* has, I think, one on
each side on the lower yards and none elsewhere, while
plans of 1711 and 1719 show English ships with none.
The Berlin Dutch model has no stirrups to the only foot-
ropes she has, on the topsail yards, and the drawing of
the Dutch *Gertruda,* of 1720 (Plate 23) shows both
lower and topsail foot-ropes without stirrups.   The German book of 1700 says nothing about them.   On the
other hand the *Royal Louis* has three a side on the lower
yards, two on the topsail yards and one on the smaller
yards.   Of course it is quite possible that the French

were the first to take to stirrups. All things considered, I think one or two a side on the lower yards and perhaps one a side on the topsail yards would be quite enough.

If stirrups are fitted they should have eyes spliced in them just big enough for the foot-ropes to go through. They should lead up abaft the yard. I do not know whether they should be unlaid and plaited and then nailed to the yards after going round two or three times as was done at the end of the 18th century. Probably a clove-hitch and a little glue will give quite a good effect, especially if the hitch is hammered down a bit.

Yard Tackles

TACKLES at the lower yard-arms, for hoisting the boats in and out, seem an obvious necessity, but were surprisingly late in appearing. The name "boat-tackles" occurs quite early in the 17th century, but it was then applied to one pair of the ordinary masthead tackles. In 1685 or thereabouts, Battine uses the same name for what is evidently the later yard-arm tackle and this is really the first clear evidence of such a fitting. The *St George* model shows them very well. The actual tackles consist of fiddle-blocks hanging from very long strops (or double pendants) from the yard-arms and of single lower blocks with long strops and hooks. The fiddle-blocks hang some 18 ft. (on the scale) below the yards; the fall starts from the strop of the lower block, which is hooked into the same ring-bolt as the foremost masthead tackle, and runs through the lower sheave of the fiddle-block, through the single block,

Fig. 190.
Yard-tackle
led to
Channels

through the upper sheave of the fiddle-block, through a leading block secured to the first deadeye abaft the ring-bolt and inboard through a port (Fig. 190).

Perhaps there were sometimes real single pendants at the yard-arms instead of the long strops shown in the *St George*. I think I should fit such pendants if I were giving yard tackles to a model of about 1680, but as a matter of fact I rather doubt if I should venture to fit them at all before 1685. When they can reasonably be

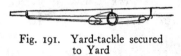

fitted they are distinctly a blessing, because they give an additional means of keeping the lower yards square. This,

Fig. 191.   Yard-tackle secured to Yard

of course, only applies in the case of a model without sails set; if the lower sails are set the yard tackles have to be lashed up to the yards out of the way (Fig. 191).

I should not fit yard tackles in a foreign model; not because I believe that other nations were blind to the convenience of such fittings, but because I know of no model other than English in which they are shown for the period at present under consideration. When they are fitted, their pendants or strops should go over the yard-arms next after the foot-ropes; then come the strops of the blocks for the lower stunsail halliards (if these are to be shown), the brace-pendants and the strops of the topsail-sheet and lift blocks, in that order.

Tacks, Sheets and Clewlines

THIS finishes the list of gear concerned with the yards and brings us to that attached to the sails. The lower corners or "clews" of the foresail and mainsail were con-trolled by the tacks, sheets and clewlines. The tacks hauled the clews down and forward, the sheets hauled them down and aft, the clewlines hauled them up to the yards ready for furling. The three are best discussed together, because they were mutually dependent.

The tack was a single rope which simply went from the clew through some kind of a fairlead and to a cleat; the sheet was double and went from the ship's side, outboard, through a block attached to the clew, back to a leading-block or sheave near its standing part and thence to a cleat; the clewline started from the yard, went through a block at the clew, back to a block on the yard and down to the deck more or less directly. The three were connected together and to the eye in the bolt-rope at the clew of the sail.

The tacks should be the same thickness as the shrouds, the sheets ¾ as thick and the clewlines half as thick as the sheets. Both tacks and sheets were usually cable-laid and strictly speaking the tacks ought to be tapered, but this is probably asking too much of the model ropemaker. The sheet block should have a length about equal to the maximum diameter of the yard and the clewline block should be about ⅔ as big. One point that requires consideration is the shape of the clewline blocks. English ships in the 18th century had them of a special shape as shown in Fig. 192; the question is, how soon did these blocks come into use and were they used in foreign ships? As to the last question, I think it is safe to say that they were not used in French or Dutch ships within the limits of time covered by this book. As to the first, I frankly do not know. The *St George* model shows them, so they evidently go back right to the beginning of the 18th century, but I personally know of no definite evidence one way or the

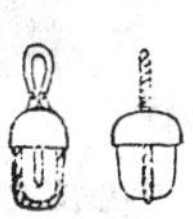

Fig. 192.
English
Clewline-
blocks in
18th century

other before that. Purely as a matter of personal judgment I should fit them after about 1680, but I should
not be in the least surprised to find either that they were
in use twenty years before or that they were quite a
novelty in 1700.

The tack, sheet-block and clewline-block depended
on the clew of the sail for their connection with one another. When sails are fitted it is necessary to consider
whether there is a bonnet or not, that is to say whether
there is a detachable portion at the foot of the sail. If
there is, the whole apparatus of tack, sheet and clewline has to be detachable also, so that it can be fitted to
the clew of the bonnet or to that of the actual "course"
as occasion requires. As far as I can judge, English
ships used bonnets on both the foresail and mainsail up
to about 1680. The Dutch seem to have given up mainsail bonnets a good deal earlier — 1660 or so —, but to
have kept foresail bonnets even later than the English.

When there is a bonnet, the sheet-block has a strop

Fig. 193. Sheet-
block Clewline-
block and Tack

with two legs with a knot on each, the
clewline-block has rather a long ordinary
strop and the tack has a big knot on it
(Fig. 193). English ships at the end of
the 18th century used a double wall and
double crown, but this may not always
have been so and any combination of crowns
and walls will meet the case. The strop of
the clewline-block is put through and over
the clew, the tack is put through the clew
with the knot aft, the two legs of the sheet-
block strop are put through the clew above
the tack, one one way and one the other, and
a seizing is put on above them (Fig. 194).

Fig. 194.
Sheet-block,
Clewline-
block and
Tack fitted
for removal

Without a bonnet there is no need for the combination to be so easily removable. In this case the clew-line-block is either actually stropped in place or secured with a seizing through two eyes in the ends of its strop (Fig. 195) and the sheet-block has an ordinary strop which is put over the clew. When there are no sails the usual practice is to put the strop of the clewline-block through the strop of the sheet-block and the tack through the strop of the clewline-block below the sheet-block (Fig. 196).

Fig. 195.
Clewline-
block seized
in place

Fig. 196.
Sheet-block,
Clewline-
block and
Tack—with-
out Sails

Having once got these three ropes connected we have to consider the question of their leads. The clewline starts from the yard at a point just more than ⅓ of the distance out from the middle of the yard to the end, goes through the block at the clew from outwards in and then to a block on the yard just ⅓ way from the middle. This block is of the ordinary shape and the same size as the block at the clew; it has a strop with two eyes and is seized round the yard. The standing part of the clewline may be secured to the yard by being rove through an eye in its own end or, more usually, by a timber hitch. In foreign ships throughout the period covered by this book and in English ships up to 1670, at any rate, the clewline went straight to the deck from the block on the yard and was belayed close to the foremost shroud. In English ships at some date between 1670 and 1700 a second block was added on the yard quite close to the mast, just outside the quarter block for the topsail sheet, and the clewline went through this too and then down to the deck beside the mast. When exactly this change took place I do not know; perhaps 1680 would not be far wrong. The two leads are shown in Fig. 197.

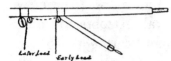

Fig. 197. Lead of Lower Clewlines

The lead of the tacks was simple; they merely passed through some kind of fairlead and were belayed. About 1625 the fore tacks went through a double fairlead, usually ornamented, attached under the knee of the head; they then passed upwards and inwards through the head, crossing one an-

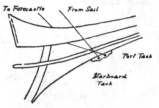

Fig. 198. Lead of Fore Tacks about 1625

other on the way, and were belayed on the forecastle; usually the starboard tack went through the hole nearest to the stem (Fig. 198). This method lasted in English ships till 1655 or thereabouts; the last example of it that I know is in an English model of 1658, in Stockholm. Dutch ships gave it up earlier, perhaps fifteen or twenty years earlier, at any rate it is not shown in Hollar's etchings of 1647. The principle of the new method was exactly the same, but the holes were made in the knee itself instead of in a piece of timber fixed to the knee (Fig. 199). Very early in the century, before heads had dropped as much as they did by 1625, Dutch ships had a stout timber fixed beside the knee of the head and pointing down and forward (Plate 2) and

Fig. 199. Lead of Fore Tacks about 1660

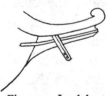

Fig. 200. Lead for Fore Tacks about 1600

took the fore tacks through holes in this (Fig. 200).

For some years the fore tacks continued to pass through
holes in the knee of the head. In Dutch
ships they continued to do so as a general
rule up to 1720 or later. In one case,
that of the *"William Rex"* model of 1698,
they pass instead through blocks attached
to the knee and go back into the ship
without crossing and recrossing (Fig.
201). Some things about this model's

Fig. 201. Fore
Tack of *"William
Rex"* model

rigging are not above suspicion, but this lead is shown
also in the French *Royal Louis* of similar date and may
well be correct, though I doubt if it
was ever common. English s h i p s
changed the lead of their fore tacks
about 1670 and took them through
what were called "dead-blocks," ornamented fairleads fitted between two
rails and two timbers of the head
(Fig. 202). The date of this change
can be fixed with fair accuracy from
the fact that Deane's drawings of 1670
(Plates 12 and 13) show t h e o l d

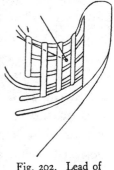

Fig. 202. Lead of
English Fore Tack
about 1690

method and the *Prince* model of the same date the new;
very likely the change came first in big ships with deep
heads.

The next improvement was also English; it consisted
in rigging a pair of "bumkins" pointing outwards, forwards and a little downwards over the lowest part of
the main head-rail on either side. These had blocks
at their ends and the tacks went through the blocks and
to the forecastle direct (Fig. 203). Probably these

bumkins came in about 1710 and took about ten years
to oust the dead-blocks altogether.   Foreign ships did
not use them much before 1740 or
so.

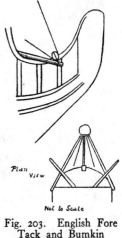

The main t a c k s a l s o p a s s e d
through fairleads, called in this case
"chesstrees." These were fitted a
little abaft the fore shrouds, usually
about as far abaft the shrouds as the
distance between two ports. In English 3-deckers, of 1660-1720, t h e y
were simply ornamental holes leading straight through the ship's side
and were on the middle deck; in earlier English ships, such as the *Prince
Royal* of 1610 and probably the *Sov-*

Fig. 203.   English Fore
Tack and Bumkin
about 1720

ereign of 1637, and in French and Dutch ships of the
end of the 17th century, it was usual to have the chesstrees on the upper deck. English 2-deckers up to 1655
or thereabouts had the same fitting, but on the upper
deck; after that they began to pass their main tacks from
aft forward through an eye in a piece of timber secured
to the outside of the bulwarks. Very often this was
simply the foremost of the fenders which ran down
from the bulwarks to the wales, but sometimes, before
1700, it was a shorter, stouter timber more or less ornamented. After 1700 the use of one of the fenders as a
chesstree was the rule in English 2-deckers. Foreign
ships varied between the direct hole, usually carved as
a lion's head, and the short chock with the hole fore-
and-aft; they do not seem to have used the fenders.
Apparently the fore-and-aft lead was more usual up to
about 1660 and the direct in-and-out lead after that; in

the middle of the 18th century they returned to the fore-and-aft method. With this lead the tack went inboard

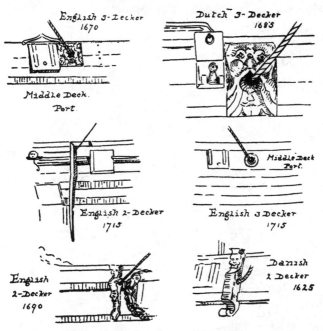

Fig. 204. Various forms of Chesstrees

at the first opportunity, either through a gun-port or a sheave fitted for the purpose. Fig. 204 gives a number of patterns of chesstrees and will be better than any amount of description.

Fig. 205.
Standing part
of Fore Sheet

The lead of the sheets varied very little. The fore sheet always went from a ring-bolt in the ship's side a little before the main channels and usually on the wale just below the upper-deck guns. Secured here with a throat seizing and a round seizing (Fig. 205) it went through the block at the clew of the sail and back to a sheave in the bulwarks above and sometimes a little before its standing part. Sometimes, particularly

about 1700, there were two sheaves here; the fore sheet
went through the upper and the spritsail sheet through
the lower.   The main sheet started in the same way

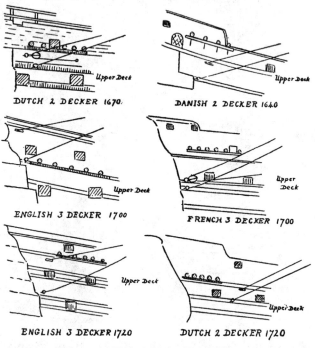

DUTCH 2 DECKER 1670.   DANISH 2 DECKER 1640

ENGLISH 3 DECKER 1700   FRENCH 3 DECKER 1700

ENGLISH 3 DECKER 1720   DUTCH 2 DECKER 1720

Fig. 206. Various leads of Main Sheet

from a ring-bolt in the side just before the quarter gallery and usually on a wale just above the middle-deck
guns of a 3-decker or the upper-deck guns of a 2-decker.
It went through the sheet-block and back above and
abaft its standing part either to a sheave in the side or
to a block secured to another ring-bolt and thence to a
hole in the side.   It is impossible to lay down any hard
and fast rule, but I think foreign ships usually preferred
a block to a sheave, while English ships — at least after
1700 — generally had sheaves.   The sketches in Fig. 206
show actual leads of different dates and countries and

the rigger must use his own judgment, remembering that a lead which fouls guns or chain-plates is probably wrong.

Bowlines

The lower bowlines varied very little. Really, the only questions to be considered are the number of parts in the bridles by which they were attached to the leeches of the sails and the positions of the blocks through which they passed before coming aft for handling. Their thickness should be about half that of the shrouds of their respective masts and the thickness of their bridles a little less.

The fore bowlines normally ran through two blocks on the bowsprit close to the lower deadeye of the forestay. These blocks were either seized directly to the

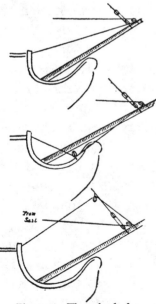

bowsprit, to the strop of the deadeye or to a pair of eye-bolts; probably the first was the most usual. They might be just before the deadeye or a very little abaft it. From them the two bowlines went to the forecastle, either direct or through a pair of blocks secured to the head; they were belayed well apart close to the two fore corners of the forecastle. Occasionally, but not often, they went from the blocks on the bowsprit up to a pair of blocks on the forestay and thence downwards to the

Fig. 207. Three leads for Fore Bowlines

forecastle.   Fig. 207 shows the three possible leads.

The main bowlines ran at one time through blocks on the bowsprit; indeed the original purpose of the bowsprit was to provide this lead.   The English "Treatise on Rigging," of about 1625, gives this as the way they were rigged and says the blocks were "hard by the stem." Perhaps it might be allowable to put them as far out as the gammoning.   In any case, with the dropping of the bowsprit that took place about this time it must have soon become impossible to lead the main bowlines to the bowsprit except by taking them so far forward that they would foul the foresail.   Another lead had to be found and the foot of the foremast seems to have been chosen.   I say "seems," because I rather fancy there may have been a period when the fore rail of the forecastle

Fig. 208.
Snatch-block
for Main
Bowlines

was used instead.   Certainly both English and Dutch models of 1700 or so, have a big snatch-block at the foot of the foremast for the main bowlines, or rather for one of them at a time (Fig. 208).   On the other hand, English lists of twenty years earlier mention two blocks for the main bowlines and I am not sure where these blocks were

placed.   They may have been secured to the foremast or to the collar of the mainstay where it enclosed the foremast, but it seems quite likely that they were put further forward, as was the case with the single snatch-block in French ships about 1750.   On the whole I should be inclined to fit blocks on the bowsprit up to about 1625 and to fit the snatch-block on the foremast after about 1665 for Dutch ships or 1680 for English. In the intervening period I should fit two separate blocks and should put them on the forecastle rail first and on the foremast or the collar of the mainstay afterwards.

The number of parts in the bowline bridles was not always the same, but usually there were three on the main and two on the foresail. A 3-part bridle was arranged as shown in Fig. 209. In English ships the connections were usually made by thimbles or bullseyes, which can be made from wooden beads, but there is evidence that the Dutch, the Danes, and perhaps the French, preferred blocks. The legs of the bridles were attached to "cringles" or loops spliced into the leech-ropes of the sail; when a model has no sails the usual thing to do with the bowline bridles is to timber-hitch them round the yard in about the position where they would be when the sail was furled (Fig. 210).

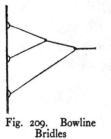

Fig. 209. Bowline Bridles

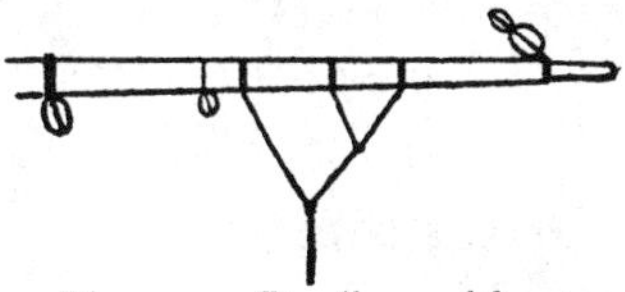

Fig. 210. Bowlines without Sails bent

When a sail had a bonnet it seems probable that the position of the bowline bridles could be varied so as to suit the "course" alone or the course and bonnet together. The simplest way to do this with a 3-part bridle would be to have the two short legs fairly near the clew of the course and to attach the long leg either above them on the course or below them on the bonnet according to circumstances. When bonnets had been given up the long leg usually came lowest.

To attach the legs to the cringles ordinary "bowline knots" should be used. This was not the case in English rigging at the end of the 18th century; a clinch was used instead and the matter is made more difficult by the fact that the French called a clinch *noeud de bouline*.

However, Blanckley, in 1750, says that a Bowline Knot
"is a knot that will not slip, by which the bowline bridle
is fastened to the cringles." I feel confident that he is
referring to the knot which is called a bowline nowadays;
the very name of that knot makes it certain that it was
used for the purpose at one time. Apparently the change
to a clinch came in the latter half of the 18th century.

Leechlines (or Martnets) and Buntlines

To gather up a square sail before furling it one uses
the clewlines, leechlines and buntlines. Of these the
clewlines haul up the lower corners of the sail and work
on its after side; while the leechlines, which haul in the
two up-and-down edges, and the buntlines, which gather
up the foot, work on the fore side. At one time the work
of the leechlines was done by the martnets; these were
different in action as well as in name, but their purpose
was the same.

Martnets were in use at the beginning of the 17th century and were superseded by the simpler leechlines about
1650. They are among the most puzzling of all fittings,
not only because of their complicated nature, but also
because they have been more abused by artists than almost any other detail of rigging. There is a clear description of one method of fitting them in the "Treatise on Rigging" and this method will certainly "work," but it does
not agree with the evidence of pictures and does little to
explain the method which the artists were trying to depict.

According to the written authority there were two
deadeyes connected by a bridle; each of them had ropes
through its three holes and these were connected at each
end to the leech of the sail, while the bridle passed
through the lower of a pair of sister-blocks. A single

block hung on a pendant from the topmast head and a fall starting from the strop of this block went through the upper sister-block, up to the pendant-block and down to the deck. Now the question occurs at once whether the two deadeyes and their two 6-part crowfeet were both on the same side of the sail or whether there was one forward and one aft. The point is this — pictures nearly always show two deadeyes and two crowfeet whichever side of the sail is shown; but at the same time, when the sail is furled and the martnets are hanging slack, they still show only two deadeyes. It seems

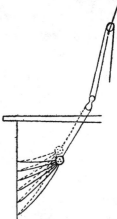

Fig. 211. English Lower Martnets about 1625

fairly certain that there were martnets on both sides of the sail and I think the description must be intended to apply to a simplified form where the bridle straddled the yard and the two (and only two) deadeyes came down one forward and one aft. If this is correct, the sketch in Fig. 211 will show how to fit martnets on this plan.

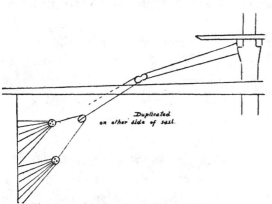

Duplicated on other side of sail.

Fig. 212. Another form of Lower Martnets

In most early 17th century pictures the fall of the martnets leads beneath the lower top instead of to a

pendant from the topmast head. With this lead it is
difficult to get enough drift to let the leech of the sail be
hauled up far enough to be any good. As far as can be
made out the arrangement was as shown in Fig. 212.
How the fall was fitted I do not know, but the probability it that its standing part was secured to the collar of

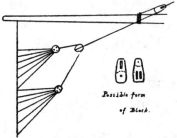

the stay and its end led down
through a block just abaft
the standing p a r t. With
yards carried lower than in
later times the martnets may
have worked well enough,
but there must have been
very little to spare and the
lead to the topmast h e a d

Fig. 213. Possible alternative method of rigging Martnets

was no doubt introduced to get over the difficulty. Another possible way of attaining the same object is shown
in Fig. 213. I have no authority for this, but it is not
seriously contradicted by the pictures and it would at
any rate give the necessary movement to the leech of
the sail.

So much for martnets. Before discussing the transi-
tion period it will be best to describe their successors, the
leechlines, in their standardised form of about 1700.
There were two cringles on either leech of the sail about
⅓ and ⅔ of the way down from the yard to the clew
and there were two leading blocks on either half of the
yard on its upper fore side. In the *St George* model, the
two blocks are fairly close together on each side of a
point ⅓ of the way in from the yard-arm cleats to the
middle of the yard; in plans of 1719 the inner block is
nearly half way in along the yard and the outer is half
way between it and the cleats. The leechlines ran from

the lower cringle, through the inner leading block, through one of a pair of sister-blocks, through the outer leading block and to the upper cringle. They were long

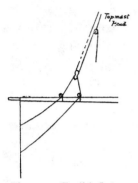

enough to let the sister-blocks stand well above the yard when the sail was set. The fall started from the topmast head above the shrouds and came down abaft the topsail to the upper of the two sister-blocks, thence to a block on a short pendant from the topmast head and so down through the topmast rigging and the top to the deck. Fig. 214 shows leechlines rigged thus. The

Fig. 214. English Lower Leechlines about 1700

Fig. 215. Shoe-blocks for Leechlines

chief variations were in what I have called the sister-blocks; the *St George* model has something very like an ordinary fiddle-block, whereas the plans of 1719 show shoe-blocks with the sheaves at right angles (Fig. 215) and Battine's lists of 1685, with their total of ten leechline blocks, seem to demand two ordinary blocks stropped together.

It is not easy to say how English leechlines should be rigged during the period 1645 - 1675. We find contemporary writers mentioning martnets, leechlines and "martlines." These last were probably the same as leechlines, for Miller, who cribbed from Hayward, calls them martlines where Hayward calls them leechlines. Hayward, writing in 1655, gives leechlines to the ships built after 1650 and martnets to the older ships, while Bond, in 1642, and Miller, in 1655, speak of martlines. One thing is certain; Hayward's leechlines were not long enough to reach to the topmast head and back.

Probably they led below the tops in the way that will
be described for Dutch ships. Deane's table of 1670
gives leechlines, but leaves their length and thickness
blank, and Keltridge, in 1675, only makes matters worse
by giving some ships odd numbers of leechline blocks.
On the whole, I think I should fit old fashioned martnets
up to about 1645, and double leechlines of the 1700 pattern after about 1670; for the intermediate period I
should fit Dutch-fashion single leechlines.

This Dutch method was very simple; a single leechline passed through a block attached to the yard or more
often through a sheave in a piece of wood bolted to the
fore side of the yard about ⅔ of
the way in from the yard-arm to
the middle; it then went through
a block seized to the collar of the
stay well back towards the mast
and down to the deck abaft the
yard (Fig. 216). French ships
used this method also and in all

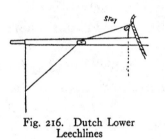

Fig. 216. Dutch Lower
Leechlines

probability Swedes and Danes did the same. The practice at Hamburg, as described in a German book of 1700,
was to fit leechlines on the English system and a Spanish
plan of 1732 shows this also; but usually, I think, foreign ships retained the Dutch method till the later lead
through blocks under the top became universal.

Dutch buntlines, in the second half of the 17th century at any rate, were fitted in the same way as the leechlines; they went from the foot of the sail, through two
blocks on the fore side of the yard between the clewline-
blocks and the quarter-blocks for the topsail sheets,
through two blocks on the collar of the stay just before
the leechline-blocks and down to the deck abaft the

yard (Fig. 217). English buntlines, from about 1680 onwards, were more complicated, there were two on each

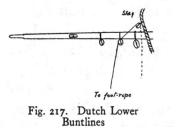

side, the inner pair of blocks on
the yard being close to the quarter-blocks or even inside them.
The cringles on the foot of the
sail were spaced further apart
than the blocks on the yard, so
that the inner pair of cringles

Fig. 217. Dutch Lower
Buntlines

came about under the outer pair of leading blocks.
There were also leading blocks under or beside the
trestle-trees in pairs. The main top had four roughly
above the fore side of the yard,
but the fore top had another
four towards the after end of
the trestle-trees. The reason
for the difference was that the
main buntlines ran forward
and the fore buntlines aft. The
main buntlines went in pairs
through the leading blocks on
the yard, through those under
the top from aft forward and
through two shoe-blocks; their
falls started from the after rail

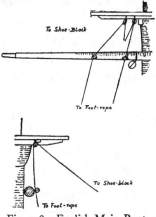

Fig. 218. English Main Buntlines about 1700

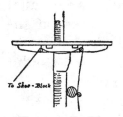

Fig. 219. English
Fore Buntlines
about 1700

of the forecastle and went through
the shoe-blocks and back to the rail
beside their standing parts (Fig. 218).
The fore buntlines were rigged in
just the same way except that they
ran from forward aft a n d h a d to
go through leading blocks at both
ends of the trestle-trees (Fig. 219).

Their falls also ran to the after rail of the forecastle.

In the early part of the 17th century there was more variation in buntlines and there is less certainty as to their fitting. Some pictures show a single buntline, while the print of the *Sovereign* seems to have no less than six on the foresail (Plate 7). In Manwayring's "Seaman's Dictionary," written about 1622, the descriptions under the two headings of "Buntlines" and "Brails," are very much the same; both are said to run from cringles on the footrope through blocks on the yard, but there seems to be a suggestion that the buntline was a single rope in the middle, while the brails were two in number and were a little way out from the middle. In the "Treatise on Rigging," of much the same date, there are said to be three buntlines, one central and one on either side and they are said to go through *a block* on the collar of the stay and to be belayed on *two cleats* on the mast. As far as the two outer buntlines are concerned there is other evidence of this lead direct to the collar of the stay without leading blocks on the yard and it would probably be quite reasonable to fit them thus in small and medium-sized ships of any country up to about 1645. With the multiple buntlines (or brails) of the *Sovereign* and other

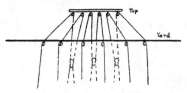

Fig. 220. Possible arrangement of English Buntlines about 1675

big ships, it seems almost certain that there must have been blocks on the yards and also under the tops or on the stays and it is probable that the buntlines worked in pairs as they did later. In 1675, Keltridge credits big ships with twelve single and three long double blocks for both fore and main buntlines; this seems to involve fitting six buntlines in pairs and passing each through a block on the yard and another under the top (Fig. 220). Apparently the fore buntlines had not yet been given the second row of leading blocks under the top.

Both leechlines and buntlines should be ⅓ of the shrouds in thickness or a trifle less. If sails are fitted, the lines should be attached to the cringles with bowline-knots or clinches, preferably the former. If there are no sails, the best thing to do with them is to put figure-of-eight knots in their ends and to haul the knots right up to the leading blocks on the yards. In cases where there are no blocks on the yards it will be best to seize the ends to the yards in about the places where they would come when the sail was brailed up. In getting the right lengths for the buntlines and leechlines it must be remembered that having the ends on the yard corresponds roughly to having the sail hauled right up. To get the length correct one must see where the double block comes both in these conditions and with the ends of the buntlines and leechlines pulled through the blocks far enough to represent their positions when the sail is set.

CHAPTER VIII

Running Rigging of the Topsails and Topgallants

THE running rigging of the upper sails falls into the same two classes as that of the courses. There is the gear belonging to the yards and that belonging to the sails. Besides these there is certain gear for hoisting or striking the masts themselves.

Top-ropes

IN English, the ropes which were used for hoisting or lowering the topmasts were called "top-ropes." Like many other fittings they became more elaborate as time went on. In their simplest form they started from an eyebolt beneath the cap of the lower mast and ran

Fig. 221.
English
Top-rope
about 1625

through a sheave cut athwartships in the heel of the topmast, through a block hooked or seized beneath the cap opposite to the standing part and down to the fourth sheave in the fore or main knight (Fig. 221). The English "Treatise on Rigging" mentions a sheave in the masthead instead of a block under the cap, but other authorities of the same date (1625) say there was a block and this seems the more likely. In foreign ships, which kept to the tie and halliard method of hoisting their lower yards and thus retained the knights with their four sheaves, this way of working the top-ropes was also retained. It did sometimes become a little more complicated, especially in big ships. There were sometimes two blocks under the cap and two sheaves in the heel of the topmast, either side by side or one above the other. In this case the top-rope started from an eyebolt well

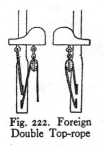

Fig. 222. Foreign Double Top-rope

forward on the cap and went in turn through one sheave, through the block opposite the standing part, through the second sheave, through the block abaft the standing part and down to the deck (Fig. 222). Probably big English ships fitted their top-ropes in much the same way in 1635 or thereabouts.

At about the same time as English ships began to use jeers for their courses to the exclusion of ties and halliards they began to fit their top-ropes in a different way. Lists of gear speak of "top-rope pendants and falls," but strictly speaking "pendant," is a misnomer; "runner" would be nearer the mark. What is meant is that there was a block on the end of the top-rope and a tackle beneath it. Such an arrangement can be traced back to 1642 at least. At this stage there would seem to have been a single top-rope; it may have gone through two sheaves and two blocks, but it had only the one tackle to actuate it. A bit later — perhaps about 1675 — two separate top-ropes were carried. They ran as described for the simple top-ropes of earlier days and were independent of one another. One went through a sheave well up on the topmast (about half way between the trestle-trees and the cap when the topmast was in place), the other had a sheave in the squared heel of the topmast and a long slot was cut to let it reach this sheave without jambing against the inside of the trestle-trees (Fig. 223). Something of the sort must always

Fig. 223. Heel of Topmast with Sheaves and Slot for Top-rope

have been necessary when there was a sheave well down in the heel; unless, as seems quite probable, the top-rope was led outside the trestle-trees instead of inside.

Each of the top-ropes on this English system had its own tackle. There was an eye spliced at its lower end and a metal-stropped block was hooked into it. A similar block, with an eye on its strop for the standing part of the fall, was hooked to a ring-bolt in the deck. In the *St George* model, the blocks are treble for the main top-rope and double for the fore. This model, as has been mentioned already, is peculiar in having sheaves in its caps instead of blocks for the top-rope "pendants." The top-ropes led down outside the trestle-trees; on the main they came

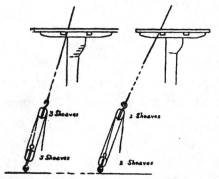

Fig. 224.   Top-rope-tackles in the *St George* model of 1701

through the hole in the middle of the top, but on the fore they came further aft and had small holes cut in the floor of the top for them. The reason for this was to let the tackles have a fair lead to the upper deck clear of the forecastle. Fig. 224 shows the lead of the tackles of fore and main top-ropes.

Speaking roughly, the thickness of a top-rope should be nearly as much as that of the lower shrouds and its fall should be about half as thick. The standing part of the pendant should be attached to the ring under the cap by means of a throat and a round seizing; its end should be left rather long. In getting the length of the top-rope one should remember that with the topmast up the tackle will be at its shortest. It will be enough to leave a drift between its blocks of something like ten feet on the scale of the model. The end of the fall can be hitched round the hook of the lower block, or better stopped to the part before it; a good surplus should be left and coiled. With foreign top-ropes leading to the knight, the end can be simply hitched round the top of the knight. Some models show the top-rope coiled and slung to the masthead and not brought down to the deck at all, but it seems best to bring it down so as to show how it really worked.

Top-ropes are seldom shown on the mizzen topmast or on the topgallants, though there should be sheaves for them in the heels of the masts. If fitted, they would probably be single ropes like those of the old style top-mast top-ropes.

Ties and Halliards

FOR the greater part of the 17th century the method of hoisting the topsails of English ships remained the same. There was a "tie" which went from the yard through a sheave in the topmast below the topmast cross-trees; this tie had a block at its end and through the block went a "runner" which was attached to one side of the ship well aft. The runner in its turn had a block at its free end and the "fall" or "halliard" worked through this block and came down on the opposite side of the ship to the standing part of the runner. At first, when topsails were small, the fall was a simple "whip" with a single block on the end of the runner and no lower

Fig. 225. Simplest form of Topsail Tie, Runner and Halliard

block (Fig. 225). As topsails grew bigger — especially in large ships — the fall became more elaborate and consisted of a 4-part tackle with a double block at the end of the runner and a single block below, or even of a 5-part tackle with a double block at the bottom and a fiddle-block on the runner (Fig. 226).

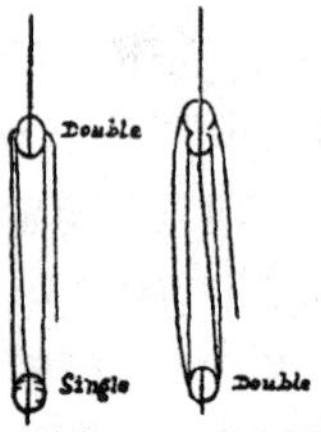

Fig. 226. More elaborate Topsail Halliards

With this type of topsail halliards the tie should be as thick as the lower shrouds, the runner ⅔ as thick and the fall ½ or less. The tie-block should have a length about equal to the diameter of the lower yard and should be spliced into the end of the tie. The other end should be secured to the yard as shown in Fig. 227 and the tie should be long enough to let the block come down as far as the lower side of the top when the yard is fully hoisted. The

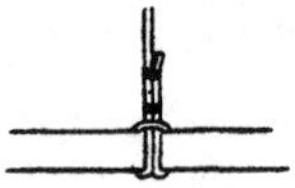

Fig. 227. Method of securing Tie to Yard

standing part of the runner should be hitched and seized, or else hooked, to an eye-bolt or ring-bolt on the inside of the bulwarks a little abaft the aftermost shroud. The runner must be long enough to let the yard go down on to the cap, but not much longer, because the block at its end will have to move twice as far as the travel of the yard. The "Treatise on Rigging" says that both the tie-block and the runner-block were spliced in, but it seems more likely that the latter was stropped and the runner seized to it — at least when the other end carried a hook. The lower block for the fall should have a hook on it and should be hooked on the other side of the ship. Normally the main topsail halliards led to the fore end of the quarter deck and the fore topsail halliards to the fore end of the waist just abaft the forecastle. The runner of the main topsail halliards should be on one side of the ship and that of the fore topsail halliards on the other.

Towards the end of the 17th century English ships began to hoist their topsails by a new method. The runner was done away with and the mechanical advantage which it gave was obtained by doubling the tie and having a block on the yard. At the same time — at any rate in big ships — the whole apparatus was duplicated, so that there were two ties and two halliards. The change was, in fact, very similar to what had happened in the case of the lower yards in the substitution of jeers for ties and halliards.

In the *St George* model, which may be taken as typical, the arrangement is as follows:— There is a double block on the yard and a single pendant block inside the topmast rigging on each side close beneath the trestle-trees. One tie starts from the masthead on the starboard side and runs through the fore sheave of the double block from forward aft; the other does exactly the reverse (Fig. 228). The halliards consist of two 4-part tackles with fiddle-blocks at the top and single blocks at the bottom; these latter are hooked to eye-bolts outboard and just before the two topmast backstays (Fig. 229). The fiddle-blocks come just about level with the topsail yards when lowered. They are stropped and the ties are seized to

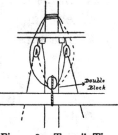

Fig. 228. Topsail Ties in the *St George* model

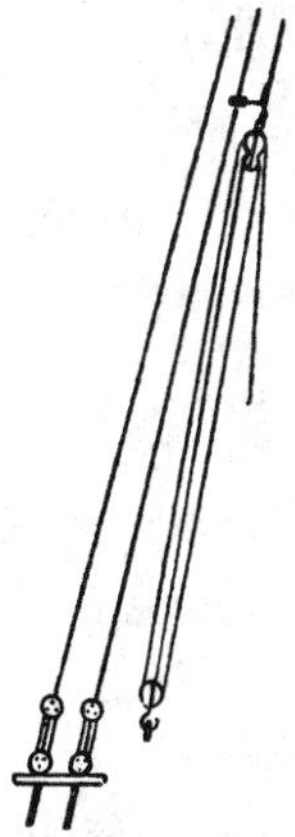

Fig. 229. Topsail Halliard in the *St George* model

them. A pair of bullseyes fitting loosely on the backstays are connected by strops to the ties just above the fiddle-blocks. The object of this was to keep the blocks from falling on deck if the ties were carried away.

No doubt there were variations on this arrangement, as there were a century later. For instance, the model of the *Royal George*, of 1715, has the upper blocks secured to the topmast caps instead of hanging below the trestle-trees. A variation, which seems quite probable, is a single tie passing through a single block on the yard and having halliards on both ends. I think it probable that there was a time (about 1680) when there might be a tie and a single halliard but no run-

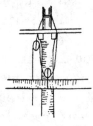

Fig. 230. Possible form of English Topsail Tie about 1680

ner. The tie might have started from the masthead and gone through a block on the yard and a sheave in the mast-head or a pendant-block on one side (Fig. 230). The objection to a single halliard was that unless it was brought down amidships, it would be helping to pull the topmast over to leeward on one tack. For some reason a halliard amid-

Fig. 231. Dutch Topsail Halliards about 1670

ships was avoided in English ships and a pair of halliards was the obvious alternative.

Dutch ships did have a single central halliard. Between 1660 and 1700 they usually had a single tie passing through a sheave in the mast with a fiddle-block on the end of it. A single block with a long strop was secured to one of the trestle-trees of the lower mast or to the eye of the maintopmast or mizzen topmast stay, and the tackle starting from the strop of this block ran in four parts with the end going down abaft the mast to the deck (Fig. 231). One model, that in Berlin, has an interesting variation; her main topsail halliards are almost a replica of those of the mainsail. She has a double tie going through two sheaves side by side and through the single upper sheave of a small duplicate of the ramhead block for the lower halliards. The block in the top is double and the halliard runs in six parts (Fig. 232).

Fig. 232.
Dutch Main
Topsail
Halliards
in the Berlin
model of 1665

French ships probably followed Dutch fashions at one time. The arrangement of the topsail halliards described by Dassié, in 1677, is exactly that of the Berlin model, except that the "ramhead" block at the main is double instead of treble. A few years later they seem to have adopted another method by which both main and fore topsails had double ties which passed through two sheaves in the mast and through the upper half of a pair of sister-blocks. A runner went through the lower half and had the usual fiddle-block and single block tackle on its end. This tackle was hooked outboard abaft the lower shrouds on one side and the standing part of the runner on the other.

Two more elaborate methods are described in a German book of 1700. In both there is a double block on the yard with a single block beneath the trestle-trees on one side and a double block on the other. The tie runs through the two sheaves of the upper double block and those of the block on the yard alternately and then goes through the single block. In the one case the tie itself comes right down to the knight from the single block,

while its other end is secured to the yard (Fig. 233);
in the other both ends carry single blocks from which the

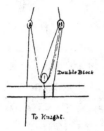

falls run in 3-part tackles
(Fig. 234). For the fore
topsail this book describes
the ordinary Dutch form of
halliards.

So far I have been dealing
with the methods of 1650 or
later. In the early part of the
17th century big ships went

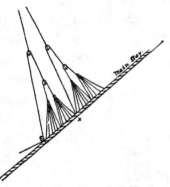

Fig. 233. German
Topsail Ties
about 1700

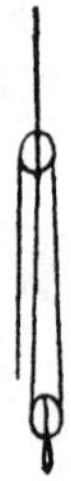

Fig. 234.
German
Topsail
Halliards
(double)
about 1700

in for complicated rigging and the topsail
halliards were one place where the boatswain

Fig. 235. Fore Topsail Halliards
from Danish print of about 1625

really let himself go. The
best example is perhaps to
be seen in the fore topsail
halliards of the ship in a
Danish print of about 1625
(Plate 5). These are drawn
out again in Fig. 235. It is
not very clear how they
worked, but there is no
doubt of the complication.
It may be that the after half
of the apparatus is merely
a backstay or that there are double ties and that there
should be another leading block at (x) for the hauling
part of the second halliard. A third possibility is that
there was a block on the yard, but in that case the yard
would never lower more than about half way with the
proportions as shown. Probably the second interpretation is correct, for the main topsail ties are certainly
double and are actuated by a pair of runners and whips

of the type described for the single halliards of English ships. Very likely English ships of this date or a little earlier would also have taken their fore topsail halliards to the main stay; the author of the "Treatise on Rigging" leaves the foremast and its gear undescribed, but there is no doubt that it was the fashion of the time to crowd as many ropes as possible on to the stays.

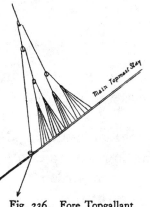

Fig. 236. Fore Topgallant Halliards from Dutch print of 1594

In the same way there was a time when the fore topgallant halliards were based on the main topmast stay. This is also shown in the Danish print and again it is doubtful whether the whole collection of blocks and crowfeet is concerned with the halliards or whether half of it represents a backstay. Probably it is all meant for halliards, for that is certainly the case in a similar tackle in a Dutch print of 1594 (Plate 1 and Fig. 236). The main topgallant was hoisted in a simpler manner; its single tie had a block on the end and a simple whip ran through this block from the two sides of the quarter-deck or poop (Fig. 237).

Occasionally this form of topgallant halliard is met with right through the 17th century. For instance, the French *Royal Louis* model of 1692, has it for both fore and main topgallants. More often, though, both English and foreign ships after about 1650 had central topgallant halliards. The tie had a block on it and there

Fig. 237. Main Topgallant Tie and Halliard about 1600

was another block on the topmast trestle-tree. Usually the tie-block was single
and the halliard ran in three
parts (Fig. 238); sometimes
—particularly in big Dutch
ships—there were fiddle-
blocks on the ties and 4-part
halliards (Fig. 239). In any
case the end came to the
deck, either to the knight
or to the rail on one side.

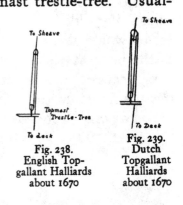

Fig. 238.
English Top-
gallant Halliards
about 1670

Fig. 239.
Dutch
Topgallant
Halliards
about 1670

By the end of the century English ships
may have begun to have a block on the
yard and a 2-part tie. If so, they had
to have the lower blocks of their topgallant halliards on the lower trestle-trees
to give enough travel to the yard. Probably it would be safer to fit the simpler
form with a single tie and two single blocks,
the lower being on the topmast trestle-
tree. However, Fig. 240 shows how to
lead the double-tie variety, if this is preferred.

Fig. 240.
Possible form
of English
Topgallant Tie
and Halliard
about 1710

Parrels

TOPSAIL and topgallant parrels were simpler than those of the courses. They had
only two rows of trucks and there were
no truss-tackles to complicate matters.
The bight of the parrel-rope should be
put round the yard and the ribs and
trucks threaded on to the two ends (Fig.
241). When the whole thing is drawn

Fig. 241.
Reeving a
Topsail Parrel

up close the ends should be taken backwards and forwards several times along the notch in the ribs. To finish off, the ends can be hitched round the several parts and stuck through with a needle. Other ways will easily suggest themselves; for instance, one can start with a noose round the yard at one side and thus have only one end to deal with. Unless the model is on a very large scale it matters very little how these smaller parrels are fitted as long as they look tidy and hold firm.

Lifts

IN English ships, right through the period dealt with in this book, the topsail lifts acted also as topgallant sheets. When fulfilling this latter duty they started from the clews of the topgallants, went through single blocks at the topsail yard-arms, then through blocks hanging on pendants from the masthead inside the stay and beneath the trestle-trees and so down the mast to the main top or fore top. In the days of very small topsails the lifts were belayed in the tops, but later they came down to the deck, passing through holes in the tops and running down beside one of the lower shrouds, about the middle shroud as a rule. The holes in the tops were roughly on the thwartship diameter and about ⅕ of the diameter in from the edge.

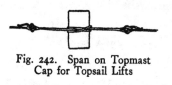

Fig. 242. Span on Topmast Cap for Topsail Lifts

When there were no topgallants, or when they were not in use, the topsail lifts started from the topmast caps. The *St George* model shows a short span with an eye in each end clove-hitched round the cap and the topsail lifts hitched to the eyes and seized (Fig. 242).

Sometimes, I think, the topsail lifts had knots or toggles on their ends and these could be put through either the eyes of the span or the clews of the topgallant as occasion demanded (Fig. 243). In rigging a model without sails one can please one-

Fig. 243. Topsail Lift toggled to Span or to Clew of Topgallant

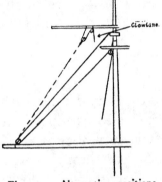

Fig. 244. Alternative positions of Topsail Lift or Topgallant Sheet

self whether to take the topsail lifts to the caps or to haul them up to the topgallant yards by means of the clewlines as shown in Fig. 244. The former is perhaps more correct, but the latter has the advantage of giving rather more to hold the topgallant yards down against their lifts and halliards and making it more obvious what the topgallant clewlines really are. The thickness of topsail lifts should be ½ that of the topmast shrouds or a little more.

This method of combining topsail lifts and topgallant sheets was not quite universal. The Danish print of about 1625, shows fiddle-blocks at the topsail yard-arms and the topgallant sheets and topsail lifts treated exactly like the corresponding ropes on the lower yards. French prints of the end of the century show the same thing in some cases. Possibly there were instances of this method all through the 17th century, but I should hesitate to show it in a model without more authority for it than I have at present.

Topgallant lifts were quite simple. They started from

the caps and ran through single blocks at the yard-arms and beneath the trestle-trees (Fig. 245).

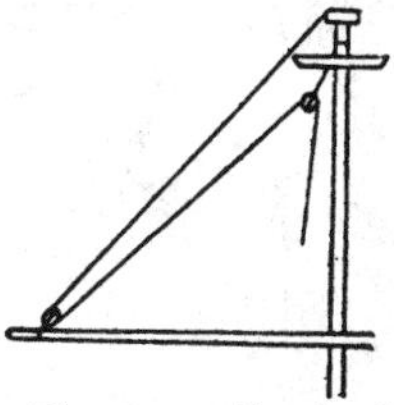

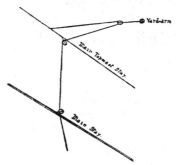

Fig. 245. Lead of Topgallant Lift

Sometimes the pendants of these latter blocks were long enough to let the blocks come well clear of the trestle-trees and even of the topgallant shrouds; sometimes they were quite short and the blocks therefore much less noticeable. Usually the topgallant lifts were belayed in the tops.

Braces

THE fore-topsail braces were exactly like the fore braces except for the fact that they ran from and to the main-topmast stay instead of the main stay. After passing through the blocks on the main-topmast stay they went down to a pair of leading blocks on the main stay and thence to the deck (Fig. 246). In English ships and, I think, in French, the point of attachment of the fore-topsail braces was further forward than that of the fore braces, so that they led down before the fore braces; in Dutch ships this was often reversed.

Fig. 246. Lead of Fore Topsail Braces

The fore-topgallant braces were based on the main-topgallant stay. Sometimes they were single ropes starting from the yard-arm; Deane shows them thus even in big ships in 1670 (Plate 12) and the Dutch model of 1665, in Berlin, has the same arrangement. More often they had pendants and were rove in the same way as the lower braces. In English ships they ran down

through leading blocks on the lower stays to a point
about the after end of the forecastle (Fig. 247). French
practice was the same, but the
Dutch sometimes took them forward to a pair of blocks about
⅓ way down the aftermost fore-
topmast shrouds and then down
through the fore top (Fig. 248).
This was a partial survival of
the method shown in Dutch and
Danish prints of the end of the
16th century and the early part of
the 17th (Plates 1 and 5), where
the fore-topgallant braces ran

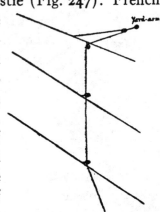

Fig. 247. Lead of Fore Topgallant Braces

through blocks secured by crowfeet to the fore-topmast
rigging and then through a pair of blocks a little way
aft on the main-
topmast stay be-
fore going to the
fore top (Fig.
249). In these
two prints the
fore topsail
braces are treat-
ed in the same
way; from the
main-topmast
stay they go to

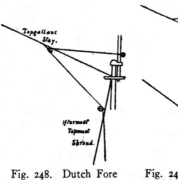

Fig. 248. Dutch Fore
Topgallant Braces
about 1670

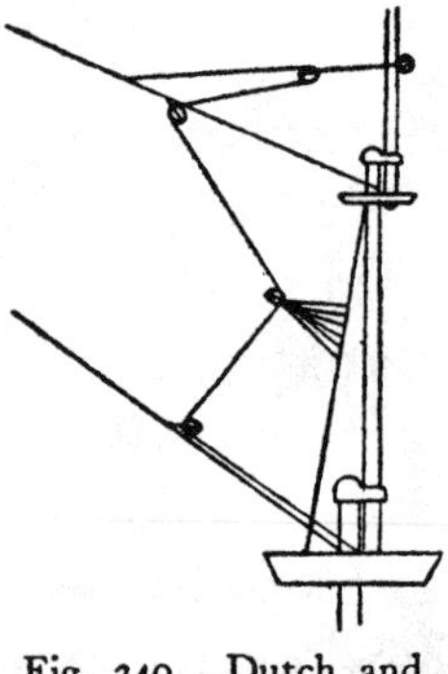

Fig. 249. Dutch and
Danish Fore Topgallant
Braces about 1600-20

blocks on the fore rigging and aft to blocks on the main
stay (Fig. 250). The only difference between them is
that the earlier print takes them straight down from the
main stay, whereas the Danish picture shows them
running forward down the stay.

One Dutch model, the *"William Rex,"* of 1698, shows

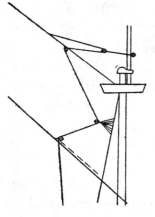

unusual leads for all three of her head braces. The fore braces start a long way aft on the main stay and return to a pair of blocks on the foremost main shrouds a little below the top. The fore-topsail braces start as usual and return to the stay as usual, though a long way aft on the stay, but instead of coming straight down to the deck they

Fig. 250. Dutch and Danish Fore Topsail Braces about 1600-20

run through a pair of blocks on the main stay not far below the mouse and then through another pair on the main shrouds below those for the fore braces. The topgallant braces after passing through the blocks on the topgallant stay go to blocks on the main topmast rigging close up to the trestle-trees. The purpose of these leads, which are shown in Fig. 251, was clearly to keep the braces clear of the stay sails. The model was rigged under expert supervision and its rigging is supposed to be intact; but it seems that Evertsen must have shown what he con-

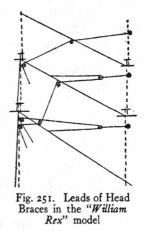

Fig. 251. Leads of Head Braces in the *"William Rex"* model

sidered ought to be done rather than what was the general practice.

Early 17th century ships had their main-topsail braces led in a remarkable way. Starting from somewhere about the mizzen top they went through the pendant blocks and back to a pair of blocks secured to the mizzen shrouds. Having reached this point one would have expected them to go straight down to the deck, but instead

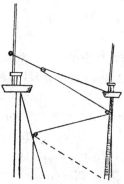

Fig. 252. Main Topsail Braces about 1630

of this they went forward again to a pair of blocks about half way up the aftermost main shrouds. Normally they went down to the deck there and this is the lead described in the "Treatise on Rigging" and shown in the print of the *Sovereign,* but the Danish print of 1625 shows a further complication by taking them aft once more to a point very little before the foot of the mizzen. Fig. 252 shows these two leads.

Other authorities confirm this lead for English ships and it seems evident that the Danes used it too, but I know of no evidence that it ever appeared in Dutch vessels. In them, I think the simpler lead down the mizzen shrouds was the rule. It might be expected that the standing parts of the braces would be made fast below the mizzen top to keep them clear of the foot of the mizzen topsail. This was done later on, but English braces started from above the top for a long time. How they were made fast does not appear, but it is probable that they were hitched or seized to the collar of the mizzen stay. It is difficult to say when they moved to a point below the top. Miller's "Complete Modellist," which is believed to date from 1655 and is certainly earlier than 1664, shows them below (Plate 9), but Deane's drawings of 1670, still have them above the top. These drawings are remarkable in another way; in three out of the set of six the main-topsail braces are brought straight down to the after end of the poop from the pendant blocks (Plate 12). Perhaps this was tried; it certainly was never the rule.

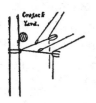

Fig. 253. English and Foreign Main Topsail Braces

When the braces were attached below the top they were fitted as follows:— a span of rope with two blocks spliced into its ends was clove-hitched round the mizzen mast between the crojack yard and the mizzen yard. It was long enough to let the two blocks stand out well clear of the mast. The standing parts of the braces had eyes in them and were seized to the legs of the span about halfway between the mast and the blocks. Foreign ships did not adopt this arrangement; they continued to start their main-topsail braces from the mizzen shrouds or the collar of the mizzen stay below the top and to bring them back to blocks on the mizzen shrouds (Fig. 253).

The main topgallant brace was based on the head of the mizzen topmast in the same way as the maintopsail brace was based on the head of the mizzen mast. The Danish print of 1625 shows it coming back to a block well down the mizzen topmast shrouds and then going forward to the main top (Fig. 254). Other pictures omit this last complication and take it to the mizzen topmast shrouds close under the cross-trees. As long as there was no mizzen topgallant there was no reason to keep the standing

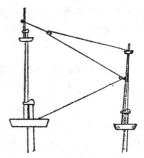

Fig. 254. Main Topgallant Brace in Danish print of about 1625

parts down below the cross-trees and they were probably
secured to the collar of the mizzen topmast stay close be-

Fig. 255.
Standing part
and Leading
block of Main
Topgallant
Brace

side the masthead. The braces returned to
blocks on the shrouds both in English and
foreign ships (Fig. 255). Sometimes, at
least in English ships, the main topgallant
braces ran singly from the yardarms to the
blocks at the mizzen topmast head and
down. Deane shows them thus in 1670
and a list of 1675 mentions no pendants.

For the thickness of braces a rough rule
is to make them half as thick as the shrouds of the corresponding masts. Their pendants should naturally be
thicker, say ¾ of the shrouds.

Sheets and Clewlines

THE clews of the upper sails do not require both tacks
and sheets, because they are hauled down to the yard
arms beneath them and the trimming of the sail is done
by means of the lower braces. It would be possible to
look on the rope controlling the lee clew as the sheet and
the other as the tack, but obviously they would have to
exchange names as the ship went about. As a matter of
fact both were called sheets whichever their duty.

Topsail sheets were thick ropes, somewhere
about ⅞ as thick as the shrouds of the corresponding lower masts. They had a knot
on the end — a crown and wall or something
of that sort — and were rove through the
clews of the topsails. When there are no
sails the only thing to do with them is to put
them through the strops of the clewline
blocks; if there are sails, the strop goes over and through

Fig. 256.
Topsail
Clew with
Clewline-
block and
Sheet

the clew of the sail before the sheet is rove through (Fig. 256). From the clew the topsail sheet went through the lower of the two blocks on the lower yard-arm from outwards in and then along the after side of the yard to a block beneath the yard near the ties or jeers; after that it went straight down to the bitts before the mast. Fig. 257 shows the lead of both topsail sheets and clewlines.

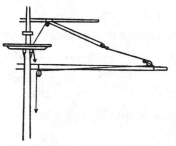

Fig. 257. Lead of Topsail Sheet and Clewline

The clewlines should be about half as thick as the topsail sheets. They should start from the topsail yard with a timber-hitch and go through the blocks at the clew of the sail and back to a pair of blocks on the yard a little inside their standing parts. From there they go through the hole in the top and down to the deck inside the lower shrouds. Early in the 17th century the clewlines led to a point on the topsail yard not very far from the middle; as time went on they moved out till they were about ⅓ of the way out along the yard. Probably they had settled down in this position by 1660 or so. One little refinement that came in in English ships towards the end of the 17th century was to have a pair of leading blocks attached to the masthead, or rather to the bights of the shrouds, to keep the clewlines clear of the floor of the top. French ships, in the middle of the 18th century, got over the same difficulty by taking the clewlines through blocks on the *outside* of the top, but I do not think this was done during the period now under consideration.

Topgallant sheets, being the same as the topsail lifts, have been dealt with already. The clewlines were often

single and started from the clews instead of from the
yard. In either case they went to a block on the yard
and down. Deane's drawings of 1670 show them single
in ships of every Rate; Battine's tables of 1685 make
them double for 3-deckers and single for smaller ships.
Deane shows them brought down direct to the top or
perhaps to leading blocks on the topmast rigging, but by
Battine's date it is probable that there were leading
blocks at the head of the topmast. Foreign ships seem
usually to have led their topgallant clewlines through
the topmast rigging over the futtock staves.

Bowlines

TOPSAIL bowlines were fitted in the same way as those
of the courses. Their bridles usually ran in four parts
on the main topsail and three on the fore. The fore top
bowline always started by going
through a pair of blocks attached
to the fore-topmast stay at about
the level of the fore yard. They
then went through two blocks attached to the bowsprit somewhere
between the collar of the forestay
and the spritsail top (Fig. 258).
After that they might do almost
anything. They might go direct to

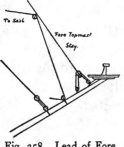

Fig. 258. Lead of Fore
Topsail Bowline from
Sail to Bowsprit

the forecastle rail or they might pass on the way through
one of the sheaves of an elongated multiple block secured to the gammoning. Instead of this they might go
to the "range"—a pin-rail across the head—or to cleats secured to the bowsprit or to the collar of the main stay near
the stem. If going to the range they might make a detour
by passing first through a pair of blocks a little way up the

fore stay. Finally they might go up to a pair of blocks beneath the fore top and down to the deck from there.

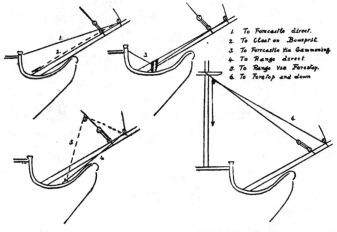

1. To Forecastle direct.
2. To Cleat on Bowsprit.
3. To Forecastle via Gammoning.
4. To Range direct.
5. To Range via Forestay.
6. To Foretop and down

Fig. 259. Various Leads of Fore Topsail Bowline from Bowsprit inboard

Fig. 259 illustrates these various methods but there were yet other possibilities. Dutch drawings of about 1675 and 1695, show the bowlines running through blocks on the topmast stay rather far up, then vertically down to blocks on the fore stay and then up to the top without going to the bowsprit at all. There is no doubt that the lead from the bowsprit to the fore top was common in Holland and the neighboring countries. With slight variations in the method of attaching the blocks to the stay and the bowsprit it occurs constantly in Dutch prints between 1594 and 1660. It is also seen in the Danish ship of 1625 and in Furttenbach's drawing of 1629, probably made from a Dutch model (Plate 4). Besides this it is described in a French book of 1677 and in a German book of 1700.

I doubt if this lead was ever fashionable in English ships. In them I think it would be best to take the fore top bowlines either straight to the forecastle or to the range *via* the forestay for the first half of the 17th century, and after about 1665 or 1670 to introduce the long blocks on the gammoning and to take the bowlines through the uppermost of their four sheaves. Really, I have very little authority for the date when this manifold block was introduced. The *St George* (1701) has it and I have found it in lists of 1675 and 1685; in the former it is called a "rack block for the bowsprit" and was 66 in. long in a 1st-Rate; in the latter it is a "long gammoning block" 70 in. long. A very detailed list of stores at Portsmouth in 1661 does not mention these blocks.

In the *St George* model there is a 3-sheaved block on the bowsprit about ⅖ of the way from the collar of the forestay to the bowsprit end. The hauling part of the fore-topmast stay tackle goes through the middle sheave and the fore topsail bowlines through the two others. They then go — as has been said — through the uppermost sheaves of the long gammoning blocks and are belayed to pins in the forecastle rail close on either side of the main stay collar. This arrangement may, I think, be taken as typical for English ships of 1690-1720. Before that I should be inclined to fit a pair of separate blocks on the bowsprit. For French ships it might be justifiable to keep to the lead to the fore top (or rather to a pair of blocks on the collar of the fore stay close under the top) up to 1680, while the *Royal Louis* model of 1692, shows exactly the same lead as the *St George*. On the whole I would suggest fitting two separate blocks on the bowsprit and a direct lead to the head or the forecastle in Dutch models between 1660 and 1700 and in French between 1675 and 1690. After these dates I should adopt the English method.

The main top bowline, as described in the English "Treatise on Rigging" and as shown in the engraving of the *Sovereign*, of 1637, led through a pair of blocks attached to the main-topmast stay and then through the two sheaves of a double block secured under the fore top (Fig. 260). By 1655, they were leading direct to the fore top and were probably rove, as they still are in the *St George*, of 1701, through a pair of blocks attached to eye-bolts under the after ends of the trestle-trees (Fig.

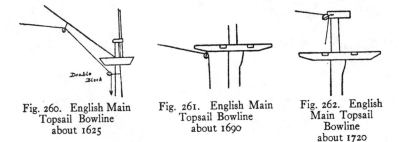

Fig. 260. English Main Topsail Bowline about 1625

Fig. 261. English Main Topsail Bowline about 1690

Fig. 262. English Main Topsail Bowline about 1720

261). In this model they come down to a pair of blocks on the forecastle some way abaft the foremast. A few years later (1710 or so) they were running through blocks fixed to eye-bolts on the fore cap (Fig. 262) or lashed to the upper part of the foremast head, as they did for the rest of the 18th century.

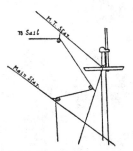

Fig. 263. Foreign Main Topsail Bowline about 1630

Foreign pictures of the early part of the 17th century, Dutch, Danish and French, show quite a different lead; the bowlines go to the main-topmast stay, the fore shrouds, the main stay and down. The Dane takes them along the main stay, the others straight down (Fig. 263). In Dutch ships this lead seems to have been replaced between 1640 and

1650 by a simpler method which shifted the blocks on the fore shrouds nearer to the top and took the bowlines straight down from there. Sometimes the blocks on the stay had such long pendants that they hardly affected the run of the bowlines and eventually—by 1700, I think—these blocks were omitted altogether and the bowlines went straight to blocks high up on the fore rigging or attached under the trestle-trees. French ships were perhaps taking their main top bowlines direct to the trestle-trees by 1680 or earlier.

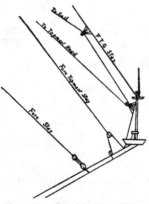

Fig. 264. Danish Fore Topgallant Bowline about 1625

Fig. 265. Usual lead of
Fore Topgallant
Bowline

The topgallant bowlines tended to imitate those of the topsails. Some of the drawings which show the fore topsail bowlines going to the fore top show the topgallant bowlines doing much the same thing a stage higher; that is to say running through blocks attached to the topgallant stay, through another pair attached to the shrouds of the spritsail topmast and then going up under the topmast cross-trees or top (Fig. 264). More often, I think, they went from the spritsail topmast shrouds to a pair of blocks on the bowsprit and thence directly inboard or to the head (Fig. 265). Sometimes, particularly in English ships, the blocks on the spritsail topmast shrouds were replaced by a pair on pendants from the spritsail topmast head and sometimes the blocks on the bowsprit were so far forward that the bowlines led through the spritsail top to get to them.

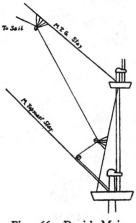

Fig. 266. Danish Main Topgallant Bowline about 1625

The main topgallant bowlines are described in the English "Treatise on Rigging" as running through blocks on the stay and blocks on the fore topmast shrouds and as being belayed in the fore top. The Danish print of similar date (1625) introduces a slight complication by taking them from the fore topmast rigging to the main topmast stay and then into the fore top along the stay (Fig. 266). Usually they ran straight down from the fore topmast head or somewhere near it; the only variation was in the way in which their blocks were secured there. The method of attaching them to the fore topmast shrouds survived well into the 18th century, especially in Dutch ships, but another method was arising by which they were secured to the after cross-tree outside the trestle-trees (Fig. 267). This appears in French and

Fig. 267. Blocks for Main Topgallant Bowlines on Fore Topmast Cross-trees

Dutch models towards the end of the 17th century. English plans of 1719 show it and I feel pretty sure that the *St George* model would have had it if she had carried topgallants.

Topgallant bowlines usually had 3-part bridles, sometimes only 2-part. The thickness of the topsail bowlines
should be about half that of the topsail sheets and their
bridles about ⅓. The topgallant bowlines should be
about half as thick as those of the topsails.

Leechlines and Buntlines

ACCORDING to the "Seaman's Dictionary," written
about 1622, martnets "commonly belong to the two
courses, yet many great ships have them to the topsails
and spritsails." The same authority explains that the
topsail martnets were based on the topgallant mastheads
as those of the courses were based on the topmast heads.
If one can fit satisfactory martnets to the courses, there
is nothing to prevent fitting the same thing to the topsails; the spritsail is quite another matter. On the whole
I think it is best to dispense with topsail martnets. The
only representations of them that I know are in a very
much retouched portrait of a Lübeck ship of the 16th century and on the main topsail of the *Sovereign*, in Payne's
print (Plate 7). They are not shown in the stern view
of this ship in Pett's portrait and even in the engraving
they are replaced by leechlines on the fore topsail. Even
the "Seaman's Dictionary" speaks of leechlines for the
topsails as the normal fitting, while the "Treatise on
Rigging" does not give either martnets or leechlines.

In the early part of the 17th century it would therefore be possible to find martnets, leechlines or neither.
After about 1640, I think, leechlines should always be
fitted. Bond gives them in 1642 and all lists after 1670
include them, though it is true that they are omitted in a
book of 1655. By the way, the print of a French ship built
in Holland in 1626 (Plate 6) has them very clearly shown.

English leechlines went at first through blocks on the yard close to the ties. There can be little doubt that they also passed through blocks at the topmast head, probably on the collar of the stay. At the end of the 17th

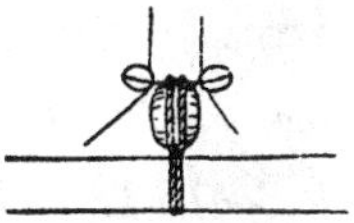

Fig. 268. Topsail
Leechline-blocks
attached to Tie-
block

century, when English ships began to have their topsail ties d o u b l e w i t h a block on the yard, it became the fashion to secure the leechline blocks to the upper part of the strop of this block (Fig. 268). In the *St George* model there are lines through these blocks coiled and hanging beneath the yard. Since there are no sails on this model it is impossible to be sure off-hand whether these are really leechlines or buntlines. A century later they would certainly be buntlines, but all the pictorial evidence of the beginning of the 18th century agrees in showing the topsail leechlines and buntlines crossing one another, the leechlines going to the middle of the yard and the buntlines some way out (Plate 22). From the way in which these lines are treated and the absence of blocks at the topmast head to take them, I imagine that they must have led simply through the two blocks and down to the top abaft the yard. As a confirmation of this we find that Battine's list of 1685, allows only two blocks for topsail leechlines, whereas Keltridge, in 1675, gives four. This would be just about the date when the new method of hoisting the topsails was coming in and it is very likely that the change in the lead of the leechlines came at the same time.

The same variation is described in a German book of 1700, often quoted already. According to this authority, if there was a block on the yard for the topsail halliards, the leechlines went through blocks on the yard and also through blocks beneath the cross-trees (we are not told how they were secured). On the other hand, when there were simple ties the leechline blocks were seized to the ties a little above the yard and the leech-lines came straight down again from there (Fig. 269). This is also what one gathers from a French book of 1677, where there are said to be a pair of blocks on the topsail ties, about one foot above the yard, for the topsail leechlines.

Fig. 269. Topsail Leechline-blocks attached to Ties

A little later French ships were taking their leechlines through blocks on the yard a little way out from the ties and then through a pair of blocks on the collar of the topmast stay (Fig. 270). Dutch ships were doing the same at the end of the 17th century and the beginning of the 18th; before that they were probably using the lead to the ties only, or, in some cases, straight to the collar of the stay without blocks on the yard at all; this is the lead shown in the Berlin model of 1665.

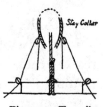

Fig. 270. Topsail Leechline leading to Stay-collar

At some periods topsail leechlines and buntlines seem to have been mutually exclusive. At the end of the 18th century the topsails had buntlines and no leechlines and it seems as if at an earlier date they often had leechlines and no buntlines. Pictures are not a very safe guide, because the buntlines might well get overlooked—especially in engravings—owing to the fact that they ran parallel to the cloths of the sails. Still it is worth mentioning that a good many prints of the first half of the 17th century show leechlines on the topsails but no buntlines. The well-known print of the *Sovereign* has very obvious bunt-lines on her foresail and leechlines on the topsail, but it shows no topsail buntlines. At least it shows no ropes running up the fore side of the sail as the lower buntlines did, but it does show a pair of ropes running from the foot of the sail towards the lower masthead (Plate 7). Such buntlines as these, if they should really be called

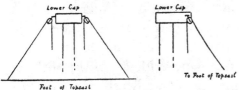

Fig. 271. English Topsail Buntlines(?) about 1715

buntlines, appear in the *St George* model of 1701 and in English plans of 1719 and there lead to a pair of blocks beneath the lower caps (Fig. 271). Their use is obvious and it may well be that they were a substitute for the ordinary buntlines; as far as I know the two fittings do not appear together.

The name "buntlines" appears in the list given by Bond, in 1642, and in other English lists right into the 18th century. It is not easy to decide how they were fitted. In Keltridge's list, of 1675, there are four s i n g l e blocks for the fore topsail and six for the main. On the other hand, lists of 1685 and 1711 give each sail two single blocks and one long double block for the topsail buntlines. This agrees exactly with what we find in the *St George* model (Fig. 272) and may be taken as proving that the ropes to the cap were indeed buntlines.

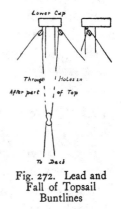

Fig. 272. Lead and Fall of Topsail Buntlines

The question is whether Keltridge's buntlines were of this sort or whether they ran up before the sail to the yard. Personally I believe they went to the lower cap, though I cannot explain how the blocks were disposed.

It is possible that each buntline ran through a block and had another on its end for a whip; in this case there must have been three buntlines on the main topsail. Another possibility is that there were blocks on the footrope of the sail and that the buntlines ran from the cap in two parts. There is a distinct suggestion of this in the print of a French ship built in Holland in 1626 (Plate 6) and English ships may sometimes have done the same thing.

As far as I know, there is no evidence of the 18th century type of topsail buntline in English ships before 1715.

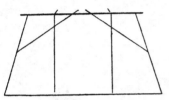

Fig. 273. Topsail Buntlines and Leechlines about 1720

They appear in some, but by no means all, of the ships in Baston's set of prints of about 1720. These show the buntlines crossing the leechlines and going through blocks well out on the yards (Fig. 273); they do not show what happened to them after that, but the probability is that they went up to the cross-trees or near them, as they did later.

Buntlines running up the fore side of the topsails seem to have come into use abroad long before they did so in England. They are shown quite clearly in a Dutch print of 1678 or earlier and in the Berlin model of 1665. Before 1660, I should omit topsail buntlines altogether, unless I fitted something from the foot of the sail to the lower masthead. I have mentioned already that this fitting appears in a Dutch-built ship of 1626 and one of Hollar's etchings of 1647 shows something similar, but most Dutch prints of the first half of the 17th century show no topsail buntlines of any kind. After 1660, I should take the buntlines straight to blocks on the collar of the topmast stay, just before and below those for the leechlines, and towards the end of the 17th century I should add blocks on the yards fairly close to the ties. French ships may have been a little later than Dutch in using topsail buntlines; at any rate there is no suggestion of them in Dassié's lists of gear in 1677. However, the *Royal Louis* model of 1692 has them and has blocks both on the yard and on the stay-collar. Buntlines, by the way, should be rather thicker than leechlines. The topgallants should have neither.

Reef-tackles

One more piece of topsail rigging remains to be described. When reefs were introduced in the topsails, it soon became necessary to have some means of hauling the upper part of the sail up to the yard and taking its weight while the reef-points were being tied. This was done by running a rope from the leech of the sail at a point level with the reef-points up through a sheave in the yard-arm and by hauling on this rope when necessary by means of a tackle. On the general question of when reefs were introduced it would be possible to write a great deal without any very definite result. There is no doubt that they were in use on the lower sails as an alternative to bonnets all through the 13th, 14th and 15th centuries. Soon after the beginning of the 16th century they disappear, but it is possible — in fact, probable — that they remained in use in small craft of which we have not much record. Roughly, 1655 is an approximate date for their reintroduction in the topsails of big ships; it may have been a few years later, but it is more likely to have been earlier.

Reef-tackles were not fittings which lent themselves to representation in drawings and we have to rely on written evidence for the date of their introduction. The earliest mention of them that I know is in Keltridge's lists of 1675; Deane does not mention them in 1670. One would imagine that they must have followed very closely on the use of reefs, but it would be dangerous to rely too much on such reasoning. I should certainly hesitate to show reef-tackles before 1670.

All the information that we get about them from the lists is that they had short "ties" and tackles with two single blocks each. Fortunately, the *St George* model shows us how they were fitted. The ties rove through sheaves in the yard-arms and ran in abaft the yards. They had single blocks spliced into their inner ends and

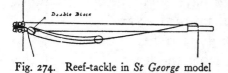

Fig. 274. Reef-tackle in *St George* model

there were two double blocks secured to the lashing of the parrel. The fall started from the outer block and ran in three parts (Fig. 274). It is shown coiled and stopped to the inner block, which may be taken to mean that it was hauled in the top and not led down to the deck. With no sail fitted, the end of the tie can be lashed beneath the yard.

Very soon after the time of the *St George*, certainly by 1715 and probably several years earlier, there came a change in the reef-tackles of English ships. Instead of working from the parrels they were led to the topmast heads. The ties had blocks on them as before and another pair of blocks hung on fairly short pendants from the topmast heads, no doubt passing

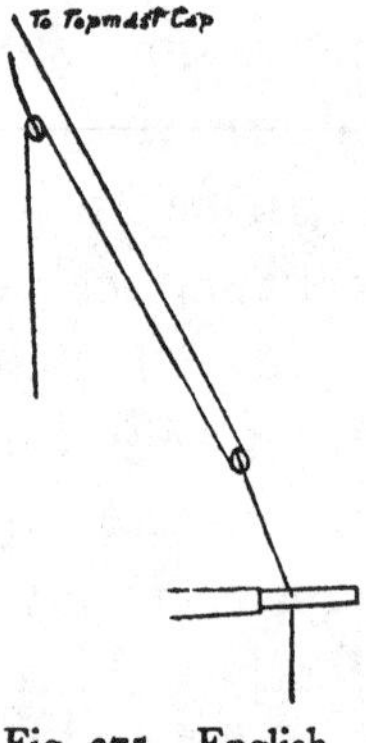

Fig. 275. English Reef-tackle about 1715

down inside the stays. The falls started from the top-mast caps and went through the tie-blocks and up again to the pendant blocks whence they ran down to the tops (Fig. 275).

French ships of about 1695 took their reef-tackles to the parrels as the English did, but they had blocks beneath the yard-arms for the ties instead of using sheaves.

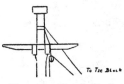

Fig. 276. Dutch Reef-
tackle about 1710

Dutch ships at the end of the 17th century, had already adopted something similar to the later English fitting with a lead to the topmast head. There were blocks at the yard-arms and ties with blocks at their ends; the falls started from the topmast heads just above the shrouds and returned to blocks close beneath the trestle-trees (Fig. 276). This is shown in models of 1698 and 1725.

CHAPTER IX

RUNNING RIGGING OF THE BOWSPRIT

ALL through the 17th century and for a long time before and after that, the bowsprit carried a single square sail, the spritsail. From 1610 to 1720, speaking approximately, all big ships and most small ones had also a spritsail topsail set on a small mast standing upright on the end of the bowsprit. Staysails on the bowsprit began to be used about 1655 or earlier and the jib, with its jib-boom prolonging the bowsprit, was in existence by 1700 or very soon after. This sail gradually ousted the spritsail topsail in its old form and as a result, by 1750, at the latest, the spritsail topmast and its sail had disappeared altogether.

It is not easy to be precise as to when a spritsail topmast should be fitted and when not. We can say that it was adopted officially in England in 1618 and abolished for all ships, except 3-deckers, in 1719. We can also say that it appears on the title-page of a Dutch book of 1600 and that Dutch East Indiamen were still carrying it in 1720-25. There is, I think, little doubt that the English *Prince Royal* carried it in 1613 and she had probably had it since 1610. On the whole, it seems safe to fit it in 3-deckers and 2-deckers of any country throughout the period 1600-1720. Small merchantmen might be without it, especially in the early years of the 17th century, but for warships — except the very smallest — it was apparently an essential. The jib will be described later among the staysails and for purposes of the present section it will be assumed that all ships carried both

spritsail and spritsail topsail throughout the period
covered by this study.

It will be best to describe the gear of the two sails
separately. The spritsail had, in essentials, the same
rigging as any other square sail. Its yard was held to
the bowsprit by a parrel or by slings, pulled out along
the bowsprit by halliards and controlled by lifts and
braces. The sail had sheets, but no tacks, and was fitted
with clewlines and buntlines.

At the beginning of the 17th century the spritsail became for the first time more or less permanently attached
to the bowsprit. Before that it had been the custom to
take it in bodily to the head, yard and all, when the sail
was not set (Plate 1). Naturally it took some little
time for the method of carrying it permanently outboard to become anything like standardised. For instance, there was the question whether it should be carried before or abaft the forestay. Usually it was before
it, but not always; the Danish print of about 1625
(Plate 5) shows it well abaft the forestay and prints of
Dutch moderate sized craft of the first half of the century often suggest the same thing. Still, by far the
greater number of pictures and prints show it slung just
before the forestay.

In that position there was not much chance of moving
it up and down the bowsprit to any extent. Even if
there had been no other obstacles (and there were usually many) there was not room enough between the forestay and the fore topmast stay for more than a very
limited travel. That being so, a parrel seems rather an
unnecessary luxury, but there is no doubt that one was
often used. The English "Treatise on Rigging" mentions a spritsail parrel as a matter of course and it is

shown in Furttenbach's ships of 1629 (Plate 4), in a German ivory model of 1620, in the Danish *Norske Löve* model, and in quite a number of prints and pictures. In most cases there are two rows of trucks and it would probably be safe to copy a topsail parrel exactly.

The *Sovereign* print of 1637, shows no parrel, but as a matter of fact it shows no slings either. Still, it is quite likely that by her time English ships had begun using slings instead of a parrel. Bond gives a sling and no parrel in his list of 1642, and later lists (when they mention anything at all) do the same. The slings should

Fig. 277. Slings of Spritsail Yard

be about the thickness of the fore shrouds or rather less. An eye should be spliced in one end and the sling should then be passed round the yard and seized to itself fairly near the eye (Fig. 277). After that it is passed over the bowsprit and round the yard again. It is then seized to itself again, close down to the yard, and its end is taken over the bowsprit and through the eye. Finally it is seized to itself once more. It is quite likely that there were sometimes eyes in both ends connected by a lashing and it is possible, though not very probable, that the two seizings just above the yard were sometimes omitted.

Early in the 17th century the spritsail yard had a tie and a halliard. How these were rigged we can only guess, but the probability is that there was a block at the bowsprit end — a sheave seems unlikely — and that the tie went through that and had a tackle on its end. By 1625 or thereabouts, there was a simple halliard and no tie. The halliard started from the bowsprit-end, went through a block at the middle of the yard and another at the bowsprit-end and led inboard as far as the gammoning where it was secured. Probably there were a pair of eye-bolts under the bowsprit for the standing part and the leading block (Fig. 278). At the end of the century the spritsail halliards ran in three parts instead of two; there was a fiddle-block under the bowsprit well out towards the end and a single block on the yard. The halliards started from the strop of this block and ended at the gammoning as before (Fig. 279). To judge from lists of blocks and lengths of halliards, this 3-part halliard was in use at least as far back as 1640.

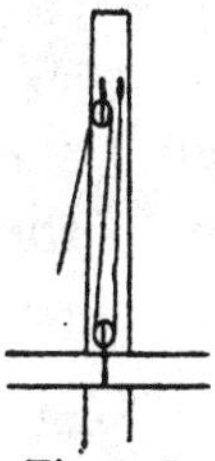

Fig. 278.
Spritsail
Halliards
about 1625

Fig. 279.
Spritsail
Halliards
about 1680

Foreign ships appear to have rigged their spritsail halliards in much the same way. The fiddle-block and single block arrangement was the most usual, but the German book of 1700 describes a 2-part tackle with its standing part made fast to the block at the bowsprit end (Fig. 280), while a French drawing of a little earlier date shows fiddle-blocks at both ends and a 4-part tackle (Fig. 281). The *Royal Louis* model has no halliards but a permanent sling formed by a lashing between a ring stropped to the yard and a ring-bolt under the bowsprit. I should hesitate to copy this in a ship of so early a date.

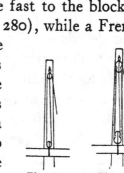
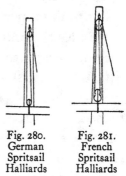

Fig. 280.
German
Spritsail
Halliards

Fig. 281.
French
Spritsail
Halliards

The lifts of the spritsail yard had the additional duty of serving as spritsail topsail sheets. When they were not doing this they were hitched to

eyes in the ends of a pair of short pendants at the
bowsprit-end. Later on these pendants were shifted to
the cap through which the spritsail topmast went (Fig.
282). I have no idea when the change took place; the

Fig. 282. Span
for Standing
parts of Sprit-
sail Lifts

safest thing is to haul the lifts up to the
spritsail topsail yard by means of the clewlines. From the pendants or the clews of
the topsail the lifts or topsail sheets went
through blocks at the spritsail yard-arms
and then to a pair of blocks secured to
eyebolts on either side of the bowsprit well out towards
the end. From there they went aft along the bowsprit.
The "Treatise on Rigging" says they were belayed to
the gammoning, but at the end of the century they were
passing through the long gammoning blocks and going
to the forecastle rail. The *St George* takes them through
the second pair of sheaves in the long blocks, the *Royal
Louis*, through the third. Dutch ships seem to have
taken them to the range in the head or to cleats on the
bowsprit near the stem-head. The German book of
1700 describes them as going through thimbles on the
collar of the forestay and thence to the forecastle.

Besides the ordinary lifts which were also used as topgallant sheets, there were what were called "standing
lifts." In English ships the method of rigging them seems
to have changed very little. A pair of deadeyes were attached to a strop on the bowsprit a few feet before the
slings of the spritsail yard and were connected by laniards
to another pair on the ends of two pendants which were
secured to the spritsail yard a little way in from the yard-
arms. The "Treatise on Rigging" calls them "horses" and
explains that they were useful as lifelines, when men had

to go out on the spritsail yard. By Bond's time (1642) they were called standing-lifts, but English plans of 1719

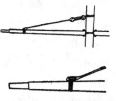

show a series of knots in them and thus confirm their use as lifelines. In the *St George* model the pendants are secured to the yard by seizings through eyes spliced in their ends (Fig. 283).

Fig. 283.   English Spritsail Standing Lifts

A German book of 1700 describes standing lifts on the English plan, but usually foreign ships had them rather differently arranged. Dutch ships dispensed with the pendants and had deadeyes on the yard not very far

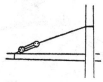

out from the slings (Fig. 284). This was at any rate the fashion between 1660 and 1700; a little

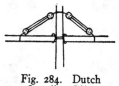

Fig. 284.   Dutch Standing Lifts about 1680

Fig. 285.   Dutch Standing Lifts about 1720

later they seem to have had something similar to the English fitting, but not running quite so far out on the yard and having the pendants on the bowsprit instead of on the yard (Fig. 285).   French ships of about 1680 took their standing lifts a long way up the bowsprit, right under the spritsail top. Sometimes they rigged them in Dutch fashion and sometimes they had pendants from both the yard and the bowsprit. The Danish *Norske Löve* model, made in 1654, has something like the first mentioned French

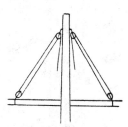

Fig. 286.   Inner Lifts to Spritsail in *Norske Löve* model

fitting, but with a pair of blocks instead of deadeyes (Fig. 286).   Standing lifts are not always shown and there may have been even more variations than have been mentioned.

The spritsail braces were in principle the same as any other braces. They had pendants from the yard-arms and the actual braces ran in two parts to the forestay. They were secured at a level about half way between the forecastle deck and the fore top and went through the pendant blocks and back to a pair of blocks either above or below their standing parts. In English ships, for the greater part of the 17th century, they usually led through a pair of blocks in the head and thence to the forecastle (Fig. 287). A possible variation, which is shown in Miller's book of 1655 (Plate 9), was to take them up the forestay to the fore top and then down to the deck.

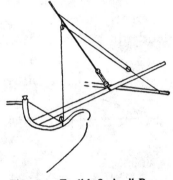

Fig. 287.   English Spritsail Braces about 1650

By 1700, the lead of the spritsail braces had become more complicated. As fitted in the *St George* it was as follows:— The standing part was secured to the yard with an eye and a seizing a little way inside the standing lift. The brace then ran through a block on a short pendant from the forestay about level with the

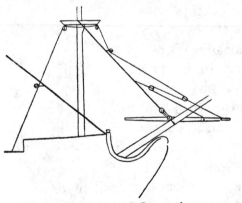

Fig. 288.   English Spritsail Braces about 1700

bowsprit-end. It returned to the pendant block and then went to another block on the forestay at the level of the fore yard. After this it went through a pair of blocks at the two ends of the trestle-tree and finally passed through a leading block on the mainstay and was belayed to a cleat on the bulwarks just abaft the fore-castle bulkhead (Fig. 288). This lead appears again in a model of the *Royal George*, of 1715, in Hanover, but the plans of 1719 show something simpler. In them, the braces start from the forestay about half way up, go to the pendant blocks and back through a pair of blocks on pendants from the forestay above

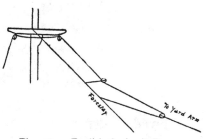

Fig. 289.   English Spritsail Braces
about 1720

the standing parts and then to blocks beneath both ends of the trestle-trees (Fig. 289).

Allowing for another pair of leading blocks on the mainstay or on the fore rigging, this would make the number of ten blocks which is given in lists of 1685 and 1711. On the other hand the list of 1675 gives six blocks, which is just what is required by the lead from the fore-stay to the head. In the same way the length given for the spritsail braces jumps suddenly from the 60 fathoms of 1655 or 58 of 1675 to 76 in 1685. This may, I think, be taken as proof that the lead to the top was officially recognized about 1680. The more elaborate lead of the models of 1701 and 1715 was probably confined to big ships and was evidently abandoned even for them.

Dutch spritsail braces, after passing through the blocks on the forestay, went through a pair of leading blocks on the bowsprit and thence to the forecastle. Usually the blocks on the stay were above the standing parts and the leading blocks well aft on the bowsprit, about mid-

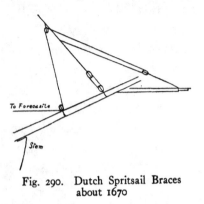

Fig. 290.   Dutch Spritsail Braces
about 1670

way between the forestay and the stem (Fig. 290). This lead was in use in Holland up to about 1700, but a German book of that year describes the simpler form of English lead to the fore top and Dutch models and drawings of about 1720 show that the change had by then come there also.   French rigging followed Dutch practice up to about 1690; the *Royal Louis,* of 1692, still has the old fashion with the extra refinement that the spritsail braces pass through the second of the sheaves in the long gammoning blocks.   The same is the case in one of the French prints of 1691, but the other shows the lead up the stay to the top.

In the same way as the lifts were duplicated to some extent by the standing lifts, the braces were assisted by the "garnets." As described in the "Treatise on Rigging," these garnets were practically braces working half way out along the yard. The standing part was

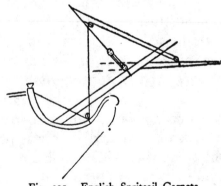

Fig. 291.   English Spritsail Garnets
about 1625

attached to the forestay below the braces and the rope went through a block on the yard, back to a block on the stay below its standing part, through a block in the head and so to the forecastle (Fig. 291). In the engraving of the *Sovereign*, the garnets are shown in three parts and running to the range in the head instead of to the

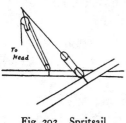

Fig. 292. Spritsail Garnets in the *Sovereign* of 1637

forecastle. Dutch prints show that the block on the stay was a fiddle-block and that the garnet was rove as shown in Fig. 292. The lead to the Range is expressly mentioned in the "Seaman's Dictionary." It is probable that the 3-part lead was the more usual, because lists make the garnets as long as the braces and they would have been shorter if they ran in two parts. Roughly speaking, spritsail garnets died out in English ships soon after 1675. Keltridge's list of that year allows garnets to all ships except the 6th-Rates, but curiously enough gives no blocks for them except in the very class, the 6th-Rates, which had no garnets. Deane gives them in 1670 and Battine, in 1685, mentions the name but leaves the dimensions blank and allows no blocks.

Garnets are very well shown (in the 3-part form) in the Dutch-built French ship of 1626 and in the Danish ship of similar date (Plates 5 and 6). Zeeman's Dutch etchings of about 1650-60, always show them, but the Danish *Norske Löve* model has none. Soon after 1660, the Dutch name for them, "trensen," was transferred to a tackle which acted as yet a third lift; in other words the upper block of the garnet was shifted to the bowsprit. The rope started from an eye-bolt under the spritsail top and ran through a block on the yard rather more than half way out and back through a block on another eye-bolt a little abaft its standing part. This is how they are shown in Dutch prints of 1678 and 1695 and in the *"William Rex,"* of 1698 (Fig. 293). Witsen's book of 1671, gives the old form, but his rigged ship is distinctly old-fashioned in many ways. After a short stay in this position the garnets went back to the forestay, but in a 2-part form like braces without pendants. They

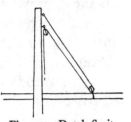

Fig. 293. Dutch Sprit-sail Garnets about 1690

appear thus in a dictionary of 1702 (Plate 21) and in a drawing of the *Gertruda,* of 1720 (Plate 23). Two-part garnets, with a short pendant from the yard, are given in a French rigging plan soon after 1680; otherwise I know of no evidence of their use in French ships. The German "Geöfnete See-Hafen," of 1700, describes the old Dutch form with fiddle-blocks on the stay. On the other hand, a Danish model of about 1690, shows no garnets.

Spritsail sheets varied almost more than any other fitting. Sometimes they had long pendants, sometimes short; sometimes the sheet-blocks had such long strops that they were practically pendants in themselves, sometimes the blocks were close up to the clews in the ordinary way and sometimes the sheets were single ropes without blocks. It is difficult to classify spritsail sheets by date or country. For example, long pendants are found in England in 1637, in Denmark in 1654, in Holland in 1665 and in Germany in 1700. Some kind of a sequence can be made out for English ships, but I doubt very much if there was any real standardisation either there or abroad before the beginning of the 18th century.

On the whole, I think we should be justified in fitting long pendants in English ships up to about 1655, 2-part sheets without pendants for the next 25 years and short pendants or long strops after that. What I call a long pendant is one long enough to let the block at its end come well aft on the fore channels. We are not told how the pendant was fitted, but it probably had the block spliced in at one end and a knot to put through the clew of the sail at the other. It went through a bullseye or thimble hanging on a short line from the foremost fore shroud; this was to keep it clear of the anchors. The sheet was made fast somewhere in the waist and returned to the same place. The "Treatise on Rigging" describes it as passing through a sheave in the side abreast of the mainmast and having its standing part "fastened there." Unfortunately, the author does not deal with the rigging of the foremast at all, so we cannot tell whether the spritsail sheet started from the same ring-bolt as the fore sheet and returned to a sheave just below that of the fore sheet, as it did about 1700. It is very likely, for that is what happens in foreign models which will shortly be described, but the print of the *Sovereign* does not show this; its spritsail sheet disappears over the bulwarks at both ends comparatively far forward in the waist (Plate 7).

In the matter of leads there was probably little difference between sheets without pendants and those with short pendants of twenty feet or less. Only one end of the sheet came very far aft. The standing part was made fast to the fore channels (plans of 1719) or to a ring-bolt in the side behind the fore shrouds (*St George* model). The hauling part went through a sheave in the waist. The *St George* has this sheave just below that for the fore sheet (Fig. 294), but the plans of 1719 and a drawing of the *Prince George*, of 1723, agree in giving the spritsail sheet a separate sheave about midway between the mainmast and the forecastle bulkhead (Fig. 295).

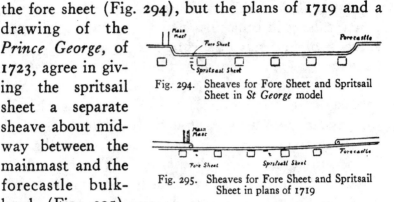

Fig. 294.   Sheaves for Fore Sheet and Spritsail
Sheet in *St George* model

Fig. 295.   Sheaves for Fore Sheet and Spritsail
Sheet in plans of 1719

On its way aft, the hauling part passed through a bullseye hanging from the fore rigging in the same way as the long pendants used to do.

Somewhere about 1690, at a guess, English riggers took to fitting very long strops to their spritsail-sheet blocks instead of using short pendants. At the same time they used for the sheets the same peculiarly shaped blocks as were coming into use for the lower clewlines. It is impossible to fix a definite date. Battine's lists give short pendants in 1685 and have no suggestion of any specially shaped blocks, whereas the *St George*, of 1701, has the long strops and the new shape of block (Fig. 296). In her case the length of the strops corresponds to about five feet; in plans of 1719 it is about ten feet.

Fig. 296.   Spritsail-Sheet
blocks with long Strops

These strops have to be fitted in a particular way. They are put through the holes in the rim of the block so that the block lies in the bight and the two ends go to the clew of the sail. Then the two ends together are made into a "spritsail-sheet knot," which goes through the clew of the sail just as if it were the knot on the end

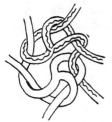

of a pendant. The knot is quite easy to make; it is simply a wall knot made with six strands instead of three and a special form of crown on top of it (Fig. 297). It seems that the strop was twisted and encouraged to get "cable-laid" before it was knotted, so that it formed what was to all intents and purposes a single pendant.

I do not think foreign ships used these special blocks at any time before 1720. In a general way they seem to have preferred simple sheets, without pendants, for most of the 17th century and to have used short pendants at the end of that century

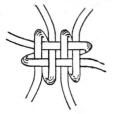

Fig. 297. Details of Spritsail-Sheet Knot

and the beginning of the 18th. Naturally, there are plenty of exceptions; for instance, the Danish ship of 1625 gives a very good example of the short (or fairly short) pendant, while the Dutch-built French ship of 1626 has either long pendants or possibly simple 1-part sheets. In the Dane, the pendant blocks appear to be spliced in as one would expect; the sheet is made fast somewhere about the fore corner of the forecastle and the hauling part goes in through the second upper-deck port abaft the fore rigging (Plate 5); there is no sign of any fair-lead for it on the way.

The Danish *Norske Löve* (1654) and the Berlin Dutch model (1665) show the long-pendant fitting in its most perfect form (Plates 8 and 11). The block is stropped and the pendant has a knot on its end, as was often the case with Dutch brace-pendants. The pendant

passes through a fair-lead hanging from one of the fore
shrouds in the Dane and appar-
ently fixed to the chain-plate
of the foremost deadeye in the
Dutchman. Its length is enough
to let the block come well abaft
the fore rigging. The sheet is
made fast to the same ring as

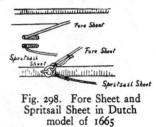

Fig. 298. Fore Sheet and
Spritsail Sheet in Dutch
model of 1665

the fore sheet and returns to a sheave just below that for
the fore sheet (Fig. 298). This same lead, long pendant and all, is described in 1700 as the standard fitting
for German ships.

More often Dutch ships of the middle part of the 17th
century did without pendants and fitted the spritsail
sheet just like those of the courses. The standing part
of the sheet was made fast somewhere in or below the
fore channels and the hauling part went through a fair-
lead hanging from the fore rigging and led inboard
through a sheave in the waist, usually just below that
for the fore sheet. Sometimes, but not so often, both
parts came aft together. This method of fitting the spritsail sheets lasted till at least 1698, since it appears in the
"William Rex," but short pendants on the spritsail clews
had been in use in some ships from 1660 or thereabouts
and seem to have come into general use soon after 1700.
French ships no doubt followed Dutch fashions up to
about 1670; after that they seem usually to have had the
short pendants.

The lead of the spritsail clewlines was simple; they
went from the yard, about ⅓ of the way out, through
the blocks at the clews, back to blocks on the yard just
inside their standing parts, through blocks in the head
and thence to the forecastle rail (Fig. 299). The "Trea-

tise on Rigging" (1625) runs them singly and starts them from the clews, but the print of the *Sovereign,* shows them double and there is little doubt that this was more usual in ships of any size, though the engraving of a Dutch-built French ship of 1626 and the *Norske Löve* model of 1654, have them

Fig. 299. Lead of Spritsail
Clewlines

single and they are described as single in the German book of 1700. Apart from this question very little variation was likely, except in the position of the final leading blocks and the place of belaying. The *Sovereign* seems to have taken her clewlines straight from the yard to the range in the head; Dutch ships were still doing this at the end of the century, but the English had definitely decided on the lead through blocks in the head to the forecastle. The *St George* model and the plans of 1719 show the third pair of blocks secured to the main rail of the head and the clewlines going straight to the forecastle from there, and this fits well with the lists of 1685 and 1675 which say the clewlines had three blocks each. It is interesting to note that the *St George,* though she has the special shaped blocks for her lower and topsail clewlines and also for her spritsail sheets, still has ordinary blocks for the spritsail clewlines. The plans of 1719 show that "clewline blocks" had been adopted there as well.

One fitting remains, the buntline or buntlines. The "Seaman's Dictionary" mentions spritsail martnets as a possibility and I have a vague memory of having once seen a representation of a spritsail leechline, but these were so rare that they may safely be ignored. The

"Treatise on Rigging" describes a single buntline running from the middle of the footrope through a block on
the bowsprit just above the middle of the yard and then

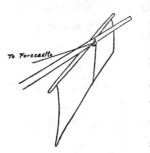

to the forecastle (Fig. 300). The
print of the *Sovereign,* which was
an exceptional ship, shows three
buntlines (Plate 7) ; there is no indication of how the outer two
worked, but it is likely, in view of
what happened later, that they
simply ran over the yard (perhaps
through staples) and aft to the
range or the forecastle.   In lists of

Fig. 300.   Spritsail
Buntline about 1625

1655 there is a very great difference in the length allowed
for buntlines in the *Sovereign* and *Resolution* and in the
rather smaller and newer ships; it seems possible that
this indicates that the smaller ships had fewer buntlines.
Bond, in 1642, speaks of a spritsail buntline "in 2 parts"
and Keltridge, in 1675, allows two double blocks for the

buntlines of all the larger ships.
Taken together these fragments
of information suggest that the
spritsail buntlines worked in
pairs as those of the courses did,
the second sheave of the double
block serving to take a whip
which actuated two buntlines
at once (Fig. 301).   In the next
list, of 1685, there was evidently
a single buntline, for the length
has dropped to half and there is
only one single block.   How
long this fashion lasted I do not

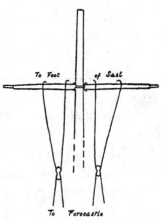

Fig. 301.   Probable arrangement of English Spritsail
Buntlines about 1675

know; it had passed by the time of the *St George* and there were then two buntlines some little distance apart, running over the yard, through one of the sheaves of the long gammoning blocks and to the forecastle rail (Fig. 302). From then, on, this was the normal English style. I doubt if it appeared in foreign ships; they seem, if they had a spritsail

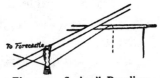

Fig. 302. Spritsail Buntlines in *St George* model of 1701

buntline at all, to have had only the one and to have taken it through a block on the bowsprit and thence to the head or the forecastle.

The rigging of the spritsail topsail was generally similar to that of the topgallants. The parrel had two rows of trucks. Nearly always the tie was single and usually it ran through a sheave in the mast. The *St George* model of 1701, has a block at the masthead instead of a sheave, but lists of 1685 and 1711 give no block for the tie, so that there was presumably a sheave. Foreign ships seem to have used a sheave always. At the end of our period English ships sometimes had a 2-part tie with a block on the yard. This is not shown in the plans of 1719, but it appears in the Hanover model of the *Royal George*, of 1715, and in Baston's print of the same ship.

The halliards were at first merely a whip starting from the cross-trees of the spritsail top and re-

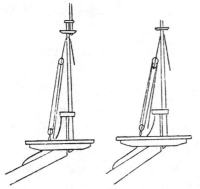

Fig. 303. English Spritsail Topsail Halliards about 1680

Fig. 304. English Spritsail Topsail Halliards about 1700

turning there. From the fact that the list of 1675 only allows one block for the spritsail topsail halliards it would seem that this fashion lasted up to then. The next list gives two single blocks, which no doubt indicates a 3-part tackle (Fig. 303). By the end of the century (as shown in the *St George*) there was a fiddle-block on the tie and a single block fixed in the spritsail top (Fig. 304). The hauling part was not brought inboard, but was belayed in the top; models show it hitched round the strop of the lower block. Foreign ships usually had

a single block on the tie and took their halliards from the spritsail top, through the tie-block, back through the top to a block on the bowsprit and then inboard (Fig. 305). Sometimes they had a fiddle block and a single block as in English ships, but even then they probably brought the end to the head or the forecastle.

Fig. 305. Dutch Spritsail Topsail Halliards about 1670

In spite of its small size, the spritsail topsail nearly always had 2-part lifts with blocks at the yard-arms. The "Treatise on Rigging" describes the standing parts and the upper blocks as being attached to the masthead and this may have been the case in the very early years of the 17th century; but there is little doubt that it was soon the rule that the standing parts were on the cap (or bent to short pendants from the cap) and the blocks on short pendants just under the cross-trees. The ends did not come inboard but were belayed in the top, probably to the chain-plates of the topmast shrouds.

English ships based their spritsail topsail braces on the forestay and had short pendants on the yard. The

standing parts were attached about level with the spritsail top and the leading blocks were a little below them.
The print of the *Sovereign* shows the spritsail topsail
braces going to the range, but
a more usual lead in later times
was to take them through a
pair of blocks fixed to eyes on
the bowsprit a little before the
gammoning and thence to the
forecastle rail close to the collar of the main stay (Fig. 306).

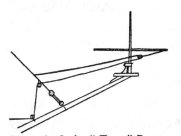

Fig. 306. Spritsail Topsail Braces

This same lead was common in foreign ships at the beginning of the 17th century, but Dutch ships of 1660-90,
sometimes based their spritsail topsail braces on the fore-
topmast stay instead of the forestay. Occasionally the
braces were single and started from the yard-arm.   In
any case, the ends came inboard; usually to the forecastle rail, but sometimes, for instance in the *"William
Rex,"* to cleats on the collar of the main stay beside the
stem-head.

Spritsail topsail sheets, being identical with the true
lifts of the spritsail yard, have been mentioned already.
The clewlines were similar to those of the topgallants
and like them were sometimes single and sometimes
double. Big English ships, of the beginning of the 18th
century, had them double, but the French *Royal Louis,*
of 1692, has them single and they are so described in the
German book of 1700. I think single clewlines would
be more usual all through the 17th century; but the
double lead was always possible. From the yard they
went down through the spritsail top (usually to a pair of
blocks on the bowsprit) and thence inboard. The *St*

George takes hers through the third pair of sheaves in the long gammoning blocks and belays them together with the spritsail topsail sheets between the spritsail clewlines and the fore tacks on the forecastle rail (Fig. 307).

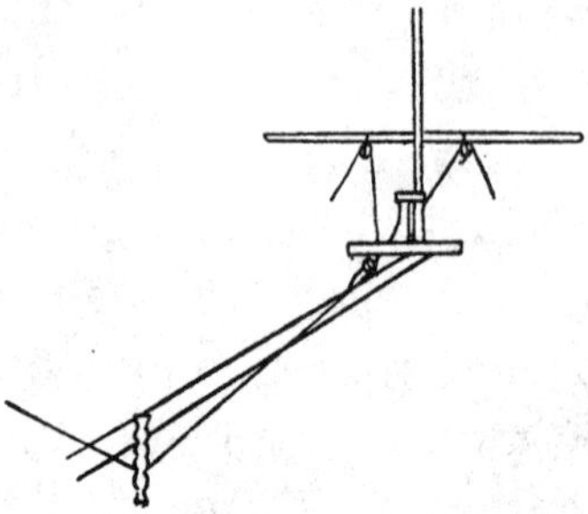

Fig. 307.   Spritsail Topsail Clewlines

So far I have mentioned no thicknesses for bowsprit rigging. For the spritsail, the halliards, lifts and brace-pendants should be rather less than half the fore shrouds. The braces, buntlines and clewlines should be about ⅓ of the fore shrouds. The sheets should be the same as the halliards or a little bigger and their pendants should be nearly ⅔ of the fore shrouds. For the spritsail topsail the various ropes should be, roughly, half those on the spritsail.

CHAPTER X

RUNNING RIGGING OF THE MIZZEN

THE mizzen mast, unlike the fore and main, had a lateen as its lower sail. This entailed almost entirely different gear. The mizzen topsail, on the other hand, was practically the same as a topgallant sail in its fittings. That is, of course, when the mizzen topsail was a square sail; the lateen mizzen topsail of the early part of the 17th century introduces problems of its own.

The lateen mizzen had its yard more or less fore and aft with the "peak," or after end, very much higher than the "nock" or fore end. It had a parrel somewhat similar to that of a square sail and it was hoisted by a tie and halliards or by jeers in much the same way; but there the resemblance finished. There was only one lift, at the after end of the yard, if there was one at all, and there were no braces so called, but a pair of tackles at the fore end of the yard with the confusing name of bowlines.

There was a single sheet and a single tack. In early days there were martnets not unlike those of the square sails, but later on there were a number of simple brails instead.

The mizzen parrel and truss had to be simple and easily adjusted, because it was the custom to shift the yard from one side of the mast to the other so as to keep the sail to leeward of the mast. The usual

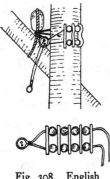

Fig. 308. English and Dutch Mizzen Parrel

231

form, which is described in English, in 1625, and in German, in 1700, and which appears in Dutch models of
1665, was as shown in Fig. 308. The parrel had two
rows of trucks and a stout parrel rope (as thick as the
mizzen shrouds). In the bight of this parrel rope there
was seized a deadeye with two holes in it, or (in the
Dutch models) a double block. The two parts of the
parrel rope were then seized to the strop of the jeer-
block, between it and the yard, so that the deadeye hung
down beside the yard. The ends passed as usual through
the ribs and trucks of the parrel and went round the
mast and then through the holes in the deadeye. They
were spliced together and a thimble was seized in the
second bight thus formed. Into this thimble the truss-
tackle was hooked. The effect was to hold, not the yard
itself, but the strop of the jeer-block close to the mast.
When there was a tie instead of jeers, the parrel-rope
and its deadeye were no doubt attached to the tie close
down to the yard.

The English account of 1625 gives the truss as a single
rope, in which case it would probably be eye-spliced

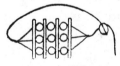

Fig. 309. Mizzen
Parrel in *Royal Louis*
model

round the bight of the parrel-rope.
In big ships, even at that date, a
tackle seems more probable and by
1650 it is certain, from a consideration of lengths and thicknesses, that
the truss was at least a 3-part tackle.
The usual practice was to have a fiddle-block hooked
into the thimble on the parrel-rope and a single block
hooked or lashed at the foot of the mast; this gave a
4-part tackle. The truss was about ¾ of the thickness
of the parrel-rope.

Another way of getting the same result is shown in

Fig. 309. Here there is a 3-row parrel. From each end of the parrel there runs a single rope which may possibly have been formed by laying together the three separate lines. One has a block spliced into its end and the other runs through this block and has a tackle on its end. This is the method employed in the French *Royal Louis,* of 1692, and is, I think, what is intended in the *St George;* models are usually rather sketchy about their parrel gear, unless they are on a very large scale. With this fitting the parrel does not seem to have been attached to the jeer-block, but to have gone round the yard a little below it with a small cleat to keep it in place.

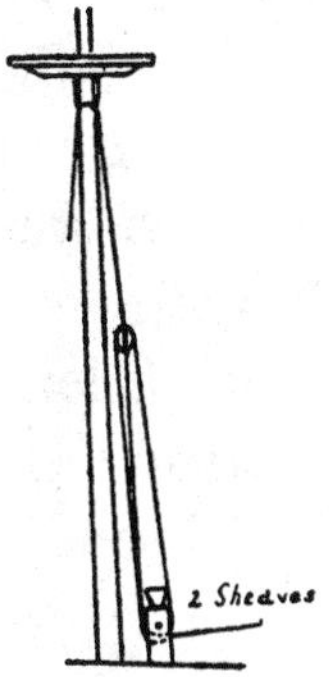

2 Sheaves

Fig. 310.
Mizzen Tie
and Halliard

The tie, when there was one, went through the sheave in the mast, from aft forward, and had a block spliced into its end (Fig. 310). The knight stood *before* the mast. According to the "Treatise on Rigging," the knight had two sheaves and the block was single. The halliards started from the block and ran in three parts, the second sheave in the knight acting merely as a lead to give a horizontal pull. No doubt big ships sometimes had two sheaves both above and below, or even three sheaves in the knight. The end was belayed round the head of the knight. Mizzen ties should be as big as the mizzen stay or bigger; the halliards should be about as thick as the shrouds.

English ships, about 1640-50, had jeers as well as a tie and halliards. At first the jeers were simple and were rigged like those of the fore and main yards in their early form — a block on the yard and another on one side of the mast with the standing part secured to the masthead on the other side (Fig. 311). Later on, when the jeers took over the whole work of hoisting the yard,

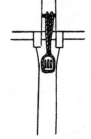

they became more elaborate. By 1670, and probably earlier, English ships of the first two Rates had a treble block hanging from the masthead and a double block on the yard. The treble block's length was about 1½ times the diameter of the yard, the double block was the same or a trifle less. The upper block was stropped with a long double strop and the eyes of this strop were lashed to the masthead above the shrouds;

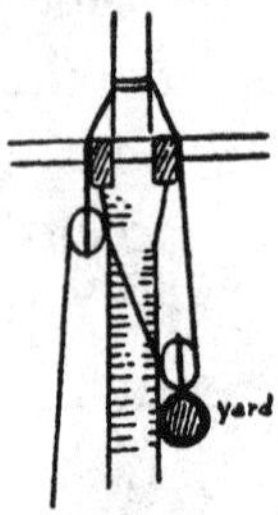

Fig. 311.
English
Mizzen Jeers
about 1650

the block hung down abaft the mast between the trestle-trees (Fig. 312). The jeers started from the yard a little below and before the block; their thickness was about the same as that of the mizzen shrouds.

Smaller ships had a simpler tackle with a double block at the masthead and a single block on the yard. That was also the fitting in foreign ships, which seem to have been rather later than English in doing

Fig. 312. Upper
Block of Mizzen
Jeers about
1700

away with tie and halliards for the mizzen yard. The St George model has the end of the jeers brought down to a "small knight" inside the poop rail and belayed there, but it was probably more usual to take it to a leading block at the foot of the mast.

The mizzen lift was more or less equivalent to the peak halliards of a modern gaff-sail. Its duty was to hold up the after end of the yard and to top it up if necessary. In the 16th century it had led to the *main* topmast head, not to the mizzen topmast. As long as the mizzen topmast was very short this lead was suitable enough, but as the topmast grew it inevitably rose above the line of the mizzen lift. What happened when the ship went about is something of a mystery; one would imagine that the lift would remove the topmast bodily, but presumably it did not. If there had been two lifts and the weather one had been slacked off the difficulty would have been more or less overcome, but there is no evidence whatever for this, whereas there is plenty for a single lift leading past the mizzen topmast about half way up.

The only possible explanation seems to be that the mizzen lift was not needed when the sail was set and could be slacked off to any extent. After all, a lug-sail requires no peak halliards, because the downward pull of the tack at the fore end of the sail keeps the after end of the yard up automatically. In confirmation of this view it may be noted that after the lift had shifted to the mizzen topmast head it was looked on as a mizzen topmast backstay rather than as a lift and that when the mizzen topmast began to have standing backstays it was often omitted altogether.

Speaking roughly, I should say that the lift (to call it by the shorter name) led to the main topmast head, up to about 1625, in English ships, and to the mizzen topmast, after that; but that from 1660 onwards — and very likely earlier — it was more often absent than present. As a matter of fact, I know of very little evidence for it after 1650, with one notable exception, the *St George* model of 1701. Probably it was not an official fitting, but a "boatswain's fancy"; that is just the sort of thing one would expect to find in a model.

When the mizzen lift led to the main topmast head

it was rigged somewhat as follows:— From the main
topmast head there was a
pendant with a block at its
end, this block coming
about half way between the
heads of the main topmast
and the mizzen topmast.
There was a more or less
elaborate crowfoot at the
peak of the mizzen yard and
the fall went from this crow-

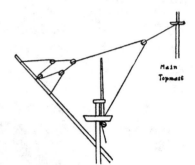

Fig. 313. Simple form of Mizzen Lift

foot through the pendant block and back to the mizzen

Fig. 314. Mizzen Lift duplicated

Fig. 315.   Elaborate form of
Mizzen Lift

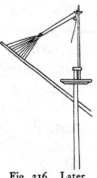

Fig. 316.   Later
form of Mizzen
Lift to Mizzen
Topmast head

top where it passed through another
block and so to the deck (Fig. 313).
Sometimes the whole apparatus was duplicated and sometimes it was more
complicated still (Figs. 314 and 315).
When it went to the mizzen topmast
head it was simpler (Fig. 316), but even
then the crowfoot or crowfeet admitted
of all sorts of variations, from a simple
span to a pair of crowfeet with any
number of parts.

The Dutch seem to have retained the mizzen lift more often than the English. It appears in the great majority of Dutch drawings or models up to 1720, at least. A print of a Dutch-built French ship, of 1626, is an early example of the lead to the mizzen topmast (Plate 6). Other foreign ships, French, Danish, Swedish and Russian, nearly always show mizzen lifts. The Danish *Norske Löve* model is perhaps the latest example of the lead to the main topmast (Plate 8); unfortunately the ship was built in 1634, twenty years before the model was made, and we have no means of knowing how far the model-maker was deliberately trying to be old fashioned.

At the fore end of the mizzen yard there were two tackles called bowlines. These had nothing to do with the bowlines of a square sail but were in reality more nearly equivalent to braces, since their duty was to control the angle which the yard made with the fore-and-aft line. In their simplest form, in small ships at the beginning of the 17th century, they were single ropes attached to the heel of the yard by being put through holes and knotted, and then leading through blocks on the aftermost main shrouds and down to the rail where they were belayed. In larger and later ships they became whips; there were a pair of blocks at the end of the yard,

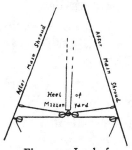

Fig. 317.   Lead of Mizzen Bowlines

either seized to the yard or to an eye-bolt in its end, and the bowlines started from the main shrouds and went back there in exactly the same way as the braces of the square sails went from the stays and back again (Fig. 317). They were comparatively thin ropes, about half as thick as the mizzen shrouds.

The mizzen sheet varied in complexity. The "Treatise on Rigging" describes it as a whip starting from the "after timber in the poop" and running through a block at the clew and a leading block near its standing part (Fig. 318). Drawings of English ships throughout the 17th century and plans of 1719 show the same thing. The *St George* model has a 3-part tackle with a double block attached to the knee at the middle of the taffrail; the sheet starts from the strop of the block at the clew

Fig. 318. Two-part
Mizzen Sheet   Fig. 319. Three-part Mizzen Sheet   Fig. 320. Four-part Mizzen Sheet

and goes through one sheave of the double block, through the block at the clew and back to the second sheave of the double block (Fig. 319). The *"William Rex"* model goes one better with a 4-part tackle and a fiddle-block at the clew (Fig. 320). I think the lead shown in the *St George* would be normal for big foreign ships about 1700 or earlier and I should be inclined to fit it in English 3-deckers also. In any case, the knee in which the ensign-staff was stepped would be the place to fit the eyes for the standing part and the block. The block at the clew had to be detachable — especially when the mizzen had a bonnet. The *St George* has a long strop with a hook and a German book of 1700 describes the same thing, but I fancy it was more usual to have two knotted legs on the strop of the block and to put these through the clew of the sail and seize them.

The mizzen had no clewlines, or very rarely. There

were brails acting on points not far from the clew, but

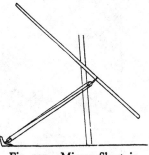
Fig. 321. Mizzen Sheet in a model without Sails

not actually on the corner of the sail. Thus, if there are no sails fitted, there is no means of showing how the mizzen sheet led except by lashing its upper block to the yard in the place where it would come when the sail was furled (Fig. 321). The sheet should be about ¾ as thick as the mizzen shrouds; its blocks should be about ¾ of the size of the jeer-blocks.

The tack was a single rope about as thick as the mizzen shrouds. When the mizzen had a bonnet, the "course" or main part of the sail was a true lateen (a triangle) and the addition of the bonnet made it into a "settee," which was something between a lateen and a lug (Fig. 322). Clearly a tack was needed to hold down the fore lower corner of this sail. In a model without sails it is best omitted, but in one with sails set it can be "put about some timber under the main shrouds," as the "Treatise on Rigging" describes it. When the mizzen bonnet

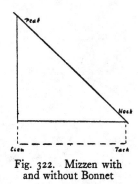
Fig. 322. Mizzen with and without Bonnet

disappeared, somewhere about 1680, the sail was usually made in the shape of the old course and bonnet combined, so that a tack was always needed.

Mizzen martnets belong to the very early years of the 17th century. They were then fitted to the upper part of the leech of the sail in much the same way as those of the foresail and mainsail, but the martnets of the two sides were independent. On each side were six "legs" passing through the three holes of a deadeye, and the falls went from the deadeyes through the two sheaves of a double block at the mizzen m a s t h e a d a n d down to the deck (Fig. 323). At this same period there were brails to haul up the foot of the sail. They had bridles attached to the footrope of the sail and

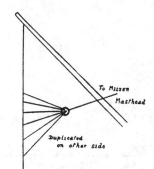

Fig. 323. Mizzen Martnets

went through blocks on the yard below the parrel and thence to the rails on either side (Fig. 324).

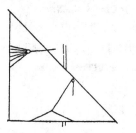

Fig. 324. Mizzen Martnets and Brails about 1625

By 1650, and probably some time b e f o r e that, martnets had disappeared and there were brails to both the foot and the leech. The number varied; in lists of 1685 there are seven a side in the first two Rates, six in the 3rd and 4th Rates, and five and three in the 5th and 6th. The *St George* of 1701 and the plans of 1719 agree in having six a side in all 3-deckers. Dutch ships usually show five a side. With an even number there were usually as many on the leech as on the foot; with an odd number I think the foot had one more than the leech. Very often the two aftermost and less often the two foremost were formed as a bridle and fall (Fig. 325). English ships u s u a l l y took the foot-brails to blocks on the main rigging (Fig.

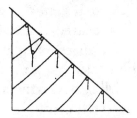

Fig. 325. Mizzen Brails about 1670

326), but the Dutch seem to have led them straight to the

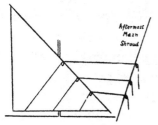

Fig. 326.   English Mizzen
Brails about 1720

rail in the same way as the after brails.

When there were two mizzens, say before 1625, the gear of the after or "bonaventure" mizzen must have been very much the same as that of the main mizzen. Sometimes its sheet led to an "outlicker" or bumkin, projecting from the stern (Plate 1). Its lifts probably went to the topmast head of the main mizzen; otherwise there would be little difference, save that its gear would be lighter and probably simpler.

The lateen mizzen topsail was a survival from the 16th century. Officially it was abandoned for the square topsail in English ships in 1618. No doubt the square topsail had been tried for some time before that; I should not hesitate to fit it at any date after 1610. How long the lateen topsail lingered on it is hard to say. Probably 1625 would be about its latest possible date. The Danish print often mentioned, and shown in Plate 5, has lateen topsails on both the mizzens. This print has been dated "about 1625," but I personally look on that date as very nearly the latest to which it could be ascribed. There is an interesting ivory model in Dresden, known to have been made in 1620; this has a lateen (or rather a settee) topsail on the main mizzen, but has also the yards for a square topsail. On the whole, I think it would be reasonable to fit a lateen topsail up to 1610 and a square topsail after 1620; for the years between the model-maker can please himself.

If he is wise, he will prefer the square kind, because

our knowledge of the gear of the lateen topsail is scanty in the extreme. As far as I know there is no print or picture that even shows it set. We can only suppose that it was hoisted in much the same way as the mizzen, that its lift went to the main topgallant mast head and its sheet to the peak of the mizzen yard; if it had a tack, it probably was made fast in the mizzen top.

With the square mizzen topsail we are on much firmer ground. I have said already that it was almost the same as a topgallant sail. The main difference lay in the fact that it had to have a yard, the "cross-jack" or "crojack" yard, to spread its foot. This yard occupied the same position on the mizzen as the lower yards did on the fore and main, but unlike them it had no sail beneath it. As a matter of fact I am not quite sure that there never was a sail beneath it, though that is the general belief. Vroom's painting of the *Prince Royal*, in 1613 (painted ten years later), shows furled sails beneath both the crojack yards, and Sir Alan Moore, in his articles on 17th century rigging, says that there is some indication that the possibility of setting a crojack course in the *Bear*, in 1618, was considered. It seems to me almost certain that some enterprising person seeing a yard doing only half duty would have tried to employ it to the full extent. Of course the mizzen would have to be topped up to let the crojack course be set and no doubt it was soon found that the game was not worth the candle. So much so, that even when the mizzen yard had disappeared, it took fifty years or so before some American captain introduced the modern crojack course. Still, I should hesitate to dismiss a representation of an early 17th century crojack course as obviously wrong, though I should not fit one unless I were copying some picture where it appears.

The crojack yard was slung aloft. It had a block
stropped to its middle and through
the block went a rope with an eye
in one end. The two ends passed
up outside the trestle-trees on opposite sides and the plain end,
after going round abaft the masthead, went through the eye and
was hitched or seized (Fig. 327).
Possibly there was sometimes
provision for lowering the yard, but
very seldom. It was, therefore, un-

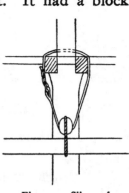

Fig. 327. Slings of
Crojack Yard

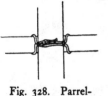

Fig. 328. Parrel-
strop of Crojack
Yard

usual to fit a parrel; a strop similar to
that of the spritsail yard was used instead (Fig. 328).

For the same reason the lifts were
often "standing" or permanent fittings,
not intended to be slacked off or hauled
up. At the beginning of the 17th cen-
tury there were no lifts at all; the topsail sheets acted
as lifts when needed, in exactly the same way as the
topgallant sheets acted as lifts for the fore and main
topsail yards. By 1640, and very likely earlier, the
crojack yard had lifts like those of the fore and main
with small blocks attached to the topsail-sheet blocks.
By 1670, these lifts were obsolete; this can be seen
from the fact that Deane's manuscript of that year gives
the name but inserts no length or thickness. Other lists
of 1675 and 1685 omit the ordinary lifts altogether.

Their place was taken by the "standing lifts," which
were pendants from the yard with deadeyes at their ends
connected by laniards to other deadeyes secured to the

mizzen cap.   The pendants were secured to the yards a

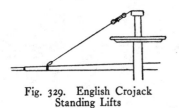

little way (two or three feet) in from the yard-arms by means of a seizing through an eye-splice (Fig. 329). The two upper deadeyes were on a span which was clove-hitched round

Fig. 329.   English Crojack Standing Lifts

the cap; at least this is what is done in the *St George* model.

The Dutch do not seem to have gone in for this type of standing lift.   As far as I can judge they did without lifts up to 1650 or 1655 and then took to fitting lifts exactly like those on the fore and main yards. It is possible t h a t t h e y changed the l e a d f r o m under the top to the cap rather earlier on the miz-

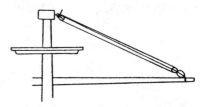

Fig. 330.   German Crojack Standing Lifts

zen than on the other masts, but I am not very sure about it.   The German book of 1700 describes a 3-part lift which started from the strop of the block on the yard and went through the two blocks and back to the cap where it was made fast behind the block (Fig. 330). This was of course simply a very elaborate form of standing lift and sounds none too probable.   The Dutch may sometimes have done the same thing, but it is more probable that they kept their crojack lifts like the others and brought them down to the pendant blocks.

For other countries, the best rule is to follow Dutch practice unless there is good evidence to the contrary. There is some indication that French ships of about 1680-5 were still taking their crojack lifts under the top, although they had begun to lead those of the fore and main to the cap or the masthead. Ten years later, all the lifts went above the tops and in the *Royal Louis*, of 1692, the crojack lifts are precisely the same as those of the other two yards, — 3-part tackles with fiddle-blocks attached to the masthead.

The crojack braces may as well be discussed together with those of the mizzen topsail yard. Neither is easy to pin down to any definite rule or sequence of rules. They might lead forward or they might lead aft and they seem to have varied without much system. Usually, English ships led their crojack braces forward to the main rigging and their mizzen topsail braces aft to the peak of the mizzen yard. This combination can be traced from the time of the *Sovereign* (1637) right on to the plans of 1719 and indeed much later. The difficulty is that there were scattered exceptions; the "Treatise on Rigging," of 1625 or thereabouts, describes the crojack braces as single ropes leading to "the aftermost timber on the poop." The stern view of the *Sovereign*, in the National Portrait Gallery, seems to show the same thing and it appears again in the 1st-Rate in Deane's plans of 1670.

Still there is no doubt that the normal practice was to take the topsail braces aft and the crojack braces forward. The topsail braces were attached to the mizzen yard quite near the peak, either directly or by means of a short span clove-hitched to the yard and with an eye-splice at each end; they went through blocks on the ends of short

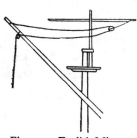

Fig. 331. English Mizzen
Topsail Braces

pendants from the topsail yard and returned to the mizzen yard where they went through another pair of blocks
attached to the yard a little below their standing parts
and so down to the deck quite near the aftermost corners
of the poop (Fig. 331).

The crojack braces, when they went forward, were
usually rigged like most other braces with short pendants; the standing part was made fast to the aftermost
shroud of the mainmast
and the leading block
was on the same shroud
a little lower down
(Fig. 332). The en-
graving of the *Sover-
eign* (Plate 7) vaguely
suggests a variation in
this lead with the brace
returning to the main
rigging *above* its stand-
ing part and then going aft again to the mizzen top and
down from there. In view of the fact that the main
topsail brace, at about this time, was doing much the
same thing in the opposite direction, I should not like
to say that such a lead was impossible, but I should
certainly want better evidence of it before copying it in
a model.

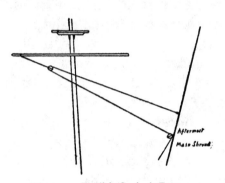

Fig. 332.   English Crojack Braces

There is no doubt that moderate-sized ships, about
1675, sometimes had single crojack braces running
straight from the yard-arms to the main rigging. However, the double brace was probably more usual in ships
of any size. Sometimes, perhaps usually, the crojack
braces were crossed, so that the starboard brace led to
the port main rigging and *vice versa*. I do not think

this was universal by any means. I would suggest that the rigger should experiment and fit the braces in whichever way seems most satisfactory.

It is difficult to make out any definite sequence in Dutch practice. One can say that both braces were leading aft at the beginning of the 17th century and that both led forward a century later, but the evidence for the period 1650-1700 is very contradictory. The ship in Furttenbach (1629), probably drawn from a Dutch model of a few years earlier (Plate 4), has both braces going as single lines to the poop. The *"Navire royale,"* a Dutch-built ship of 1626 (Plate 6), has the crojack braces going aft singly and the topsail braces taken in two parts to the mizzen yard in the ordinary English fashion. A rather similar ship depicted on a series of tiles, now in the Rijks Museum in Amsterdam — probably of somewhat later date — shows the crojack braces running singly to the main rigging. Zeeman's etchings of about 1650-60 (Plate 10) have a variation by which the

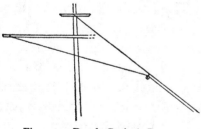

Fig. 333.   Dutch Crojack Braces
about 1655

crojack braces run through leading blocks on the mizzen stay and then forward down the stay (Fig. 333). The ship in Witsen's book of 1671, with her braces arranged exactly as in the ship of 1626, cannot be taken as evidence for anything later than 1650 and perhaps not as late as that. A print of 1678, which was copied by Van Yk, in 1697, takes the topsail braces *forward* to the upper part of the aftermost main shrouds in two parts, but unfortunately omits the crojack braces or rather shows them so badly that it is impossible to say which way they went. Probably both pairs of braces went forward to the main rigging, as a general rule, after about 1665, but it must be mentioned that the ship in Allard's book of 1695, has her crojack braces running in two parts to the quarter. This lead is contradicted by the "Dutch flagship," in the 1705 edition of the same book, and I doubt if it was ever usual. After 1700 it is safe to say that both the topsail and the crojack braces went forward (Fig. 334). I do not think they were crossed as often as in English ships and it seems that they were sometimes fitted without pendants.

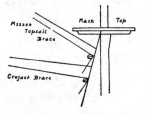

Fig. 334. Dutch Crojack and Mizzen Topsail Braces about 1700

French ships, as one might expect, varied between English and Dutch fashions. Dassié, in his book of 1677, takes the topsail braces in two parts to the mizzen yard and those of the crojack singly to the main rigging. A plan of about 1680-5, follows English practice exactly and so does the *Royal Louis* model of 1692, but one of the prints of similar date takes both braces forward just as a Dutch ship would do. After this date it would probably be right to take them forward without exception. As far as the evidence goes one can say that other countries tended to follow the Dutch lead, though a Russian print of 1701 (Plate 18) shows normal English practice. The Danish *Norske Löve* has both braces led aft in two parts, the topsail brace to the mizzen yard and the crojack braces to the poop; this may be right, but there are signs that her rigging has been tampered with at some time and it is quite possible that a mistake has been made in replacing the braces of the crojack. One little variation, that sometimes occurred in French and possibly in Dutch ships, was to seize the crojack brace-pendant to the yard so that what was left was equivalent to a very short pendant fitted well in along the yard (Fig. 335). For thickness it can be said that the crojack braces should be about ⅖ or ½ the mizzen shrouds and the topsail braces ⅓; the pendants should naturally be rather heavier.

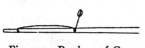

Fig. 335. Pendant of Crojack Brace seized to Yard

The mizzen topsail had a parrel "framed as other parrels," in the words of the "Treatise on Rigging." According to the same authority it had a tie and no halliards, that is to say, the tie simply went through the sheave in the topmast and down to the deck. This may have been the case in small ships early in the century, but there is no doubt that halliards were soon added in ships of any size. Bond, writing in 1642, gives halliards "in 3 parts"; probably this means that there was a block on the end of the tie and another in the mizzen top (Fig. 336). On the other hand, it is possible that the lower block was sometimes down at the deck level, in the mizzen channels or abaft them. Towards the end of the 17th century, as the mizzen topsail grew, it became the rule in English ships to give it a double tie with a block on the yard. The end of the tie went through a sheave in the mast or a block under the trestle-trees and had a fiddle-block spliced into it. The halliards started from a block hooked to the ship's side (to starboard in the St George) and ran in four parts (Fig. 337). I do not

Fig. 336. English Mizzen Topsail Halliards about 1640

pretend to know when this change came, but should expect it to have been after 1680.

Dutch ships usually had a single tie with a fiddle-block on its end and a single block in the mizzen top; the end of the halliards sometimes came down to the deck on one side near the mizzen shrouds. As far as I know neither Dutch nor English ever had tie, runner and halliards for their mizzen topsails, but I have seen this arrangement in a French ship of somewhere about 1680. Another French picture of much the same date shows the Dutch plan, while the *Royal Louis*, of 1692, has the English method of the end of the century, a double tie and long halliards on one side. The Danish *Norske Löve* model has a single tie with a fiddle-block which came well down the mizzen shrouds when the sail was hoisted and a single block in the mizzen channels on the starboard side for the halliards (Plate 8); later Danish ships seem usually to have followed the Dutch fashion.

Fig. 337. English Mizzen Topsail Halliards about 1700

As far as lifts, sheets and clewlines are concerned the mizzen topsail can be looked on as a topgallant sail, except that its sheets, when they no longer had to act as crojack lifts as well, were led like those of the other topsails, through blocks at the yard-arms and down through other blocks near the middle of the yard. The French *Royal Louis* model (1692) has a double block at the middle of the yard with the two sheets going through it in opposite directions, but this fitting, though it may have been the rule in France, was not used in Dutch or English ships till very much later.

Only the bowlines remain to be mentioned. These

led to the main shrouds above the crojack braces and just below the futtock staves.   In English ships they were sometimes crossed as the braces were; in Dutch ships it seems to have been quite the exception to cross them.

As in the case of fore and main royals, it is not necessary to say much about a mizzen topgallant sail. Such a sail was certainly possible about 1630, but it was probably more or less a "lash up" on the mizzen flagstaff. The engraving of the *Sovereign* (Plate 7) is the only evidence that I know of a real separate mizzen topgallant mast before the middle of the next century. Still, if a mizzen topgallant is to be fitted, it is merely a matter of copying the other topgallants on a smaller scale.

CHAPTER XI

STAYSAIL AND STUNSAIL GEAR

FOR nearly half of the period under consideration in this book there is no need to worry about either staysails or stunsails. It is true that stunsails were used occasionally from at least as far back as the middle of the 16th century and that the "Treatise on Rigging," which is believed to date from about 1625, includes them and describes them as "set on either side of your fore and main sails." Still, I think I am right in saying that no picture or model shows them and no list of stores mentions them before 1650. The earliest official reference that I know for both stunsails and staysails is in a list of the stores of the English ships returning from Jamaica in 1655, though they are mentioned in a Dutch poem of 1634, and the earliest representation of a staysail (in a 3-masted ship) that I have seen is in a drawing by Van de Velde, of some Dutch ships, in 1658.

It seems, therefore, that 1660 is about the date when one ought to begin to provide for both staysails and stunsails when rigging a model. Taking stunsails first, as being the simpler, I think, as I have said in Chapter IV., that English ships had stunsails at the main after 1660 or 1655 and on the fore as well after about 1690. Dutch ships seem to have had them on both masts after about 1665 and the French were apparently not far behind.

The stunsail booms have been dealt with already and unless the actual sails themselves are to be carried there is not very much gear that can reasonably be shown. A block beneath the lower yard for the lower stunsail

halliards, one beneath the topsail yard for the topsail
stunsail halliards, one above the end of the stunsail boom
for the topsail stunsail sheet and perhaps one below it

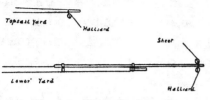

Fig. 338. Blocks for Stunsails

for outer halliards
for the lower stunsail,
is all that is needed
(Fig. 338). If the stun-
sails themselves are to
be carried, the lower
booms will have to be

hooked in the channels and will have to have blocks at
their ends for the lower stunsail sheets. They will also
need guys of some kind to keep them in place. The stunsails will probably have to have yards, and the sheets,
tacks and halliards will have to be rove and made fast.

I will not attempt to describe how this should be done.
It would be possible to explain the methods of 1800, but
I have no idea how far these would be applicable in 1700
or earlier. As I have said already, I do not recommend
actually fitting stunsails, because this involves setting
the foresail and mainsail and a model hardly ever looks
well with this done. If the model-rigger insists on stunsails, he can follow the rigging and seamanships books
of about 1800, or, Mr. Davis's recent "Ship Model
Builder's Assistant," in the hope that their instructions,
though meant for a much later period, will not take him
far wrong.

As a matter of fact, I am not at all sure that all these
early stunsails did have
yards. In about 1760,
French drawings show the
lower stunsails merely
hoisted by the two corners

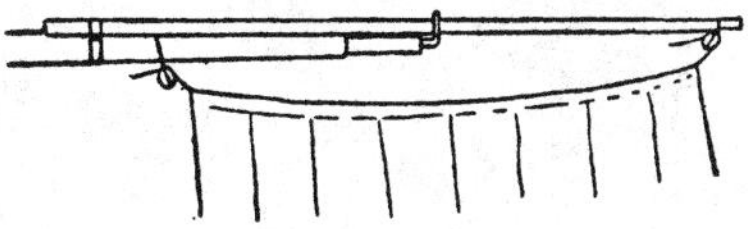

Fig. 339. French Lower Stunsail
about 1760

(Fig. 339). On the other hand, it is quite likely that lower stunsails, in about 1700, were narrow at the head like the topsail stunsails. In that case it is at least possible that both they and the topsail stunsails were "jib-headed" or triangular and hoisted to the blocks beneath the yards without any extra spread. At all events, their heads were probably quite narrow and the yards therefore quite short.

With regard to staysails, the first thing to be decided is which stays are to carry them. In a general way it can be said that there should (or might) be mizzen, main, main-topmast and fore-topmast staysails from 1660 to 1690 and that after that, mizzen-topmast and main-topgallant staysails might be added. From 1705, or a few years earlier, there might be a jib, though this was by no means universal.

For the moment the jib can wait, while we consider what gear is required for the regular staysails. The amount shown on models without sails, is usually simply the halliards and (if necessary) the false stays to which the staysails were laced. I say "if necessary," because in the case of some stays — particularly the mizzen stay — which had no braces or bowlines leading to them, it was possible to lace the staysail to the stay itself and a false stay was not wanted.

The false stays had eye-splices at their upper ends and 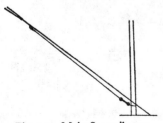 were seized underneath the stays. They were set up by means of deadeyes or hearts; the former seems to have been more usual in English ships, the latter in Dutch. For the main staysail stay there was a

Fig. 340. Main Staysail-stay

collar with a heart or deadeye on the foremast just below the line of the main stay (Fig. 340). The upper end of the false stay was seized to the stay not far below the mouse. For the main-topmast staysail the false stay was not taken so far up; about ¾ of the way up the stay will be enough. It is set up to a deadeye on the collar of the fore-stay (Fig. 341). Some Dutch ships led the false stay beneath the top and set it up to a collar on the mast

Fig. 341. Main Topmast Staysail-stay

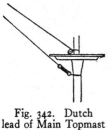

Fig. 342. Dutch lead of Main Topmast Staysail-stay

just below the cheeks (Fig. 342). I do not think this was universal, even in Dutch ships, and I am confident that in ships of other countries the lead above the top was much more usual. The fore-topmast staysail stay was secured about ⅔ of the way up the fore topmast stay. Its lower deadeye or heart was attached to the bow-sprit a little abaft the real stay (Fig. 343). Sometimes it had a long collar to take it clear of other gear. In the *St George* model, the false stay goes just *before* the stay, but this arrangement — especially with the spritsail topmast back stay running to the stay — seems so unpractical that it looks like a mistake.

Fig. 343. Fore Topmast Staysail-stay

Staysail halliards were usually 2-part tackles. There was a single block seized to the stay just above where the false stay was attached and another block hooked into the head of the sail. The halliard started from the strop of the fixed block and went through the block on the sail, back to the block on the stay and down to the deck (Fig. 344). Occasionally the main staysail had a 3-part tackle with a fiddle-block on the stay. When there are no sails it is best to hook the lower block to a strop attached to the foot of the false stay and to bring the hauling part of the halliard back there to be secured (Fig. 345).

Fig. 344. Staysail Halliards

If there are sails they have to be given sheets; if not, it is best to dispense with staysail sheets. When they

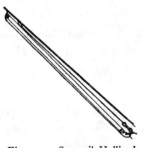

Fig. 345. Staysail Halliards secured beneath Staysail-stay

are fitted they are put through the clew of the sail and seized so as to form two separate sheets. Those of the main staysail come to the side, a little before those of the main-topmast staysail, both of them a little before the mainmast. The fore topmast staysail might have double sheets with pendants from the clew; it led to somewhere just about the fore corner of the fore-castle (Fig. 346).

Staysails were laced to their stays with thin lines passed the opposite way to the lay of the rope (Fig. 347). They had simple tacks and probably had "down-haulers." These details are taken from books of about 1800, but it is probable

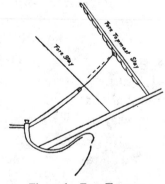

Fig. 346. Fore Topmast Staysail Sheet

that they would be equally true a century earlier.

The jib was in shape and in action very much like a staysail, but was set flying, that is to say without a stay, as can be seen from its original name, the "flying jib." It was carried between the fore-topmast head and the end of the jib-boom, which was a comparatively light spar prolonging the bowsprit. The new sail was officially recognised in

Fig. 347. Lacing of a Staysail

England in 1705, so it is probable that it had been tried at least as far back as 1700. Still, as long as the sprit-sail topmast survived, it was more or less a "lash up." The jib-boom was merely lashed to the bowsprit, usually

Fig. 348. Early Jib-boom attached beneath Bowsprit

underneath, but sometimes on one side. Its heel came aft as far as the spritsail yard or very near it and it ran through the spritsail top and projected beyond the end of the bowsprit about half its own length (Fig. 348). Probably it had a sheave near the end for the jib tack. I doubt if there was a traveller, but there must have been some means of fetching the sail inboard and it seems likely that there was a line from the tack of the sail to the sprit-sail top for this purpose; the tack itself was also probably belayed in the top (Fig. 349).

Fig. 349. Probable arrangement of Jib Tack and Inhauler

The halliards were no doubt similar to those of a stay-sail; there would be a block at the head of the sail and another at the fore-topmast head (Fig. 350). With a

sail fitted, the halliards can be attached to the head and
the tack to the foot; without a sail it is best to bring the
halliard-block right down and hook it
to the tack. Sheets can only be shown
when there is a sail. They may have
been in two parts with pendants, but
were more likely single. One led on
either side of the various stays and they
went to the fore corners of the forecastle.

Fig. 350. Jib
Halliards

It is not easy to say when a jib and jib-boom should
or should not be fitted. English men-of-war certainly
had them after 1705, but I am not at all sure that foreigners were quite so quick in taking up the new sail.
It is not shown in any of the drawings or models of
Dutch East Indiamen of 1720-5 or in a French 3-decker
in a series of etchings of 1710.

CHAPTER XII

SAILS

IF a model is to have sails, they should be as like the real thing as possible. This means, to my mind, that they should be made of woven material with seams, or at all events imitation seams, at the right distance apart and with a "bolt-rope" stitched all round. They should not be stiffened with size, distorted by means of wires through the hems and seams, glued to metal sheets, or treated in any other way in which no real sail ever was or ever could have been treated. Artificially "bellying" sails may look artistic on a purely decorative model, but on a real scale-built model they are an abomination.

Many people consider it a mistake to put sails on a model. They argue that the sails hide the rigging and it is certainly true that it is harder to pick out small details of rigging on a model with sails than on one without. On the other hand, there are things such as buntlines, leechlines and bowlines whose very purpose is obscure (except to people with considerable knowledge of ships) unless the sails are fitted. Perhaps it would be fair to say that for the expert there is more to be seen in a model without sails, but that for the general public sails add interest and make the purpose of the rigging more intelligible.

For my own part I have a feeling—perhaps quite illogical—that sails should be fitted only when the hull is really complete. They seem to me out of place on an English 17th-century "Navy Board" model with its hull unplanked below the waterline and its decks partly open, but on a foreign model of the same period, with the bottom planked and the decks complete, rigging seems to demand sails as well. That is, if the model is big enough for them; I should not advise fitting sails on a model whose scale is less than ¼ inch to the foot.

The best, almost the only, material for sails is linen. Silk does not last well enough; it may look nice for years, but suddenly it will go to pieces all over. Make the sails of linen stitched with linen thread and they will last as long as the yards that carry them.

Cutting out a sail is not an easy job. If it were only a matter of cutting and hemming a piece of material of a given shape, it would be simple enough; but there is more in it than that. Sails were made with a certain amount of "bag" in them and this was obtained by taking up a certain amount of the canvas all round the edge as it was sewn to the bolt-rope. Obviously it is the length of the bolt-rope on the four sides that has to be taken from the dimensions of the spars; the actual linen has to be cut and hemmed so as to be a certain amount larger. What the practice was in the 17th century, I do not know. Towards the end of the 18th, the rule in English sail-making was to take up to the extent of 1 part in 12 at the head and foot of square sails and 1 in 24 on the leeches. There were slight variations, but this is near enough and gives a simple rule to follow. Mizzens and staysails should have the same amount of "take-up" on the head, but are better with none on the foot or leech, because it is certain that they can never have much strain put on them in a model to pull them out.

Another matter that needs consideration is how far

out on the yard the actual sail is to extend. It must not
be made the full width between the cleats, because its
head-cringles will project a bit on each side and these
have to be lashed outwards to the cleats by means of the
earrings to keep the sail spread. Probably it will be
satisfactory to make the finished surface of the canvas
about eighteen inches short (on the scale) at each side
for the larger sails and less for the smaller, but not less
than six inches in any case. If there are no cleats on the
yard, one must work from the place where they would
be; that is to say, the place where the first of the various
strops and eyes on the yard-arm comes.

In the same way, both in width at the foot and in
depth, it is necessary to allow for the fact that the clew
will project a bit and that the sheets have to lead in a
definite direction. The yards must be hoisted to the
proper height and carefully squared; then it will be possible to allow a reasonable drift between the clews and
the sheet-blocks and to get the dimensions of the sail
with some accuracy. This refers to topsails and topgallants; courses at the time under consideration were
nearly always the same width at the foot as at the head,
and with them it is only a matter of getting the depth
right.

I have said that the yards must be hoisted to the
proper height, but so far I have given no indication of
what that height is. To tell the truth, it is a good deal
easier to leave the matter vague. Early in the 18th century, English ships hoisted their lower yards till their
upper sides were about 1/16 to 1/18 of the full length
of the yard below the trestle-trees. It seems to me probable that early in the 17th century yards were not hoisted
so high and it certainly appears that Dutch ships of the

latter part of the century hoisted their yards very much less. In their case it will be enough to hoist them to a point about 1/12 or even 1/10 of their length below the trestle-trees. In English ships I should be inclined to lift the yards gradually in accordance with the date, from about 1/12 of their length down in 1620 to 1/18 in 1720.

This question of the height to which the yards are hoisted affects the shape of the feet of the upper sails, particularly the topsails. When the lower yards are well up, the topsails can be cut straight on the foot, but with the yards lower the topsails have to be "roached" or hollowed on the foot to keep them clear of the stays and their crowfeet. How much this should be done is best settled by experiment, but something not far from 1/20 of the width will be about the maximum. Possibly it may be desirable to do the same thing to the feet of

Fig. 351. Foot of Course in English Plans of 1719

the lower sails to let them clear the boats, etc. If so, they will probably be square amidships and drop about 1 in 5 for the last ⅕ of their width on either side (Fig. 351). This is what English sails were doing in 1719. In cutting a topsail with a hollow foot, I should make the foot an arc of a circle.

If a sail is to have a bonnet, the whole thing is made in one piece and cut in half afterwards, or rather the bottom third is cut off to form the bonnet. This makes it necessary to allow for two extra hems, at the foot of the "course" and the head of the bonnet. The width of the hems or "tablings," varied with the size of the sail. About four inches for the leeches and foot of a mainsail or foresail, three inches for a topsail, spritsail or

mizzen and two inches for smaller sails will be somewhere near right for big ships; the head tabling should
be about 1 inch more.

The tablings must, of course, be included in the meas-
urements before the sail is cut out, but the actual hemming must not be done till the seams have been made,
because that was the order of things in making a real
sail and the opposite course makes the seams run wrong
where they run into the leech-tablings of sails with sloping or "gored" leeches.

In a general way, sail-cloth in the 17th century seems
to have been 28 in. wide. The seams at the beginning
of the 18th century were two inches wide in the courses
and topsails of big ships; before that they had been nar-
rower. For model work a two-inch seam will be found
quite small enough unless the scale is very large. Strictly
speaking, the distance from the middle of one seam to
the next should be 27 or 27¼ in., but in any model on a
scale of less than 1/24, I should suggest putting them
24 in. apart for the sake of ease in measuring; the difference will not be noticeable.

In a model sail, as in the real thing, the selvage of
the material should run parallel with the seams. In the
case of a square sail this means that the head is at right
angles to the selvage. Starting, then, from a line exactly across the material, the shape of the finished sail
(hemmed, but not attached to the bolt-rope) can be
marked out. Then the middle lines of the seams should
be marked. The cloths should be equally disposed about
the middle line of the sail, but it does not matter whether
there is a middle seam or a middle cloth; this is simply
a matter of considering which will best avoid narrow
patches at the corners or narrow strips down the leeches.

With the middle lines of the seams indicated, the actual stitching can be done. For this and for other stitching concerned with the sails, linen thread of a fairly light brown colour should be used. The stitching of the seams has to extend far enough beyond the lines of the finished sail to be sure to cover as much of the hems as will show. Fold the material on the right of one of the lines at a distance corresponding to one inch on the scale and then, starting at the top, stitch or "over-sew" all the way down. Fold the opposite way on the other side of the line and repeat the process. The result will be a series of diagonal stitches and one of straight stitches on each side of the sail (Fig. 352). The stitches should be as small and as close together as can be managed. In reality they ought only to be about $\frac{1}{3}$ of an inch apart on a full-sized sail; this is, of course, an impossible standard to reach on a model.

Fig. 352.
Stitching
of a dummy
Seam

When all the seams have been stitched, for the full depth of the sail, including the tablings or hems, it is time to cut the sail out, but first a tacking thread should be run in along the line on any slanting or curved edge to prevent the material from stretching out of shape. When once this is done, the sail can be cut and hemmed all round; the hem goes on the after side of a square sail and on the starboard side of a fore-and-aft sail.

If there are to be reef-points, there have to be reef-bands to strengthen the sail where they come. These are sewn on the fore side of the sail (or the port side of a mizzen) and have a width equal to $\frac{1}{4}$ of a cloth or seven inches, but are put on double, so that the strip to be cut has to correspond to 14 inches on the scale. The strips

should be taken from the selvages of the linen and should
be folded so that the fold is just nearer the inside of the
strip than it is to the selvage. Then the nar-
rower part is sewn to the sail close up to the
fold and the wider part is turned down over it
and sewn along the bottom (Fig. 353). Other
strengthening pieces, such as "leech-pieces,"
"buntline pieces," etc., are best omitted in mod-

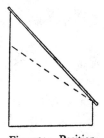

Fig. 353.
Method of
attaching
Reef-bands

el sails. Some of them were certainly in use in
the 17th century, but they do not add much to
the appearance of the sail and they certainly
tend to make it clumsy and hard to set or clew up nicely.

The question of reefs has been mentioned already. It
is difficult to give exact dates for their introduction or
multiplication in the various sails. Speaking roughly it
may be said that the fore and main topsails should have
a single reef after 1660 and might perhaps have one after
1655; that they might have a second reef after 1670 and
would probably have it after 1680. The mizzen topsail
seems to have acquired a single reef about 1700 and a
second about 1710, when it also became possible for the
larger topsails to have a third reef. The foresail and
mainsail probably had a single reef as soon as they lost
their bonnets, somewhere about 1680 in English ships.
The case of the mizzen was similar; as
long as it had a bonnet it did not need a
reef, but without a bonnet it had a row of
reef-points starting from close up to the
yard at the fore end and running at a
slight angle to the yard, so as to reduce
the sail more and more towards the peak
(Fig. 354). This change may, I think,
be dated somewhere about 1680 also.

Fig. 354. Position
of Reef in a
Mizzen

Now comes the sewing on of the bolt-rope. In thickness this should be about ¾ of the shrouds for the sails on the lower masts and as thick as the topmast shrouds in the case of the topsails. Other sails can have bolt-ropes in proportion to their sizes. This is the stage where the linen has to be "taken up" to the extent laid down already. This can be done by holding the material in front and sewing it to the rope and not *vice versa*. The result is a slight fullness in the material and this can be increased or decreased as required. The bolt-rope goes on the after side of square sails and the port side of fore-and-aft sails, but it is so near the edge that this is hardly noticeable. There ought to be a stitch to every strand of the bolt-rope and cross-stitches at such places as the clews and head-cringles. At these latter the stitching must, however, be left till later, because there is some splicing to be done first.

The following description of fittings on the bolt-rope must be looked on as merely what I have found by experiment to be best on a model, and not necessarily ac-

Fig. 355.
Bolt-rope forming Clew

curate except in general appearance. The bolt-rope on a square sail should be put on in two pieces. One forms the head-rope and the other the foot-rope and the two leech-ropes. The clews can be formed simply by leaving a loop in the bolt-rope and putting a seizing at the waist of this loop (Fig. 355), but the head-cringles at the upper corners have to be made rather differently. They are best made by carrying the head-rope beyond the head of the sail, turning it down and splicing it downwards into the leech-ropes in exactly the same way as an eye-splice is made. The leech-ropes are then spliced inwards into the head-rope just where they met at the corner of the

Fig. 356.
Head-cringle
of a Square
Sail

sail (Fig. 356). In the case of the junction of the head-rope and leech-rope of a bonnet, the matter is a little more complicated, because the leech-rope has to go on past the head-rope and to be finished off with a knot as part of the apparatus for attaching the bonnet to the "course." The way to do this is to unlay the head-rope, pass it strand by strand through the leech-rope and then lay the strands together again before splicing them into the leech-rope lower down (Fig. 357). The course of a sail which is to have a bonnet, has a clew just like that of a n y o t h e r square sail. The mizzen, if a true lateen, is best roped with the bolt-rope starting and finishing at the "nock" or lower end of the yard. The foot-rope can be spliced

Fig. 357.
Head-cringle
of a Bonnet

into the head-rope close to the sail and
the head-rope in turn spliced into the
foot-rope with a little slack to f o r m a
clew (Fig. 358). At the other corners
there can be simple loops in
the bolt-rope. If the mizzen is
a "settee," with a short luff,

Fig. 358.
Nock-cringle of
Lateen Mizzen

there can be simple loops at the peak, the
tack and the clew, while at the nock the head-rope and luff-rope can be spliced together as shown in Fig. 359, so that one of them forms a cringle or loop outside the other.

Fig. 359.
Nock-cringle
of Settee
Mizzen

Before the sails are bent or attached to the yards they must be given cringles on the bolt-rope for such things as bowlines, and — if they are to have reefs — the reef-points must be fitted. The number and distribution of the cringles must be suited to that of the bowlines, leechlines (or martnets) and buntlines; but besides these there have to be cringles at the ends of each reef-band and a pair just below the lowest reef-band for the reef-tackles. To make these cringles, take one strand of a rope slightly thinner than the bolt-rope, pass it through the bolt-rope at each end, lay it up to re-form the rope as a loop and tuck the ends into the bolt-rope like the strands in a splice (Fig. 360). If working on a small scale, it is best to dispense with cringles and attach the various lines directly to the bolt-rope.

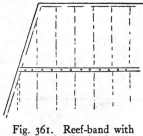

Fig. 360. Cringle for Bowline or Leechline

Whether reef-points in their early days were made of plaited rope, as they were later, I do not know, but I do know that it is best to use ordinary rope on a model. There should be two reef-points to each cloth, as shown in Fig. 361. It will be impossible to sew in gromets at the holes and they will simply have to be pierced with a needle; the reef-points will then be put through and kept in place by means of knots tied close up to the sail on either side. Some early representations of reefing gears show holes in the reef-bands without any reef-points; Plate 15 is a case in point. What exactly this means is uncertain. There may have been detachable reef-points or there may have been a long lacing some-

Fig. 361. Reef-band with holes for Reef-points

what similar to what was used in attaching a bonnet.
Without further evidence it will be best to avoid this
fitting in a model.

Bending sails is a straightforward, but very tedious,
job. First they have to be stretched out beneath the
yards by means of the earrings, which are simply laniards spliced into the head-cringles.
Two or three turns are taken outside the foot-ropes, the brace-pendants and the strops of the topsail-
sheet blocks, and the rest of the ear-
ring, some five or six turns, is taken
straight up round the yard (Fig.

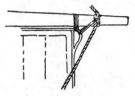

Fig. 362. Method of
passing Earrings

362). Then come the robands; these
are thin lines taken through holes in
the head-tabling just below
the bolt-rope and up round
the yard, two to each cloth.
On the larger sails they are
led as in Fig. 363 and on the
topgallants as in Fig. 364.
The more complicated type
of roband is impossible to
describe, but is easy enough to fit and the drawing ought
to make it clear how it goes; the use of a needle makes
the operation very much easier.

Fig. 363. Roband
of Courses or
Topsails

Fig. 364.
Roband of
Topgallants

For attaching a bonnet a lacing was used. This was
put on to the head of the
bonnet as shown in Fig. 365.
As before, there were two
holes to each cloth. The
loops went on the after side
of the bonnet and were put

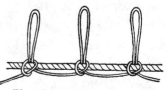

Fig. 365. Lacing on Head of
Bonnet

through corresponding holes in the foot of the course and then led through one another (Fig. 366). To secure the lacing the last loop and the end were tied together. This lacing should be put

Fig. 366. Method of securing lacing of Bonnet to Course

on in four or more parts, so that either the attaching or the letting go of the bonnet might begin at several places at once. To complete the fixing of a bonnet its head-cringle is seized to the clew of the course and the knot at the end of its leech-rope is held by a twisted strop from the leech-rope of the course above it (Fig. 367).

Fig. 367. Head-cringle of Bonnet and Clew of Course

One fitting remains, the gaskets, by which the furled sail was secured. These were attached to the yard by means of staples and strops. The gasket was spliced or seized into one end of the strop and after passing round the sail was put through the other end of the strop and taken several times under itself (Fig. 368). In a model it will be simpler to dispense with the strops and to make eyes on the standing ends of the gaskets (Fig. 369). There were not very many gaskets;

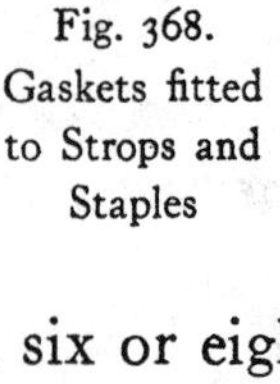

Fig. 368. Gaskets fitted to Strops and Staples

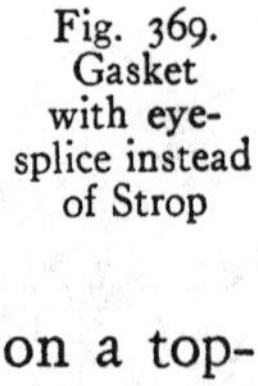

Fig. 369. Gasket with eye-splice instead of Strop

eight or twelve on a lower yard, six or eight on a topsail yard and four on a topgallant yard will be quite a good allowance. The upper sails, by the way, were stowed with their bunts lashed to the mastheads and their clews projecting, not distributed beneath the yards.

If a model has sails, I advise hauling the foresail and mainsail up to the yards by means of the clewlines, buntlines and leechlines. The spritsail is best treated in the same way or even furled altogether. The mizzen will be a difficulty; it is a pity not to have it set, because it forms such a characteristic feature of old-time ships, but it will be found very hard to get it to set properly. Still, it can be done with patience and ingenuity, and anyone who has managed to rig a model and fit it with sails is bound to have developed both these qualities.

PRINCIPAL AUTHORITIES

I. Printed Books by Contemporary Writers

MANWAYRING, SIR HENRY. *The Sea-mans Dictionary* . . . , 1644, etc. Written about 1622. Modern edition, 1922 (*Navy Records Society*).

ANONYMOUS. *A Treatise on Rigging.* Written about 1625. Modern edition, 1921 (*Society for Nautical Research*).

BOTELER, NATHANIEL. *Six Dialogues about Sea Services* . . . , 1685. Written about 1634.

BOND, HENRY. *The Boate Swaines Art* . . . , 1642, etc. Frequently reprinted without being brought up to date.

SMITH, JOHN. *The Seaman's Grammar* . . . , 1653, etc. An enlargement by another hand of the author's *Accidence* . . . *for all Young Sea-men*, of 1626, etc.

HAYWARD, EDWARD. *The Sizes and Lengths of Riggings for all the States Ships and Frigats* . . . , 1655. Reissued, 1660, with changed title-page, but otherwise the same.

MILLER, THOMAS. *The Compleat Modellist* . . . , 1655, or 1656. Second edition, 1664; probably identical.

BUSHNELL, EDMUND. *The Compleat Ship-wright*, 1664.

SUTHERLAND, WILLIAM. *The Ship-builder's Assistant* . . . , 1711, etc.

———— *Britain's Glory: or Ship-Building Unvail'd*, . . . , 1717, etc.

WITSEN, NICOLAES. *Aeloude en Hedendaegsche Scheeps-Bouw en Bestier*, 1671.

ANONYMOUS. *Hollandsche Scheepsbouw*, 1678, etc.

———— *De Volmaakte Boots-man* . . . , 1680, etc.

WINSCHOOTEN, WIGARD. *Seeman* . . . , 1681.

ALLARD, CAREL. *Nieuwe Hollandse Scheeps-Bouw* . . . , 1695. Enlarged in 1705 and again in 1716.

VAN YK, CORNELIS. *De Nederlandsche Scheeps-Bouw-Konst* . . . , 1697.

FOURNIER, GEORGES. *Hydrographie* . . . , 1643. Second edition, 1667.

DASSIÉ, LE SIEUR. *L'Architecture Navale* . . . , 1677.

AUBIN, —. *Dictionnaire de Marine*, 1702. Second edition, 1736.

ANONYMOUS. *L' Art de Bâtir les Vaisseaux* . . . , 1719.

FURTTENBACH, JOSEPH. *Architectura Navalis*, 1629.

ANONYMOUS. *Der geöfnete See-Hafen* . . . , 1700.

CRESCENTIO, BARTOLOMEO. *Nautica Mediterranea* . . . , 1607.

PANTERO PANTERA, —. *L'Armata Navale* . . . , 1614.

CANO, THOME. *Arte para Fabricar* . . . *Naos* . . . , 1611.

II. MODERN PRINTED BOOKS

SOCIETY FOR NAUTICAL RESEARCH. *The Mariner's Mirror*, 1911 — in progress. Particularly articles by MOORE, ALAN, *Rigging in the 17th Century*, 1912-14; and HÄGG, J. *Some Details from the Model of the* . . . *Amaranthe*, 1913.

CHATTERTON, E. KEBLE. *Ship Models*, 1923.

NANCE, R. MORTON. *Sailing Ship Models*, 1924.

LAUGHTON, L. G. CARR. *Old Ship Figure-Heads and Sterns* . . . , 1925.

CULVER, HENRY B. *Contemporary Scale Models* . . . of the 17th Century, 1926.

PÂRIS, EDMOND. *Le Musée de Marine du Louvre*, 1883.

———— *Souvenirs de Marine* . . . , 6 vols., 1882-1908.

DE LA RONCIÈRE, C. *Histoire de la Marine française*, Vol. 4, 1910, and Vol. 5, 1920.

KÖSTER, AUGUST. *Modelle alter Segelschiffe*, 1926.

DURO, C. FERNANDEZ. *Disquisiciones Nauticas*, Vol. 5, 1880, and Vol. 6, 1881.

ARTIÑANO, GERVASIO DE. *La Arquitectura Naval Española,* 1920.

HÄGG, J. AND ZETTERSTEN, A. *Örlogskeppet Amarant.* In *Tidskrift i Sjöväsendet,* 1903.

III. MANUSCRIPTS, ETC.

DEANE, ANTHONY. *Doctrine of Naval Architecture,* 1670.

KELTRIDGE, WILLIAM. *His Book,* 1675.

BATTINE, EDWARD. *The Method of Building . . . Ships of Warr . . . ,* 1689.

GARROTE, FRANCISCO ANTONIO. *Nueva Fabrica de Baxeles . . . ,* 1691. (Modern copy).

Prints and Etchings by and after HOLLAR, ZEEMAN, VAN DER MEULEN, BASTON, SAILMAKER, etc.

Drawings and Paintings by VAN DE VELDE, etc.

Rigging-Plans of the 1719 Establishment, etc.

Plans and Notes from the Model of the *St George,* of 1701, etc.

INDEX

A CATALOG OF SELECTED

DOVER BOOKS

IN ALL FIELDS OF INTEREST

A CATALOG OF SELECTED DOVER
BOOKS IN ALL FIELDS OF INTEREST

CONCERNING THE SPIRITUAL IN ART, Wassily Kandinsky. Pioneering work by father of abstract art. Thoughts on color theory, nature of art. Analysis of earlier masters. 12 illustrations. 80pp. of text. 5⅜ x 8½.   23411-8

ANIMALS: 1,419 Copyright-Free Illustrations of Mammals, Birds, Fish, Insects, etc., Jim Harter (ed.). Clear wood engravings present, in extremely lifelike poses, over 1,000 species of animals. One of the most extensive pictorial sourcebooks of its kind. Captions. Index. 284pp. 9 x 12.   23766-4

CELTIC ART: The Methods of Construction, George Bain. Simple geometric techniques for making Celtic interlacements, spirals, Kells-type initials, animals, humans, etc. Over 500 illustrations. 160pp. 9 x 12. (Available in U.S. only.)   22923-8

AN ATLAS OF ANATOMY FOR ARTISTS, Fritz Schider. Most thorough reference work on art anatomy in the world. Hundreds of illustrations, including selections from works by Vesalius, Leonardo, Goya, Ingres, Michelangelo, others. 593 illustrations. 192pp. 7⅛ x 10¼.   20241-0

CELTIC HAND STROKE-BY-STROKE (Irish Half-Uncial from "The Book of Kells"): An Arthur Baker Calligraphy Manual, Arthur Baker. Complete guide to creating each letter of the alphabet in distinctive Celtic manner. Covers hand position, strokes, pens, inks, paper, more. Illustrated. 48pp. 8¼ x 11.   24336-2

EASY ORIGAMI, John Montroll. Charming collection of 32 projects (hat, cup, pelican, piano, swan, many more) specially designed for the novice origami hobbyist. Clearly illustrated easy-to-follow instructions insure that even beginning papercrafters will achieve successful results. 48pp. 8¼ x 11.   27298-2

THE COMPLETE BOOK OF BIRDHOUSE CONSTRUCTION FOR WOODWORKERS, Scott D. Campbell. Detailed instructions, illustrations, tables. Also data on bird habitat and instinct patterns. Bibliography. 3 tables. 63 illustrations in 15 figures. 48pp. 5¼ x 8½.   24407-5

BLOOMINGDALE'S ILLUSTRATED 1886 CATALOG: Fashions, Dry Goods and Housewares, Bloomingdale Brothers. Famed merchants' extremely rare catalog depicting about 1,700 products: clothing, housewares, firearms, dry goods, jewelry, more. Invaluable for dating, identifying vintage items. Also, copyright-free graphics for artists, designers. Co-published with Henry Ford Museum & Greenfield Village. 160pp. 8¼ x 11.   25780-0

HISTORIC COSTUME IN PICTURES, Braun & Schneider. Over 1,450 costumed figures in clearly detailed engravings–from dawn of civilization to end of 19th century. Captions. Many folk costumes. 256pp. 8⅜ x 11¾.   23150-X

CATALOG OF DOVER BOOKS

STICKLEY CRAFTSMAN FURNITURE CATALOGS, Gustav Stickley and L. & J. G. Stickley. Beautiful, functional furniture in two authentic catalogs from 1910. 594 illustrations, including 277 photos, show settles, rockers, armchairs, reclining chairs, bookcases, desks, tables. 183pp. 6½ x 9¼.   23838-5

AMERICAN LOCOMOTIVES IN HISTORIC PHOTOGRAPHS: 1858 to 1949, Ron Ziel (ed.). A rare collection of 126 meticulously detailed official photographs, called "builder portraits," of American locomotives that majestically chronicle the rise of steam locomotive power in America. Introduction. Detailed captions. xi+ 129pp. 9 x 12.   27393-8

AMERICA'S LIGHTHOUSES: An Illustrated History, Francis Ross Holland, Jr. Delightfully written, profusely illustrated fact-filled survey of over 200 American lighthouses since 1716. History, anecdotes, technological advances, more. 240pp. 8 x 10¾.
                                                                               25576-X

TOWARDS A NEW ARCHITECTURE, Le Corbusier. Pioneering manifesto by founder of "International School." Technical and aesthetic theories, views of industry, economics, relation of form to function, "mass-production split" and much more. Profusely illustrated. 320pp. 6⅛ x 9¼. (Available in U.S. only.)   25023-7

HOW THE OTHER HALF LIVES, Jacob Riis. Famous journalistic record, exposing poverty and degradation of New York slums around 1900, by major social reformer. 100 striking and influential photographs. 233pp. 10 x 7⅞.   22012-5

FRUIT KEY AND TWIG KEY TO TREES AND SHRUBS, William M. Harlow. One of the handiest and most widely used identification aids. Fruit key covers 120 deciduous and evergreen species; twig key 160 deciduous species. Easily used. Over 300 photographs. 126pp. 5⅜ x 8½.   20511-8

COMMON BIRD SONGS, Dr. Donald J. Borror. Songs of 60 most common U.S. birds: robins, sparrows, cardinals, bluejays, finches, more—arranged in order of increasing complexity. Up to 9 variations of songs of each species.
                                                            Cassette and manual 99911-4

ORCHIDS AS HOUSE PLANTS, Rebecca Tyson Northen. Grow cattleyas and many other kinds of orchids—in a window, in a case, or under artificial light. 63 illustrations. 148pp. 5⅜ x 8½.   23261-1

MONSTER MAZES, Dave Phillips. Masterful mazes at four levels of difficulty. Avoid deadly perils and evil creatures to find magical treasures. Solutions for all 32 exciting illustrated puzzles. 48pp. 8¼ x 11.   26005-4

MOZART'S DON GIOVANNI (DOVER OPERA LIBRETTO SERIES), Wolfgang Amadeus Mozart. Introduced and translated by Ellen H. Bleiler. Standard Italian libretto, with complete English translation. Convenient and thoroughly portable—an ideal companion for reading along with a recording or the performance itself. Introduction. List of characters. Plot summary. 121pp. 5¼ x 8½.   24944-1

TECHNICAL MANUAL AND DICTIONARY OF CLASSICAL BALLET, Gail Grant. Defines, explains, comments on steps, movements, poses and concepts. 15-page pictorial section. Basic book for student, viewer. 127pp. 5⅜ x 8½.   21843-0

THE CLARINET AND CLARINET PLAYING, David Pino. Lively, comprehensive work features suggestions about technique, musicianship, and musical interpretation, as well as guidelines for teaching, making your own reeds, and preparing for public performance. Includes an intriguing look at clarinet history. "A godsend," *The Clarinet,* Journal of the International Clarinet Society. Appendixes. 7 illus. 320pp. 5⅜ x 8½.   40270-3

HOLLYWOOD GLAMOR PORTRAITS, John Kobal (ed.). 145 photos from 1926-49. Harlow, Gable, Bogart, Bacall; 94 stars in all. Full background on photographers, technical aspects. 160pp. 8⅜ x 11¼.   23352-9

THE ANNOTATED CASEY AT THE BAT: A Collection of Ballads about the Mighty Casey/Third, Revised Edition, Martin Gardner (ed.). Amusing sequels and parodies of one of America's best-loved poems: Casey's Revenge, Why Casey Whiffed, Casey's Sister at the Bat, others. 256pp. 5⅜ x 8½.   28598-7

THE RAVEN AND OTHER FAVORITE POEMS, Edgar Allan Poe. Over 40 of the author's most memorable poems: "The Bells," "Ulalume," "Israfel," "To Helen," "The Conqueror Worm," "Eldorado," "Annabel Lee," many more. Alphabetic lists of titles and first lines. 64pp. 5$_{3/16}$ x 8¼.   26685-0

PERSONAL MEMOIRS OF U. S. GRANT, Ulysses Simpson Grant. Intelligent, deeply moving firsthand account of Civil War campaigns, considered by many the finest military memoirs ever written. Includes letters, historic photographs, maps and more. 528pp. 6⅛ x 9¼.   28587-1

ANCIENT EGYPTIAN MATERIALS AND INDUSTRIES, A. Lucas and J. Harris. Fascinating, comprehensive, thoroughly documented text describes this ancient civilization's vast resources and the processes that incorporated them in daily life, including the use of animal products, building materials, cosmetics, perfumes and incense, fibers, glazed ware, glass and its manufacture, materials used in the mummification process, and much more. 544pp. 6⅛ x 9¼. (Available in U.S. only.)
                                     40446-3

RUSSIAN STORIES/RUSSKIE RASSKAZY: A Dual-Language Book, edited by Gleb Struve. Twelve tales by such masters as Chekhov, Tolstoy, Dostoevsky, Pushkin, others. Excellent word-for-word English translations on facing pages, plus teaching and study aids, Russian/English vocabulary, biographical/critical introductions, more. 416pp. 5⅜ x 8½.   26244-8

PHILADELPHIA THEN AND NOW: 60 Sites Photographed in the Past and Present, Kenneth Finkel and Susan Oyama. Rare photographs of City Hall, Logan Square, Independence Hall, Betsy Ross House, other landmarks juxtaposed with contemporary views. Captures changing face of historic city. Introduction. Captions. 128pp. 8¼ x 11.   25790-8

AIA ARCHITECTURAL GUIDE TO NASSAU AND SUFFOLK COUNTIES, LONG ISLAND, The American Institute of Architects, Long Island Chapter, and the Society for the Preservation of Long Island Antiquities. Comprehensive, well-researched and generously illustrated volume brings to life over three centuries of Long Island's great architectural heritage. More than 240 photographs with authoritative, extensively detailed captions. 176pp. 8¼ x 11.   26946-9

NORTH AMERICAN INDIAN LIFE: Customs and Traditions of 23 Tribes, Elsie Clews Parsons (ed.). 27 fictionalized essays by noted anthropologists examine religion, customs, government, additional facets of life among the Winnebago, Crow, Zuni, Eskimo, other tribes. 480pp. 6⅛ x 9¼.   27377-6

FRANK LLOYD WRIGHT'S DANA HOUSE, Donald Hoffmann. Pictorial essay of residential masterpiece with over 160 interior and exterior photos, plans, elevations, sketches and studies. 128pp. 9¼ x 10¾.   29120-0

THE MALE AND FEMALE FIGURE IN MOTION: 60 Classic Photographic Sequences, Eadweard Muybridge. 60 true-action photographs of men and women walking, running, climbing, bending, turning, etc., reproduced from rare 19th-century masterpiece. vi + 121pp. 9 x 12.   24745-7

1001 QUESTIONS ANSWERED ABOUT THE SEASHORE, N. J. Berrill and Jacquelyn Berrill. Queries answered about dolphins, sea snails, sponges, starfish, fishes, shore birds, many others. Covers appearance, breeding, growth, feeding, much more. 305pp. 5¼ x 8¼.   23366-9

ATTRACTING BIRDS TO YOUR YARD, William J. Weber. Easy-to-follow guide offers advice on how to attract the greatest diversity of birds: birdhouses, feeders, water and waterers, much more. 96pp. 5³⁄₁₆ x 8¼.   28927-3

MEDICINAL AND OTHER USES OF NORTH AMERICAN PLANTS: A Historical Survey with Special Reference to the Eastern Indian Tribes, Charlotte Erichsen-Brown. Chronological historical citations document 500 years of usage of plants, trees, shrubs native to eastern Canada, northeastern U.S. Also complete identifying information. 343 illustrations. 544pp. 6½ x 9¼.   25951-X

STORYBOOK MAZES, Dave Phillips. 23 stories and mazes on two-page spreads: Wizard of Oz, Treasure Island, Robin Hood, etc. Solutions. 64pp. 8¼ x 11.   23628-5

AMERICAN NEGRO SONGS: 230 Folk Songs and Spirituals, Religious and Secular, John W. Work. This authoritative study traces the African influences of songs sung and played by black Americans at work, in church, and as entertainment. The author discusses the lyric significance of such songs as "Swing Low, Sweet Chariot," "John Henry," and others and offers the words and music for 230 songs. Bibliography. Index of Song Titles. 272pp. 6½ x 9¼.   40271-1

MOVIE-STAR PORTRAITS OF THE FORTIES, John Kobal (ed.). 163 glamor, studio photos of 106 stars of the 1940s: Rita Hayworth, Ava Gardner, Marlon Brando, Clark Gable, many more. 176pp. 8⅜ x 11¼.   23546-7

BENCHLEY LOST AND FOUND, Robert Benchley. Finest humor from early 30s, about pet peeves, child psychologists, post office and others. Mostly unavailable elsewhere. 73 illustrations by Peter Arno and others. 183pp. 5⅜ x 8½.   22410-4

YEKL and THE IMPORTED BRIDEGROOM AND OTHER STORIES OF YIDDISH NEW YORK, Abraham Cahan. Film Hester Street based on *Yekl* (1896). Novel, other stories among first about Jewish immigrants on N.Y.'s East Side. 240pp. 5⅜ x 8½.   22427-9

SELECTED POEMS, Walt Whitman. Generous sampling from *Leaves of Grass*. Twenty-four poems include "I Hear America Singing," "Song of the Open Road," "I Sing the Body Electric," "When Lilacs Last in the Dooryard Bloom'd," "O Captain! My Captain!"—all reprinted from an authoritative edition. Lists of titles and first lines. 128pp. 5³⁄₁₆ x 8¼.   26878-0

CATALOG OF DOVER BOOKS

THE BEST TALES OF HOFFMANN, E. T. A. Hoffmann. 10 of Hoffmann's most important stories: "Nutcracker and the King of Mice," "The Golden Flowerpot," etc. 458pp. 5⅜ x 8½. 21793-0

FROM FETISH TO GOD IN ANCIENT EGYPT, E. A. Wallis Budge. Rich detailed survey of Egyptian conception of "God" and gods, magic, cult of animals, Osiris, more. Also, superb English translations of hymns and legends. 240 illustrations. 545pp. 5⅜ x 8½. 25803-3

FRENCH STORIES/CONTES FRANÇAIS: A Dual-Language Book, Wallace Fowlie. Ten stories by French masters, Voltaire to Camus: "Micromegas" by Voltaire; "The Atheist's Mass" by Balzac; "Minuet" by de Maupassant; "The Guest" by Camus, six more. Excellent English translations on facing pages. Also French-English vocabulary list, exercises, more. 352pp. 5⅜ x 8½. 26443-2

CHICAGO AT THE TURN OF THE CENTURY IN PHOTOGRAPHS: 122 Historic Views from the Collections of the Chicago Historical Society, Larry A. Viskochil. Rare large-format prints offer detailed views of City Hall, State Street, the Loop, Hull House, Union Station, many other landmarks, circa 1904-1913. Introduction. Captions. Maps. 144pp. 9⅜ x 12¼. 24656-6

OLD BROOKLYN IN EARLY PHOTOGRAPHS, 1865-1929, William Lee Younger. Luna Park, Gravesend race track, construction of Grand Army Plaza, moving of Hotel Brighton, etc. 157 previously unpublished photographs. 165pp. 8⅞ x 11¾. 23587-4

THE MYTHS OF THE NORTH AMERICAN INDIANS, Lewis Spence. Rich anthology of the myths and legends of the Algonquins, Iroquois, Pawnees and Sioux, prefaced by an extensive historical and ethnological commentary. 36 illustrations. 480pp. 5⅜ x 8½. 25967-6

AN ENCYCLOPEDIA OF BATTLES: Accounts of Over 1,560 Battles from 1479 B.C. to the Present, David Eggenberger. Essential details of every major battle in recorded history from the first battle of Megiddo in 1479 B.C. to Grenada in 1984. List of Battle Maps. New Appendix covering the years 1967-1984. Index. 99 illustrations. 544pp. 6½ x 9¼. 24913-1

SAILING ALONE AROUND THE WORLD, Captain Joshua Slocum. First man to sail around the world, alone, in small boat. One of great feats of seamanship told in delightful manner. 67 illustrations. 294pp. 5⅜ x 8½. 20326-3

ANARCHISM AND OTHER ESSAYS, Emma Goldman. Powerful, penetrating, prophetic essays on direct action, role of minorities, prison reform, puritan hypocrisy, violence, etc. 271pp. 5⅜ x 8½. 22484-8

MYTHS OF THE HINDUS AND BUDDHISTS, Ananda K. Coomaraswamy and Sister Nivedita. Great stories of the epics; deeds of Krishna, Shiva, taken from puranas, Vedas, folk tales; etc. 32 illustrations. 400pp. 5⅜ x 8½. 21759-0

THE TRAUMA OF BIRTH, Otto Rank. Rank's controversial thesis that anxiety neurosis is caused by profound psychological trauma which occurs at birth. 256pp. 5⅜ x 8½. 27974-X

A THEOLOGICO-POLITICAL TREATISE, Benedict Spinoza. Also contains unfinished Political Treatise. Great classic on religious liberty, theory of government on common consent. R. Elwes translation. Total of 421pp. 5⅜ x 8½. 20249-6

MY BONDAGE AND MY FREEDOM, Frederick Douglass. Born a slave, Douglass became outspoken force in antislavery movement. The best of Douglass' autobiographies. Graphic description of slave life. 464pp. 5⅜ x 8½.   22457-0

FOLLOWING THE EQUATOR: A Journey Around the World, Mark Twain. Fascinating humorous account of 1897 voyage to Hawaii, Australia, India, New Zealand, etc. Ironic, bemused reports on peoples, customs, climate, flora and fauna, politics, much more. 197 illustrations. 720pp. 5⅜ x 8½.   26113-1

THE PEOPLE CALLED SHAKERS, Edward D. Andrews. Definitive study of Shakers: origins, beliefs, practices, dances, social organization, furniture and crafts, etc. 33 illustrations. 351pp. 5⅜ x 8½.   21081-2

THE MYTHS OF GREECE AND ROME, H. A. Guerber. A classic of mythology, generously illustrated, long prized for its simple, graphic, accurate retelling of the principal myths of Greece and Rome, and for its commentary on their origins and significance. With 64 illustrations by Michelangelo, Raphael, Titian, Rubens, Canova, Bernini and others. 480pp. 5⅜ x 8½.   27584-1

PSYCHOLOGY OF MUSIC, Carl E. Seashore. Classic work discusses music as a medium from psychological viewpoint. Clear treatment of physical acoustics, auditory apparatus, sound perception, development of musical skills, nature of musical feeling, host of other topics. 88 figures. 408pp. 5⅜ x 8½.   21851-1

THE PHILOSOPHY OF HISTORY, Georg W. Hegel. Great classic of Western thought develops concept that history is not chance but rational process, the evolution of freedom. 457pp. 5⅜ x 8½.   20112-0

THE BOOK OF TEA, Kakuzo Okakura. Minor classic of the Orient: entertaining, charming explanation, interpretation of traditional Japanese culture in terms of tea ceremony. 94pp. 5⅜ x 8½.   20070-1

LIFE IN ANCIENT EGYPT, Adolf Erman. Fullest, most thorough, detailed older account with much not in more recent books, domestic life, religion, magic, medicine, commerce, much more. Many illustrations reproduce tomb paintings, carvings, hieroglyphs, etc. 597pp. 5⅜ x 8½.   22632-8

SUNDIALS, Their Theory and Construction, Albert Waugh. Far and away the best, most thorough coverage of ideas, mathematics concerned, types, construction, adjusting anywhere. Simple, nontechnical treatment allows even children to build several of these dials. Over 100 illustrations. 230pp. 5⅜ x 8½.   22947-5

THEORETICAL HYDRODYNAMICS, L. M. Milne-Thomson. Classic exposition of the mathematical theory of fluid motion, applicable to both hydrodynamics and aerodynamics. Over 600 exercises. 768pp. 6⅛ x 9¼.   68970-0

SONGS OF EXPERIENCE: Facsimile Reproduction with 26 Plates in Full Color, William Blake. 26 full-color plates from a rare 1826 edition. Includes "The Tyger," "London," "Holy Thursday," and other poems. Printed text of poems. 48pp. 5¼ x 7.   24636-1

OLD-TIME VIGNETTES IN FULL COLOR, Carol Belanger Grafton (ed.). Over 390 charming, often sentimental illustrations, selected from archives of Victorian graphics—pretty women posing, children playing, food, flowers, kittens and puppies, smiling cherubs, birds and butterflies, much more. All copyright-free. 48pp. 9¼ x 12¼.   27269-9

PERSPECTIVE FOR ARTISTS, Rex Vicat Cole. Depth, perspective of sky and sea, shadows, much more, not usually covered. 391 diagrams, 81 reproductions of drawings and paintings. 279pp. 5⅜ x 8½. 22487-2

DRAWING THE LIVING FIGURE, Joseph Sheppard. Innovative approach to artistic anatomy focuses on specifics of surface anatomy, rather than muscles and bones. Over 170 drawings of live models in front, back and side views, and in widely varying poses. Accompanying diagrams. 177 illustrations. Introduction. Index. 144pp. 8⅜ x11¼. 26723-7

GOTHIC AND OLD ENGLISH ALPHABETS: 100 Complete Fonts, Dan X. Solo. Add power, elegance to posters, signs, other graphics with 100 stunning copyright-free alphabets: Blackstone, Dolbey, Germania, 97 more–including many lower-case, numerals, punctuation marks. 104pp. 8⅛ x 11. 24695-7

HOW TO DO BEADWORK, Mary White. Fundamental book on craft from simple projects to five-bead chains and woven works. 106 illustrations. 142pp. 5⅜ x 8. 20697-1

THE BOOK OF WOOD CARVING, Charles Marshall Sayers. Finest book for beginners discusses fundamentals and offers 34 designs. "Absolutely first rate . . . well thought out and well executed."–E. J. Tangerman. 118pp. 7¾ x 10⅝. 23654-4

ILLUSTRATED CATALOG OF CIVIL WAR MILITARY GOODS: Union Army Weapons, Insignia, Uniform Accessories, and Other Equipment, Schuyler, Hartley, and Graham. Rare, profusely illustrated 1846 catalog includes Union Army uniform and dress regulations, arms and ammunition, coats, insignia, flags, swords, rifles, etc. 226 illustrations. 160pp. 9 x 12. 24939-5

WOMEN'S FASHIONS OF THE EARLY 1900s: An Unabridged Republication of "New York Fashions, 1909," National Cloak & Suit Co. Rare catalog of mail-order fashions documents women's and children's clothing styles shortly after the turn of the century. Captions offer full descriptions, prices. Invaluable resource for fashion, costume historians. Approximately 725 illustrations. 128pp. 8⅜ x 11¼. 27276-1

THE 1912 AND 1915 GUSTAV STICKLEY FURNITURE CATALOGS, Gustav Stickley. With over 200 detailed illustrations and descriptions, these two catalogs are essential reading and reference materials and identification guides for Stickley furniture. Captions cite materials, dimensions and prices. 112pp. 6½ x 9¼. 26676-1

EARLY AMERICAN LOCOMOTIVES, John H. White, Jr. Finest locomotive engravings from early 19th century: historical (1804–74), main-line (after 1870), special, foreign, etc. 147 plates. 142pp. 11⅜ x 8¼. 22772-3

THE TALL SHIPS OF TODAY IN PHOTOGRAPHS, Frank O. Braynard. Lavishly illustrated tribute to nearly 100 majestic contemporary sailing vessels: Amerigo Vespucci, Clearwater, Constitution, Eagle, Mayflower, Sea Cloud, Victory, many more. Authoritative captions provide statistics, background on each ship. 190 black-and-white photographs and illustrations. Introduction. 128pp. 8⅞ x 11¾. 27163-3

LITTLE BOOK OF EARLY AMERICAN CRAFTS AND TRADES, Peter Stockham (ed.). 1807 children's book explains crafts and trades: baker, hatter, cooper, potter, and many others. 23 copperplate illustrations. 140pp. 4⅝ x 6. 23336-7

VICTORIAN FASHIONS AND COSTUMES FROM HARPER'S BAZAR, 1867–1898, Stella Blum (ed.). Day costumes, evening wear, sports clothes, shoes, hats, other accessories in over 1,000 detailed engravings. 320pp. 9⅜ x 12¼. 22990-4

GUSTAV STICKLEY, THE CRAFTSMAN, Mary Ann Smith. Superb study surveys broad scope of Stickley's achievement, especially in architecture. Design philosophy, rise and fall of the Craftsman empire, descriptions and floor plans for many Craftsman houses, more. 86 black-and-white halftones. 31 line illustrations. Introduction 208pp. 6½ x 9¼. 27210-9

THE LONG ISLAND RAIL ROAD IN EARLY PHOTOGRAPHS, Ron Ziel. Over 220 rare photos, informative text document origin (1844) and development of rail service on Long Island. Vintage views of early trains, locomotives, stations, passengers, crews, much more. Captions. 8⅞ x 11¾. 26301-0

VOYAGE OF THE LIBERDADE, Joshua Slocum. Great 19th-century mariner's thrilling, first-hand account of the wreck of his ship off South America, the 35-foot boat he built from the wreckage, and its remarkable voyage home. 128pp. 5⅜ x 8½. 40022-0

TEN BOOKS ON ARCHITECTURE, Vitruvius. The most important book ever written on architecture. Early Roman aesthetics, technology, classical orders, site selection, all other aspects. Morgan translation. 331pp. 5⅜ x 8½. 20645-9

THE HUMAN FIGURE IN MOTION, Eadweard Muybridge. More than 4,500 stopped-action photos, in action series, showing undraped men, women, children jumping, lying down, throwing, sitting, wrestling, carrying, etc. 390pp. 7⅞ x 10⅝. 20204-6 Clothbd.

TREES OF THE EASTERN AND CENTRAL UNITED STATES AND CANADA, William M. Harlow. Best one-volume guide to 140 trees. Full descriptions, woodlore, range, etc. Over 600 illustrations. Handy size. 288pp. 4½ x 6⅜. 20395-6

SONGS OF WESTERN BIRDS, Dr. Donald J. Borror. Complete song and call repertoire of 60 western species, including flycatchers, juncoes, cactus wrens, many more–includes fully illustrated booklet. Cassette and manual 99913-0

GROWING AND USING HERBS AND SPICES, Milo Miloradovich. Versatile handbook provides all the information needed for cultivation and use of all the herbs and spices available in North America. 4 illustrations. Index. Glossary. 236pp. 5⅜ x 8½. 25058-X

BIG BOOK OF MAZES AND LABYRINTHS, Walter Shepherd. 50 mazes and labyrinths in all–classical, solid, ripple, and more–in one great volume. Perfect inexpensive puzzler for clever youngsters. Full solutions. 112pp. 8⅛ x 11. 22951-3

PIANO TUNING, J. Cree Fischer. Clearest, best book for beginner, amateur. Simple repairs, raising dropped notes, tuning by easy method of flattened fifths. No previous skills needed. 4 illustrations. 201pp. 5⅜ x 8½. 23267-0

HINTS TO SINGERS, Lillian Nordica. Selecting the right teacher, developing confidence, overcoming stage fright, and many other important skills receive thoughtful discussion in this indispensible guide, written by a world-famous diva of four decades' experience. 96pp. 5⅜ x 8½. 40094-8

THE COMPLETE NONSENSE OF EDWARD LEAR, Edward Lear. All nonsense limericks, zany alphabets, Owl and Pussycat, songs, nonsense botany, etc., illustrated by Lear. Total of 320pp. 5⅜ x 8½. (Available in U.S. only.) 20167-8

VICTORIAN PARLOUR POETRY: An Annotated Anthology, Michael R. Turner. 117 gems by Longfellow, Tennyson, Browning, many lesser-known poets. "The Village Blacksmith," "Curfew Must Not Ring Tonight," "Only a Baby Small," dozens more, often difficult to find elsewhere. Index of poets, titles, first lines. xxiii + 325pp. 5⅜ x 8¼. 27044-0

DUBLINERS, James Joyce. Fifteen stories offer vivid, tightly focused observations of the lives of Dublin's poorer classes. At least one, "The Dead," is considered a masterpiece. Reprinted complete and unabridged from standard edition. 160pp. 5³⁄₁₆ x 8¼. 26870-5

GREAT WEIRD TALES: 14 Stories by Lovecraft, Blackwood, Machen and Others, S. T. Joshi (ed.). 14 spellbinding tales, including "The Sin Eater," by Fiona McLeod, "The Eye Above the Mantel," by Frank Belknap Long, as well as renowned works by R. H. Barlow, Lord Dunsany, Arthur Machen, W. C. Morrow and eight other masters of the genre. 256pp. 5⅜ x 8½. (Available in U.S. only.) 40436-6

THE BOOK OF THE SACRED MAGIC OF ABRAMELIN THE MAGE, translated by S. MacGregor Mathers. Medieval manuscript of ceremonial magic. Basic document in Aleister Crowley, Golden Dawn groups. 268pp. 5⅜ x 8½. 23211-5

NEW RUSSIAN-ENGLISH AND ENGLISH-RUSSIAN DICTIONARY, M. A. O'Brien. This is a remarkably handy Russian dictionary, containing a surprising amount of information, including over 70,000 entries. 366pp. 4½ x 6⅛. 20208-9

HISTORIC HOMES OF THE AMERICAN PRESIDENTS, Second, Revised Edition, Irvin Haas. A traveler's guide to American Presidential homes, most open to the public, depicting and describing homes occupied by every American President from George Washington to George Bush. With visiting hours, admission charges, travel routes. 175 photographs. Index. 160pp. 8¼ x 11. 26751-2

NEW YORK IN THE FORTIES, Andreas Feininger. 162 brilliant photographs by the well-known photographer, formerly with *Life* magazine. Commuters, shoppers, Times Square at night, much else from city at its peak. Captions by John von Hartz. 181pp. 9¼ x 10¾. 23585-8

INDIAN SIGN LANGUAGE, William Tomkins. Over 525 signs developed by Sioux and other tribes. Written instructions and diagrams. Also 290 pictographs. 111pp. 6⅛ x 9¼. 22029-X

ANATOMY: A Complete Guide for Artists, Joseph Sheppard. A master of figure drawing shows artists how to render human anatomy convincingly. Over 460 illustrations. 224pp. 8⅜ x 11¼. 27279-6

MEDIEVAL CALLIGRAPHY: Its History and Technique, Marc Drogin. Spirited history, comprehensive instruction manual covers 13 styles (ca. 4th century through 15th). Excellent photographs; directions for duplicating medieval techniques with modern tools. 224pp. 8⅜ x 11¼. 26142-5

DRIED FLOWERS: How to Prepare Them, Sarah Whitlock and Martha Rankin. Complete instructions on how to use silica gel, meal and borax, perlite aggregate, sand and borax, glycerine and water to create attractive permanent flower arrangements. 12 illustrations. 32pp. 5⅜ x 8½. 21802-3

EASY-TO-MAKE BIRD FEEDERS FOR WOODWORKERS, Scott D. Campbell. Detailed, simple-to-use guide for designing, constructing, caring for and using feeders. Text, illustrations for 12 classic and contemporary designs. 96pp. 5⅜ x 8½. 25847-5

SCOTTISH WONDER TALES FROM MYTH AND LEGEND, Donald A. Mackenzie. 16 lively tales tell of giants rumbling down mountainsides, of a magic wand that turns stone pillars into warriors, of gods and goddesses, evil hags, powerful forces and more. 240pp. 5⅜ x 8½. 29677-6

THE HISTORY OF UNDERCLOTHES, C. Willett Cunnington and Phyllis Cunnington. Fascinating, well-documented survey covering six centuries of English undergarments, enhanced with over 100 illustrations: 12th-century laced-up bodice, footed long drawers (1795), 19th-century bustles, l9th-century corsets for men, Victorian "bust improvers," much more. 272pp. 5⅜ x 8¼. 27124-2

ARTS AND CRAFTS FURNITURE: The Complete Brooks Catalog of 1912, Brooks Manufacturing Co. Photos and detailed descriptions of more than 150 now very collectible furniture designs from the Arts and Crafts movement depict davenports, settees, buffets, desks, tables, chairs, bedsteads, dressers and more, all built of solid, quarter-sawed oak. Invaluable for students and enthusiasts of antiques, Americana and the decorative arts. 80pp. 6½ x 9¼. 27471-3

WILBUR AND ORVILLE: A Biography of the Wright Brothers, Fred Howard. Definitive, crisply written study tells the full story of the brothers' lives and work. A vividly written biography, unparalleled in scope and color, that also captures the spirit of an extraordinary era. 560pp. 6⅛ x 9¼. 40297-5

THE ARTS OF THE SAILOR: Knotting, Splicing and Ropework, Hervey Garrett Smith. Indispensable shipboard reference covers tools, basic knots and useful hitches; handsewing and canvas work, more. Over 100 illustrations. Delightful reading for sea lovers. 256pp. 5⅜ x 8½. 26440-8

FRANK LLOYD WRIGHT'S FALLINGWATER: The House and Its History, Second, Revised Edition, Donald Hoffmann. A total revision—both in text and illustrations—of the standard document on Fallingwater, the boldest, most personal architectural statement of Wright's mature years, updated with valuable new material from the recently opened Frank Lloyd Wright Archives. "Fascinating"—*The New York Times*. 116 illustrations. 128pp. 9¼ x 10¾. 27430-6

CATALOG OF DOVER BOOKS

PHOTOGRAPHIC SKETCHBOOK OF THE CIVIL WAR, Alexander Gardner. 100 photos taken on field during the Civil War. Famous shots of Manassas Harper's Ferry, Lincoln, Richmond, slave pens, etc. 244pp. 10⅝ x 8¼.   22731-6

FIVE ACRES AND INDEPENDENCE, Maurice G. Kains. Great back-to-the-land classic explains basics of self-sufficient farming. The one book to get. 95 illustrations. 397pp. 5⅜ x 8½.   20974-1

SONGS OF EASTERN BIRDS, Dr. Donald J. Borror. Songs and calls of 60 species most common to eastern U.S.: warblers, woodpeckers, flycatchers, thrushes, larks, many more in high-quality recording.   Cassette and manual 99912-2

A MODERN HERBAL, Margaret Grieve. Much the fullest, most exact, most useful compilation of herbal material. Gigantic alphabetical encyclopedia, from aconite to zedoary, gives botanical information, medical properties, folklore, economic uses, much else. Indispensable to serious reader. 161 illustrations. 888pp. 6½ x 9¼. 2-vol. set. (Available in U.S. only.)   Vol. I: 22798-7
          Vol. II: 22799-5

HIDDEN TREASURE MAZE BOOK, Dave Phillips. Solve 34 challenging mazes accompanied by heroic tales of adventure. Evil dragons, people-eating plants, blood-thirsty giants, many more dangerous adversaries lurk at every twist and turn. 34 mazes, stories, solutions. 48pp. 8¼ x 11.   24566-7

LETTERS OF W. A. MOZART, Wolfgang A. Mozart. Remarkable letters show bawdy wit, humor, imagination, musical insights, contemporary musical world; includes some letters from Leopold Mozart. 276pp. 5⅜ x 8½.   22859-2

BASIC PRINCIPLES OF CLASSICAL BALLET, Agrippina Vaganova. Great Russian theoretician, teacher explains methods for teaching classical ballet. 118 illustrations. 175pp. 5⅜ x 8½.   22036-2

THE JUMPING FROG, Mark Twain. Revenge edition. The original story of The Celebrated Jumping Frog of Calaveras County, a hapless French translation, and Twain's hilarious "retranslation" from the French. 12 illustrations. 66pp. 5⅜ x 8½.
          22686-7

BEST REMEMBERED POEMS, Martin Gardner (ed.). The 126 poems in this superb collection of 19th- and 20th-century British and American verse range from Shelley's "To a Skylark" to the impassioned "Renascence" of Edna St. Vincent Millay and to Edward Lear's whimsical "The Owl and the Pussycat." 224pp. 5⅜ x 8½.
          27165-X

COMPLETE SONNETS, William Shakespeare. Over 150 exquisite poems deal with love, friendship, the tyranny of time, beauty's evanescence, death and other themes in language of remarkable power, precision and beauty. Glossary of archaic terms. 80pp. 5³⁄₁₆ x 8¼.   26686-9

THE BATTLES THAT CHANGED HISTORY, Fletcher Pratt. Eminent historian profiles 16 crucial conflicts, ancient to modern, that changed the course of civilization. 352pp. 5⅜ x 8½.   41129-X

THE WIT AND HUMOR OF OSCAR WILDE, Alvin Redman (ed.). More than 1,000 ripostes, paradoxes, wisecracks: Work is the curse of the drinking classes; I can resist everything except temptation; etc. 258pp. 5⅜ x 8½. 20602-5

SHAKESPEARE LEXICON AND QUOTATION DICTIONARY, Alexander Schmidt. Full definitions, locations, shades of meaning in every word in plays and poems. More than 50,000 exact quotations. 1,485pp. 6½ x 9¼. 2-vol. set.
Vol. 1: 22726-X
Vol. 2: 22727-8

SELECTED POEMS, Emily Dickinson. Over 100 best-known, best-loved poems by one of America's foremost poets, reprinted from authoritative early editions. No comparable edition at this price. Index of first lines. 64pp. 5 3/16 x 8¼. 26466-1

THE INSIDIOUS DR. FU-MANCHU, Sax Rohmer. The first of the popular mystery series introduces a pair of English detectives to their archnemesis, the diabolical Dr. Fu-Manchu. Flavorful atmosphere, fast-paced action, and colorful characters enliven this classic of the genre. 208pp. 5 3/16 x 8¼. 29898-1

THE MALLEUS MALEFICARUM OF KRAMER AND SPRENGER, translated by Montague Summers. Full text of most important witchhunter's "bible," used by both Catholics and Protestants. 278pp. 6⅝ x 10. 22802-9

SPANISH STORIES/CUENTOS ESPAÑOLES: A Dual-Language Book, Angel Flores (ed.). Unique format offers 13 great stories in Spanish by Cervantes, Borges, others. Faithful English translations on facing pages. 352pp. 5⅜ x 8½. 25399-6

GARDEN CITY, LONG ISLAND, IN EARLY PHOTOGRAPHS, 1869–1919, Mildred H. Smith. Handsome treasury of 118 vintage pictures, accompanied by carefully researched captions, document the Garden City Hotel fire (1899), the Vanderbilt Cup Race (1908), the first airmail flight departing from the Nassau Boulevard Aerodrome (1911), and much more. 96pp. 8⅞ x 11¾. 40669-5

OLD QUEENS, N.Y., IN EARLY PHOTOGRAPHS, Vincent F. Seyfried and William Asadorian. Over 160 rare photographs of Maspeth, Jamaica, Jackson Heights, and other areas. Vintage views of DeWitt Clinton mansion, 1939 World's Fair and more. Captions. 192pp. 8⅞ x 11. 26358-4

CAPTURED BY THE INDIANS: 15 Firsthand Accounts, 1750-1870, Frederick Drimmer. Astounding true historical accounts of grisly torture, bloody conflicts, relentless pursuits, miraculous escapes and more, by people who lived to tell the tale. 384pp. 5⅜ x 8½. 24901-8

THE WORLD'S GREAT SPEECHES (Fourth Enlarged Edition), Lewis Copeland, Lawrence W. Lamm, and Stephen J. McKenna. Nearly 300 speeches provide public speakers with a wealth of updated quotes and inspiration–from Pericles' funeral oration and William Jennings Bryan's "Cross of Gold Speech" to Malcolm X's powerful words on the Black Revolution and Earl of Spenser's tribute to his sister, Diana, Princess of Wales. 944pp. 5⅜ x 8⅜. 40903-1

THE BOOK OF THE SWORD, Sir Richard F. Burton. Great Victorian scholar/adventurer's eloquent, erudite history of the "queen of weapons"–from prehistory to early Roman Empire. Evolution and development of early swords, variations (sabre, broadsword, cutlass, scimitar, etc.), much more. 336pp. 6⅛ x 9¼. 25434-8

AUTOBIOGRAPHY: The Story of My Experiments with Truth, Mohandas K. Gandhi. Boyhood, legal studies, purification, the growth of the Satyagraha (nonviolent protest) movement. Critical, inspiring work of the man responsible for the freedom of India. 480pp. 5⅜ x 8½. (Available in U.S. only.)   24593-4

CELTIC MYTHS AND LEGENDS, T. W. Rolleston. Masterful retelling of Irish and Welsh stories and tales. Cuchulain, King Arthur, Deirdre, the Grail, many more. First paperback edition. 58 full-page illustrations. 512pp. 5⅜ x 8½.   26507-2

THE PRINCIPLES OF PSYCHOLOGY, William James. Famous long course complete, unabridged. Stream of thought, time perception, memory, experimental methods; great work decades ahead of its time. 94 figures. 1,391pp. 5⅜ x 8½. 2-vol. set.
Vol. I: 20381-6   Vol. II: 20382-4

THE WORLD AS WILL AND REPRESENTATION, Arthur Schopenhauer. Definitive English translation of Schopenhauer's life work, correcting more than 1,000 errors, omissions in earlier translations. Translated by E. F. J. Payne. Total of 1,269pp. 5⅜ x 8½. 2-vol. set.   Vol. 1: 21761-2   Vol. 2: 21762-0

MAGIC AND MYSTERY IN TIBET, Madame Alexandra David-Neel. Experiences among lamas, magicians, sages, sorcerers, Bonpa wizards. A true psychic discovery. 32 illustrations. 321pp. 5⅜ x 8½. (Available in U.S. only.)   22682-4

THE EGYPTIAN BOOK OF THE DEAD, E. A. Wallis Budge. Complete reproduction of Ani's papyrus, finest ever found. Full hieroglyphic text, interlinear transliteration, word-for-word translation, smooth translation. 533pp. 6½ x 9¼.   21866-X

MATHEMATICS FOR THE NONMATHEMATICIAN, Morris Kline. Detailed, college-level treatment of mathematics in cultural and historical context, with numerous exercises. Recommended Reading Lists. Tables. Numerous figures. 641pp. 5⅜ x 8½.
24823-2

PROBABILISTIC METHODS IN THE THEORY OF STRUCTURES, Isaac Elishakoff. Well-written introduction covers the elements of the theory of probability from two or more random variables, the reliability of such multivariable structures, the theory of random function, Monte Carlo methods of treating problems incapable of exact solution, and more. Examples. 502pp. 5⅜ x 8½.   40691-1

THE RIME OF THE ANCIENT MARINER, Gustave Doré, S. T. Coleridge. Doré's finest work; 34 plates capture moods, subtleties of poem. Flawless full-size reproductions printed on facing pages with authoritative text of poem. "Beautiful. Simply beautiful."–*Publisher's Weekly.* 77pp. 9¼ x 12.   22305-1

NORTH AMERICAN INDIAN DESIGNS FOR ARTISTS AND CRAFTSPEOPLE, Eva Wilson. Over 360 authentic copyright-free designs adapted from Navajo blankets, Hopi pottery, Sioux buffalo hides, more. Geometrics, symbolic figures, plant and animal motifs, etc. 128pp. 8⅜ x 11. (Not for sale in the United Kingdom.)   25341-4

SCULPTURE: Principles and Practice, Louis Slobodkin. Step-by-step approach to clay, plaster, metals, stone; classical and modern. 253 drawings, photos. 255pp. 8⅛ x 11.
22960-2

THE INFLUENCE OF SEA POWER UPON HISTORY, 1660–1783, A. T. Mahan. Influential classic of naval history and tactics still used as text in war colleges. First paperback edition. 4 maps. 24 battle plans. 640pp. 5⅜ x 8½.   25509-3

CATALOG OF DOVER BOOKS

THE STORY OF THE TITANIC AS TOLD BY ITS SURVIVORS, Jack Winocour (ed.). What it was really like. Panic, despair, shocking inefficiency, and a little heroism. More thrilling than any fictional account. 26 illustrations. 320pp. 5⅜ x 8½.
20610-6

FAIRY AND FOLK TALES OF THE IRISH PEASANTRY, William Butler Yeats (ed.). Treasury of 64 tales from the twilight world of Celtic myth and legend: "The Soul Cages," "The Kildare Pooka," "King O'Toole and his Goose," many more. Introduction and Notes by W. B. Yeats. 352pp. 5⅜ x 8½.
26941-8

BUDDHIST MAHAYANA TEXTS, E. B. Cowell and others (eds.). Superb, accurate translations of basic documents in Mahayana Buddhism, highly important in history of religions. The Buddha-karita of Asvaghosha, Larger Sukhavativyuha, more. 448pp. 5⅜ x 8½.
25552-2

ONE TWO THREE . . . INFINITY: Facts and Speculations of Science, George Gamow. Great physicist's fascinating, readable overview of contemporary science: number theory, relativity, fourth dimension, entropy, genes, atomic structure, much more. 128 illustrations. Index. 352pp. 5⅜ x 8½.
25664-2

EXPERIMENTATION AND MEASUREMENT, W. J. Youden. Introductory manual explains laws of measurement in simple terms and offers tips for achieving accuracy and minimizing errors. Mathematics of measurement, use of instruments, experimenting with machines. 1994 edition. Foreword. Preface. Introduction. Epilogue. Selected Readings. Glossary. Index. Tables and figures. 128pp. 5⅜ x 8½.   40451-X

DALÍ ON MODERN ART: The Cuckolds of Antiquated Modern Art, Salvador Dalí. Influential painter skewers modern art and its practitioners. Outrageous evaluations of Picasso, Cézanne, Turner, more. 15 renderings of paintings discussed. 44 calligraphic decorations by Dalí. 96pp. 5⅜ x 8½. (Available in U.S. only.)   29220-7

ANTIQUE PLAYING CARDS: A Pictorial History, Henry René D'Allemagne. Over 900 elaborate, decorative images from rare playing cards (14th–20th centuries): Bacchus, death, dancing dogs, hunting scenes, royal coats of arms, players cheating, much more. 96pp. 9¼ x 12¼.
29265-7

MAKING FURNITURE MASTERPIECES: 30 Projects with Measured Drawings, Franklin H. Gottshall. Step-by-step instructions, illustrations for constructing handsome, useful pieces, among them a Sheraton desk, Chippendale chair, Spanish desk, Queen Anne table and a William and Mary dressing mirror. 224pp. 8⅛ x 11¼.
29338-6

THE FOSSIL BOOK: A Record of Prehistoric Life, Patricia V. Rich et al. Profusely illustrated definitive guide covers everything from single-celled organisms and dinosaurs to birds and mammals and the interplay between climate and man. Over 1,500 illustrations. 760pp. 7½ x 10⅛.
29371-8

Paperbound unless otherwise indicated. Available at your book dealer, online at **www.doverpublications.com**, or by writing to Dept. GI, Dover Publications, Inc., 31 East 2nd Street, Mineola, NY 11501. For current price information or for free catalogues (please indicate field of interest), write to Dover Publications or log on to **www.doverpublications.com** and see every Dover book in print. Dover publishes more than 500 books each year on science, elementary and advanced mathematics, biology, music, art, literary history, social sciences, and other areas.